# MANAGING AFRICAN CONFLICTS:
# THE CHALLENGE OF MILITARY INTERVENTION

# MANAGING AFRICAN CONFLICTS: THE CHALLENGE OF MILITARY INTERVENTION

EDITORS

L du Plessis
Director: Centre for Military Studies
University of Stellenbosch

M Hough
Director: Institute for Strategic Studies
University of Pretoria

© 2000 by Human Sciences Research Council/CEMIS & ISSUP

All rights reserved. No part of this publication may be reproduced or transmitted in any form or by any means, electronic or mechanical, including photocopy, recording or any information storage and retrieval system, without permission in writing from the publisher.

ISBN 0-7969-1959-3

Cover design: Tanya Jansen,
College for Educational Technology, Centurion

Cover photographs: Peter Hammond, Newlands

Layout and design: Mari Nel

Published by:
HSRC Publishers
Private Bag X41
Pretoria

Printed by:
Quality Duplicating
(012) 567 4604

# Contributors

Doctor (Colonel) Louis du Plessis is Director of the Centre for Military Studies of the University of Stellenbosch. He specialises in trends in security analysis and in African conflicts and conflict management.

Professor (Doctor) Michael Hough is Director of the Institute for Strategic Studies of the University of Pretoria. He is Professor of Political Science and specialises in African politics and security issues.

Professor (Doctor) Amadu Sesay is Professor of International Relations at the Obafemi Awolowo University, Ile-Ife, Nigeria. He specialises in relations between Europe and Africa and in the nature of African regionalism.

Professor (Doctor) George Barrie is Professor of Public Law at the Rand Afrikaans University in Johannesburg. He specialises in topical international law.

Professor (Doctor) Anton du Plessis is Professor of International Relations at the University of Pretoria. He specialises in the theory and practice of world politics.

Heinrich Matthee is a senior researcher at the Western Cape branch of the Centre for Military Studies of the University of Stellenbosch. He specialises in African conflicts and in information processing in modern warfare.

Doctor Theo Neethling is a senior researcher at the Gauteng branch of the Centre for Military Studies of the University of Stellenbosch. He specialises in international peace support missions and in the roles of armed forces.

ADDRESSES

Centre for Military Studies (Cemis)
South Africa 012 674 4820
louis@cemis.co.za

Institute for Strategic Studies (Issup)
South Africa 012 420 2407
wmartin@postino.up.ac.za

# Contents

|    | Introduction<br>*Louis du Plessis*<br>*Michael Hough* | 1 |
|----|---|---|
| 1. | Military Intervention:<br>Nature and Scope<br>*Anton du Plessis* | 3 |
| 2. | International Law and Forcible Intervention:<br>A Millennium Assessment<br>*George Barrie* | 73 |
| 3. | African Conflict at the Turn of the Century:<br>Manifestations, Propensity and Management<br>*Louis du Plessis* | 119 |
| 4. | Military Intervention in sub-Saharan Africa:<br>A Historical Overview<br>*Michael Hough* | 167 |
| 5. | West African Military Interventions in the 1990s:<br>The Case of ECOWAS in Liberia and Sierra Leone<br>*Amadu Sesay* | 193 |
| 6. | Central African Military Interventions in the 1990s:<br>The Case of the DRC<br>*Heinrich Matthee* | 253 |
| 7. | Southern African Military Interventions in the<br>1990s: The Case of SADC in Lesotho<br>*Theo Neethling* | 287 |
| 8. | Conclusion:<br>The Challenge of Military Intervention<br>*Louis du Plessis* | 333 |

# Introduction

Louis du Plessis
and Michael Hough

In the last years of the twentieth century military interventions by states in the conflicts occurring in other countries dominated television news on Africa. Military units from Nigeria or Gambia, Ghana or Guinea were patrolling the streets of Monrovia, the capital of Liberia. Armoured vehicles from South Africa and Botswana lumbered up and down the main streets of Lesotho's capital, Maseru. Soldiers from Zimbabwe and Angola assisted those from the Democratic Republic of the Congo (DRC) to defend the Congolese capital against rebel insurgents supported by Ugandan, Rwandan and Burundian forces. Those who observed the camouflaged uniforms, and wished to understand something more of these events, were inevitably puzzled by many questions. Some of these questions were:

- Why are the armed forces of so many African states intervening in the domestic affairs of their neighbours?

- What are these armed forces actually doing on foreign soil?

- Why are so many African conflicts continuing from year to year, thereby inevitably inviting and attracting intervention?

- And finally: What kinds of theoretical and legal conceptual frameworks will help observers understand the nature of such military interventions?

Not only academic interest, but also a deep empathy for a volatile continent, motivated a few scholars from Africa to debate these issues and to put their observations and ideas on paper with the aim of stimulating further discussion and analysis.

In this work the emphasis falls on the underlying societal reasons for African conflict and intervention; on the history of intervention by extracontinental, as well as by other African armed forces; on the policies, risks and costs involved; and on the international political and legal framework within which such intervention occurs. Thus the issue is not intervention by armed forces in the domestic politics of their own countries, for example through *coup d'états*, but direct military intervention by one or more states in the domestic conflicts of other countries. Military intervention is also distinguished from peace missions under international law.

The general patterns are illustrated by way of case studies of the three most comprehensive examples of military intervention in African conflict areas at the end of the previous century. These are the West African interventions of the Economic Community of West African States (ECOWAS) in Liberia and Sierra Leone under the leadership of Nigeria; the Central African interventions by several states in the DRC; and the Southern African intervention of the Southern African Development Community (SADC) in Lesotho under the leadership of South Africa. In the final chapter the case studies are summarised within a global, continental and regional context; the primary negative and positive results are identified; and the complex nature of military intervention in African conflicts is highlighted.

# Chapter 1

# MILITARY INTERVENTION: NATURE AND SCOPE

## Anton du Plessis

## 1. INTRODUCTION

Considering the events and ideas of the 1990s, the notion that intervention is a pervasive, in-built and significant feature of the international system that lies at the heart of all debate about international order has become a truism of contemporary world politics.[1] In the aftermath of the Cold War the world has seen the re-emergence of intervention as a phenomenon and a topic of debate that poses challenging questions to scholars and practitioners alike.[2] This is amply illustrated, firstly, by the contention that the post-Cold War era is an "era of intervention" propelled by modest forms of interventionism;[3] and secondly, by the notion that wars of intervention are expected to be the most common type of war in the next decades, since the conduct of future warfare will be conditioned by the possibility of intervention by the most substantial military powers.[4] Whereas the former is associated with a proclaimed vision of a "new world order" and the interventionist foreign policy doctrine that accompanies it,[5] the latter describes the nature of geostrategy in a globalising and turbulent strategic realm characterised by the erosion of the traditional Westphalian, or state-centric system.[6] Since intervention represents both a factual situation and an issue of contemporary world politics, and since its intrinsic nature and context have undergone subtle albeit significant changes,[7] it is imperative to study this phenomenon and its persistence over time, in sub-Saharan Africa in particular. Whereas the primary aim of this chapter is to provide a conceptual and theoretical introduction, attention is later given to the definition, typology, context, anatomy, policy dimensions and risk of military intervention.

## 2. DEFINITION AND TYPOLOGY OF MILITARY INTERVENTION

Military intervention is a particular type of intervention and any attempt to define the former requires an understanding of the latter. Yet paradoxically, despite its salience and description of an age-old phenomenon, the concept of intervention suffers from ambiguity and a lack of definitional clarity.[8] Some clarification is nonetheless required.

The general nature of intervention is derived from the Latin verb *intervenere* which can mean to step between, to disrupt and to interfere. In international law, intervention was first defined by Emmerich de Vattel in 1758 as a breach of the sovereignty of a target state.[9] In its broadest sense the first meaning or essential feature of intervention, also indicative of its finite and temporary character, is that it pertains to "the interference by one state in the affairs of another state, thereby temporarily interrupting the normal bilateral pattern between these two".[10] In its mild form interference is virtually indistinguishable from normal foreign policy activity, although more extreme forms can be tantamount to subversion. Thus intervention deviates from the internationally acknowledged norms of peaceful co-existence and non-intervention.[11] More recently, intervention has acquired a second general meaning, where it refers to a spectrum of actions undertaken in the name of peace and security. This special form of activity requires elaborate rationales and is based on a defined body of international law and precedent.[12]

From this it is evident that the descriptive and operational utility of the concept weakens due to the ambivalent and complex nature of intervention, the notion that all conflict between states is intervention,[13] and the fact that the concept covers an ever-widening spectrum of phenomena and fields of activity. It ranges from the limited legalistic notion of variform unsanctioned foreign attempts at reshaping the internal politics of sovereign states by means of dictatorial or coercive interference in their spheres of jurisdiction,[14] through undesirable activity that is not approved by the international community,[15] to the more inclusive notion of collective foreign political engagement sanctioned by multilateral institutions in pursuit of universal values and involving the entire spectrum of coercive techniques.[16] Intervention thus becomes the proverbial "twilight area" where power, self-interest, international law and morality meet as constitutive elements of the international system.[17] As a result a definitive notion or universally acceptable definition of the concept is singularly absent, making most attempts to define intervention somewhat static and futile.[18] More is to be gained by investigating the phenomenon than by defining the word.

Although the problem of definition applies to military intervention as well, the delimitation of the latter is only necessary. Notwithstanding the fact that it constitutes only a small segment of the intervention field, military intervention represents the most basic and traditional type of intervenient behaviour most closely associated with war.[19] It involves (military) force as an instrument of foreign policy, but is also specifically concerned with perceived national interests and foreign policy objectives. As a higher profile form of intervention, military intervention thus not only deviates from the norm of non-intervention, but also from the normal pattern of relations between the target state and the intervener.[20] Not even the contemporary peaceful intervention roles of military forces or the alleged declining role of the military instrument detract from military intervention still being regarded as a prominent feature, albeit not the norm, of the international system.[21]

Specific conditions, however, distinguish military intervention from any other use of force.[22] For example, military intervention requires an asymmetry in power between the intervener and the target state — that is the intervener should be more powerful; that the use of force should be limited with regard to the force levels involved and the duration of the operation; that as an instrument of foreign policy it should be used to achieve a specific goal determined by politics; and that it should have the potential to escalate the conflict between the intervener and the intervened on an assumed "ladder of escalation", above coercive diplomacy but below limited war. Furthermore, a specific distinction can be made between (classical) war and military intervention.[23] The principal domain or epicentre of war is interstate, but that of military intervention is intrastate; the central objective of war is territorial conquest aimed at transforming the international order, while that of military intervention is to affect the domestic affairs of a state by maintaining or changing its political authority structure; and the basic strategy of war is primarily military and secondarily political, whereas that of military intervention is primarily political and secondarily military. Bearing these essential features in mind, Otte provides the following descriptive definition of military intervention:[24]

> Military intervention is the planned limited use of force for a transitory period by a state (or a group of states)

against a weaker state in order to change or maintain the target state's domestic structure or to change its external policies; it is the continuation of politics with the limited addition of means of military force in order to re-establish the normal pattern of bilateral relations by forcing the opponent into compliance. Military intervention is a rigid instrument that does not leave any room for concessions to be made to the intervened and that embraces the risk of escalation.

From this it is evident that military intervention is complex and highly context-dependent, that it fulfils an international order function, and that as an instrument of statecraft involving (military) force, it remains essentially of a political nature.[25] Although this definition encapsulates the generic features of military intervention, most other definitions of military intervention tend either to broaden or limit the concept by respectively making it more inclusive or exclusive. In addition, stipulative adjectives such as "foreign", "external" and "overt" are added, thereby producing very specific operational definitions and also a typology of military intervention. Two main groups of definitions can be distinguished in those attributing either a limited or a comprehensive scope to military intervention.

Tillema, for example, adopts the more limited approach by defining foreign overt military intervention as the "form of intervenient behavior... (that) includes all authoritative military operations that directly involve a state in foreign combat or unilaterally and irrevocably commit regular military forces to combat should resistance be met".[26] In operational terms this translates into direct combatant or combat-preparatory military operations conducted upon foreign territory by units of a state's regular military forces.[27] These combat-related interventions include conventional deployments of ground combat units that involve actions ranging from alert patrol, through riot quelling, to battle; as well as less intense actions ranging from small unit raids, through aerial bombing, to artillery, gunnery and rocketry. Accordingly, as an operative "act of war" stripped of moral and legal connotations "(a)ll combat-ready foreign military operations undertaken by regular military forces, and only such operations, constitute overt military intervention".[28] This delimitation specifically excludes operations conducted by a state within its own integral territory; less blatant interfering acts ranging from covert operations, through shows of force and military assistance, to peace support operations that do not directly involve overt military intervention as defined above; and incidents confined to small arms cross-border fire and engagements or encounters among aircraft and naval vessels. Military intervention is hereby also visibly distinguished from the private (mercenary) use of force, from civil military action and from the intervenient use of armed force by non-state actors such as terrorist groups and national liberation movements. Thus foreign overt military intervention is "distinctive military behavior that is necessary and sufficient to initiate contemporary armed conflict and that is a necessary but not sufficient condition for contemporary international war.... (and thus) a recognizable form of intervention that is not necessarily limited in magnitude, legality and lethal consequence".[29]

In principle, Vertzberger's conceptual definition of foreign military intervention corresponds with that of Otte, inasmuch as he defines it as "coercive state-organized and state-controlled, convention-breaking, goal-orientated activities by one sovereign state in the territory of another, activities directed at its political authority structure with the purpose of preserving or changing that structure, affecting thereby its domestic political process, and/or certain of its foreign policies by usurping its autonomous decisionmaking authority through the use of extensive military force".[30] Similar to Tillema, his operational definition also limits the scope of foreign military intervention to combat and combat-ready activities by relating it to the following indicators, namely "the direct, overt commitment of uniformed, combat-ready military formations, including ground forces... to conduct, when necessary, conventional ground warfare operations that are, in expressed purpose, continuous but limited in time".[31] The use of military advisers or irregular forces in covert operations is also specifically excluded since these and other intervenient actions, not being large-scale and overt, are regarded as military "involvement" and not military intervention.[32] Schraeder, however, does not exclude covert forms of military intervention.[33] As an expansion of the combat-related conceptualisation he specifically identifies paramilitary intervention as a distinct subtype which he defines as "economic and military aid to an armed insurgency intent on overthrowing a government deemed inimical to (own) foreign policy interests..."[34] It is used in situations where direct or overt intervention would be counterproductive, and it represents a proxy utilisation of armed force in a covert mode.

Freedman also adopts a more conventional approach by defining military intervention as "the use of armed force to influence the character and course of a developing conflict which is neither taking place upon nor directly threatening national territory, and does not touch upon any specific obligation to allies".[35] Implicitly he does, however, open the possibility for broader interpretations by elevating conflict to a position where it becomes the focal point of military intervention, irrespective of whether it occurs within a single state or involves a number of states. Depending on its development, the conflict can involve sporadic fighting to large-scale battles. In this respect military intervention is nonetheless distinguished from other contingencies involving armed force. This distinction is based on the absence of truly vital interests and the lack of a strategic imperative since neither the intervener nor its allies are directly at risk.[36]

Dunér, on the other hand, by concentrating on the anatomy of intervention in civil (internal) wars, presents a more wide-ranging definition of military intervention. At first glance he appears to limit external military intervention "to acts which affect one party's military fighting or capacity to fight the opposing party".[37] Since he focuses on the level of involvement — that is on the amount of force and the instruments used — the level of intervention actually refers to the closeness or immediacy of intervention acts to the battle situation. Paradoxically, by including the phrases "military fighting" and "capacity to fight" in his definition, he actually broadens the scope of military intervention by making provision for intervenient acts of a direct and an indirect nature, ranging through combat involvement, paracombat involvement and supporting activities.[38] According to this viewpoint, and based on the levels and instruments he includes, military intervention extends well beyond combat and combat-ready involvement to include a variety of activities and forms of interference considered by others to be military "involvement".

This definitional expansion is taken yet a step further by the distinction made between coercive[39] and peaceful intervention. By implication the former includes military instruments, and therefore corresponds with the conventional view of coercive military intervention involving combat and combat-ready actions. Peaceful (military) intervention, however, departs significantly from the traditional notion since it is predominantly non-combat and non-forcible in nature. It makes provision for the intervenient use of military forces in a peaceful capacity, as part of a multilateral security regime that encompasses a broad spectrum of peace-orientated approaches to conflict and humanitarian assistance involving peace support operations.[40] In this respect the distinctive role of the armed forces is helping to bring about a peace while the fighting continues; providing relief for those caught up in the fighting; and helping to keep the peace once it has been agreed.[41] Although some of these (military) activities actually predate the 1990s, for example peacekeeping, this development is more specifically linked to initiatives proposed by the United Nations (UN) Secretary-General, Boutros Boutros-Ghali, in his 1992 *An Agenda for Peace*.[42] As envisaged, multilateral peaceful intervention is based upon collective security regimes. It specifically provides for non-combat military intervention in the form of preventive deployments, peacekeeping and (pre- and post-conflict) peace building, as well as for (potential) combat and therefore forcible military intervention in the form of peace enforcement.[43] Thus military intervention is extended beyond the traditional confines of the predominantly (but not exclusively) unilateral combatant and coercive use of military force, to the domain of multilateral, non-combatant peaceful intervention in the form of peace support operations conducted under the auspices of inter-governmental organisations.

Since it is used in an ambivalent manner, the concept of humanitarian intervention is also problematic. Although it is often related and sometimes even regarded as synonymous with peaceful intervention, it is actually a particular variation of coercive military intervention that differs merely in respect of the humanitarian cause that it serves. Arend and Beck define humanitarian intervention as "the use of armed force by a state (or states) to protect citizens of the target state from large-scale human rights violations there".[44] People suffering human rights abuses are the unit level of analysis, rather than the state as is usually the case. Although humanitarian intervention is ostensibly directed at an over-strong and repressive state government that violates human rights on a massive scale, it can in theory be directed at non-governmental actors such as ethnic groups indulging in ethnic genocide. It is, however, also argued that the present context of humanitarian intervention includes vicious internal conflicts associated with over-weak or contested governments, and that it is no longer confined to human rights violations but extends to upholding international humanitarian law and providing humanitarian assistance. It is furthermore contended that it lies at a range of possibilities ambiguously related to non-forcible peacekeeping and a range of non-military cross-border enterprises.[45]

Strictly speaking, humanitarian intervention should be distinguished from intervention to protect nationals, intervention to facilitate self-determination, and humanitarian relief operations linked to the collective use of force under the UN Charter or mandated by regional organisations.[46] Although humanitarian motives are often cited to justify intervention, genuine instances of humanitarian intervention are rare, if they have occurred at all.[47] By definition humanitarian intervention falls within the narrower conceptualisation and is limited to the use of military force for altruistic humanitarian objectives, the humanitarian rationale being predominant.[48] Humanitarian intervention is, however, often (erroneously) associated with peaceful intervention, illustrative of the more comprehensive approach. As such it is used "in a very broad sense to cover non-forcible action for humanitarian reasons",[49] approaching what should preferably be called humanitarian assistance or humanitarian relief operations supportive of or supplementary to peaceful intervention.

A major problem with peaceful intervention and the more liberal interpretation of humanitarian intervention, is that the use of both runs counter to the previously held norm of non-intervention and the related tenets and rules of international law that govern justified intervention. Apart from the presumed non-combatant nature of these types of intervention, four additional characteristics distinguish them from their coercive, combat-related counterparts. Firstly, they give concrete expression to the emerging norm of intervention in the pursuit of peace and humanitarian concerns, particularly where ethnic genocide and the gross violation of human rights occur. This provides an additional (post-1989) reason for justifiable intervention. Secondly, as collective intervention, multilateral peace support operations require a mandate from the UN in the form of a Security Council resolution (and similar resolutions from other intergovernmental organisations), as well as impartiality or neutrality on the part of the intervening forces. This is noticeably different from overt foreign military intervention that is undertaken as a one-sided action (irrespective of whether one or more states intervene), at the explicit invitation and on behalf of a party to the conflict. Thirdly, these interventions must also be mandated and legitimised by broad acceptance by the international community of states, that is the "critical mass of nations".[50] Finally, these interventions do not always comply with the established legal precepts that govern overt foreign military intervention. In some instances no request for intervention was made in advance by the government or governing authority of the target territory, particularly where peace enforcement was involved.[51] In these instances collective military intervention was unilaterally initiated by and undertaken under the

### TABLE I: TYPOLOGY OF MILITARY INTERVENTION

| AUTHOR(S) | TYPOLOGY | DESCRIPTION | APPROACH |
|---|---|---|---|
| Tillema, H K | Overt foreign military intervention | Overt, combat and combat-ready, coercive | Limited |
| Vertzberger, Y Y I | Foreign military intervention | Overt, combat and combat-ready, coercive | Limited |
| Schraeder, P J | Paramilitary intervention | Covert, combat and combat-ready, supportive, coercive, proxy | Limited |
| Freedman, L | Military intervention | Conflict and combat-related(fighting) | Limited |
| Dunér, B | External military intervention | Overt, combat and combat-ready, paracombat, supportive, direct and indirect, coercive | Comprehensive |
| *An Agenda for Peace* | Peaceful intervention | Overt, combat and non-combat, peace support, direct, coercive and co-operative | Comprehensive |
| Various | Humanitarian intervention | By definition overt, combat and combat-ready and coercive, but often linked to peaceful intervention and confused with humanitarian assistance and relief | Limited, but often regarded as comprehensive |

auspices of an intergovernmental organisation, to be condoned, mandated and sanctioned after the event by the said organisation. This means that actions and means are used that are morally justified and not illegal, but are not yet legally regulated and are therefore non-legal.[52]

Considering these divergent definitions and types of military intervention, suffice it to conclude that both the theorist and practitioner should take cognisance of the various possibilities (summarised in Table 1). An eclectic approach is recommended where the choice of a particular definition and subtype(s) is dependent on the purpose of their application and on personal preferences. Notwithstanding the existence of more inclusive definitions, the discussion in the subsequent chapters is limited to the combat-related conceptualisation of foreign military intervention as an intervenient act of a forcible nature. This is not to imply that other forms of military "intervention and/or involvement" are inapplicable to or non-existent in sub-Saharan Africa. They do, however, fall beyond the scope and purpose of this work.

## 3. THE CONTEXT OF MILITARY INTERVENTION

Since the historical and legal dimensions are covered by later chapters, it is sufficient to discuss briefly the political, military and ethical context of contemporary military intervention.

### 3.1 Political context

Intervention by means of military force emanates from and penetrates the political context. The political context is indicative of the geopolitical prospects and constraints that impact on military intervention. Bearing in mind that military intervention is neither a new phenomenon, nor tied to any particular international system,[53] an overview is given of the pre-Cold War, the Cold War and the post-Cold War eras.

Concerning the pre-Cold War era (pre-1945), it is important to note that military intervention predates the modern state system, and examples can be traced back to antiquity. But it has become more prevalent since the 17th century, reaching an apex during the 19th century. In an era of European major power conflict and alliance formation, military intervention was generally recognised as a function of the prevailing multilateral balance of power system and an instrument of statecraft with profound effect. During this period the basis was also laid for the body of international law governing intervention that duly evolved. Of equal significance was the development of the political "rules of the game" — namely that since military intervention served the interests of major powers, it was not to be used by major powers among themselves but as an accepted and "civilised" way of dealing with "less civilised" and weaker states peripheral to the "Concert of Europe"; that as a co-operative venture military intervention was not a purely military exercise, but one that demanded diplomatic preparation; and that support for the legitimacy of intervention was important.[54] As an antecedent and precursor of contemporary world politics, the pre-Cold War era typified the politics of power and dominance. It thereby cloaked military intervention in international political realism and institutionalised it as a prerogative of major powers.

The most enduring features of the Cold War era (1945-1989) were a dominant bipolar structure based on the superpower status of the United States of America (USA) and the Soviet Union; acute ideological divisions underpinning rigid alliance systems; a structural balance based on self-restraint and nuclear deterrence; major power "cold" war in the central Euro-Atlantic theatre and "hot" proxy conflict through surrogates in the peripheral Third World; increasing military stratification due to nuclear proliferation and technology warfare; growing economic polarisation between North and South; the proliferation of intrastate war; and the ascendancy of high risk foreign policy options in pursuit of national interests.[55] Thus the Cold War period differed significantly from the era preceding it.

The Cold War did not leave military intervention unaffected. On the one hand, such intervention had to contend with the ramifications of change. In particular it had to accommodate the advent of nuclear weapons and subsequent changes in warfare; the postcolonial political pluralism and changes in international politics; the desire to contain ideological expansion; the utility of military force residing in its threat or limited use; and the Third World as a surrogate forum for superpower competition.[56] On the other hand, it had to contend with international law and humanitarian inputs that urged caution and non-involvement. Since respect for sovereignty was the norm, governments alone decided on the implementation of the human rights regime and were not held accountable for their human rights record (apartheid South Africa being a notable exception). Within the central balance, respect for sovereignty prevented humanitarian intervention and entailed respect for the territorial integrity of existing states.[57] Outside or peripheral to the central balance these principles were often subjugated to political expediency, with the result that overt and proxy military intervention became fairly common.

In assessing external intervention in the Third World, Bull summarises the unfavourable conditions that existed during the post-1945 period. These conditions are the growth in the will and capacity of Third World countries to resist intervention; the decline in the will and capacity of the Western world to intervene openly and directly in the Third World; the growing power of the Soviet Union and its allies and their commitment as the champion of the oppressed and unliberated, making Western intervention more difficult and risk laden; the emergence of a global equilibrium unfavourable to intervention; and the emergence of a new climate of legitimacy limiting intervention. In response to these constraints new interveners emerged from the ranks of the communist fold and the Third World (for example the Soviet Union, the People's Republic of China, Vietnam, India, Indonesia, Libya and Cuba); changes occurred in the form of intervention, with the introduction of non-forcible, indirect, clandestine and covert intervention; and intervention between rich and poor, strong and weak, centre and periphery became a reflection and a very part of the structure of the international system.[58]

Urged on by the strategic impetus of the Cold War, military intervention became an extension of geopolitical interventionism. It was furthermore regarded as a viable instrument of foreign policy that found constant application. Since it became less practical in its traditional form (the Suez fiasco providing proof of this), proxy warfare in the Third World gave ample opportunity for the elaborate "game" of new military intervention, particularly in its covert form. As such, military intervention gained prominence, was used more frequently and became more dangerous.[59] However, as used during this era, it often foundered or became protracted. Although this was in part due to structural constraints imposed by the bipolar international system, the real reason was that it engendered a combination of indigenous national resistance and counterintervention organised by opposed geopolitical actors.[60] Although this did not dissuade states from using military intervention, it increased the long term cost-risks thereof and also raised the political-ideological stakes of involvement and the threshold of disengagement.

The post-Cold War political era (post-1989) reflects geopolitical transition and an emergent world order characterised by a dramatic increase in state and non-state actors; high levels of ideological homogeneity; increasing globalisation; a multipolar global structure dominated by the US as the sole remaining superpower; democratic peace; multilateralism; and neofunctional integration. It is, however, also characterised by the increasing marginalisation of the South; the exacerbation of the internal weaknesses of many Third World countries; the prevalence of regional conflicts and internal war, enhanced by the resurgence of virulent ethnic nationalism and religious fundamentalism; the proliferation of weapons of mass destruction; and the fear of unbounded rogue states and terrorist organisations.[61] With the disappearance of a single dominant security threat and growing instability in a less predictable international environment, the post-Cold

War era is one without a discernible profile where international actors have to contend with an amorphous security concept, a new set of security problems and a compromised security agenda.[62]

This environment has had a threefold effect on military intervention. Firstly, it has induced a shift in interventionary diplomacy away from geopolitical interventionism towards support for humanitarian claims to alleviate human suffering. The new humanitarian interventionism of the 1990s was expressed strongly in US foreign policy and enacted and channelled through the UN and the North Atlantic Treaty Organisation (NATO).[63] Since then it has found similar expression in the foreign policies and activities of several regional powers and organisations. It is a development that has furthermore compromised the norm of non-intervention, since international law, and humanitarian and liberal-democratic regimes not only demand but also create opportunities for the application of the emergent norm and new forms of intervention. Although welcomed from a purely normative legal-moral perspective, this approach has been vehemently criticised,[64] and has also foundered because of the stand-off between the authority to intervene and the lack of resources and political will to do so.[65]

Secondly, notwithstanding attitudes of collective responsibility and compassion, and the growing demand for humanitarian intervention, major powers are increasingly reluctant to become embroiled in military intervention beyond the confines of their geopolitical and national interests. The critical geopolitics of humanitarian intervention, typifying an anti-interventionary mood, often discourages action at the regional or global level.[66] This stance is reinforced by the prohibitive financial costs of such action, and by the fact that intervention is deemed feasible only in territorially clearly defined units.

Humanitarian intervention, in contrast, is most particular to divided or disintegrating territorial units fraught with dangers and a high risk of complete failure.[67] Thus parallel to the emergence of new interventionism there has also been an avoidance of intervention, even in the face of extreme humanitarian emergencies. The UN position is not unrelated to this predicament, being one of uncertainty and an amalgam of contradictions with no clearly defined solution. Hence the role of the UN is dictated by the permanent members of the Security Council. The major powers are neither prepared to accept the undermining of the UN by other states — and thus uphold the UN role to preserve its symbolic position[68] — nor inclined to respond automatically to and meet all requests for humanitarian intervention.

Thirdly, since the post-Cold War environment has seen the re-emergence of all those traditional imperatives and elements of international order and security that were reduced in importance during the Cold War,[69] it is conducive to the continuation of geopolitically driven military intervention at a regional level. It is, for example, an environment where nation, statehood, sovereignty and territoriality have again become important; where it is necessary to balance the external encouragement of nationalistic tendencies toward self-determination with adequate protection of human rights;[70] where the vestiges of former colonial empires remain in the interests of and continue to require the support of former colonial powers, most of whom have had a long history of using military intervention; where the most-developed countries are still dependent on essential raw materials, including oil; and where the internal and external pressures for the use of military intervention have increased in response to the threat posed by ethnic unrest, non-democratic regimes and the proliferation of missile technology and weapons of mass destruction.[71] It is also an environment where the borders between soldiering and statecraft have become blurred. Despite initial expectations to the contrary, the weak prohibitions of the post-Cold War environment have increased the incentives and opportunities for military intervention.

## 3.2 Military context

The military context pertains to the nature of warfare and expected patterns of conflict that impact on military intervention. Considering that violence between and within states is still common and also bearing in mind that military activity is always spasmodic and variable, Freedman argues that "contemporary trends have served to invalidate traditional models of war".[72] This viewpoint is based on the notions that the structure of international politics has a greater influence on warfare than changes in military technology; that there is rarely a straight symmetry between political aims and military means; that wars create their own political stakes beyond the immediate concerns of the belligerents; that the connections between a particular conflict and the rest of the international community are a crucial part of the military art; and that the preferred way of fighting all wars is from a safe distance, using military instruments and forms of combat of sharp and efficient direction that provide high political pay-offs at a low human cost. However, there still exists a feared form of warfare that tends to be vicious and militia-based. This strategy is also increasingly geared to conditions of external, and possibly Western, military involvement. As a result states are extremely wary of entering into conflict – their first requirement of entrance is a credible exit strategy. Since military involvement has become more discretionary, belligerents must work hard to persuade external powers either to get in or stay out.[73]

In considering the relationship between the nature of warfare and military intervention, three factors can be noted. Firstly, it is obvious that the present and future nature of warfare is not only more conducive to military intervention, but that military intervention is in fact becoming an integral part of this form of warfare. As such the distinction between limited war, military intervention and coercive diplomacy becomes extremely difficult, if not impossible, to maintain – also considering the fact that political semantics and rhetoric add to, rather than clarify, this confusion. Secondly, since it is argued that the aim will not be the total destruction or complete rout of opponents, but rather minimum destruction, minimum bloodshed and the partial defeat of opponents, military intervention in a preventive or responsive mode provides an alternative involving the coercive use of military force short of limited war. Thirdly, the distinctiveness of separate political and military domains associated with the more traditional conceptualisation of warfare is seriously compromised. Although the link between politics and military strategy is not in dispute, the point is that the salience of military intervention in warfare not only introduces a more prominent and decisive role to politics in warfare, but in fact politicises warfare to a level not previously experienced.

The patterns of conflict are expected to enhance these trends. Blacker identifies six clusters of conflicts: wars of national liberation; wars of territorial conquest or aggrandisement; wars over natural resources; wars caused or exacerbated by ethnic, racial and/or religious differences; proxy wars; and small- to large-scale military interventions undertaken or led by superpowers.[74] Apart from the fact that these clusters are not peculiar to any particular international system and persist over time, they do not by definition exclude military intervention. They also easily fit into the basic distinction made between interstate and intrastate war, or more specifically between international, civil and mixed conflict. Military intervention is primarily (although not exclusively) associated with civil and mixed conflict. A civil conflict exists when a state is experiencing domestic unrest, taking the form of low intensity unrest, civil war, wars of secession and wars of unification.[75] Mixed conflicts have both international and civil dimensions and result from the military intervention by a state (or states) in a civil conflict, either in support of the government or the rebel group(s). As most civil conflicts involve outside intervention, mixed conflict can also be associated with the counterintervention of a third party.[76]

Since 1945 the majority of international conflicts have been internal wars. This trend will most likely continue well into the future because civil and mixed conflicts, involving substate groups fighting for political, economic, social and personal reasons where national governments are unable to govern their territories effectively, are expected to be the norm. These conflicts will mostly be found in a grouping of "third tier" states, that is in ungovernable and failed states.[77] As a result the international security environment is expected to be sharply bifurcated. At its centre, deterrence and therefore peace will prevail. If conflict does arise, it is expected to relate to civil unrest caused by prolonged economic recession, chronic unemployment, social alienation, etc.; the struggle for greater regional autonomy within, or political independence from, existing state structures; and explosions in tensions between indigenous populations and national minorities. In the periphery and the third tier, the potential for conflict is likely to be much greater. Although similar conditions as in the centre will exist, these will be exacerbated by high levels of persistent civil strife; nationalism — ethnic nationalism in particular; resource scarcity and a demand for raw materials; and religious fundamentalism. The potential for conflict in the periphery is also expected to be much higher, owing to the declining ability and willingness of the US, the UN and other international or regional organisations to secure order. The most serious and threatening challenges are, however, expected to occur at the juncture of this fault line between centre and periphery.[78] As a result the present increase in intrastate conflict (internal and civil wars) is most likely to continue, bearing in mind that interstate conflict at a regional level also cannot be totally excluded.

In considering the relationship between military intervention and the patterns and sources of conflict, a further three factors can be noted. Firstly, it is obvious that the very nature of expected conflict favours military intervention as a preventive or coercive response. These conflicts and their root causes create the typical conditions under which the use of military intervention is currently considered and justified along humanitarian and liberal-democratic lines. Secondly, since most of these conflicts and their causes are essentially non-military, the intrinsic political nature of military intervention makes this type of intervenient action more suitable for dealing with the political complexities of the conflict. Thirdly, although altruistic and humanitarian concerns are prominent, the fact cannot be ignored that military intervention remains an instrument of statecraft that can further self-interest in the context of political realism. In this respect it should be borne in mind that the purported altruistic rationale of military intervention may serve as a pretext for the pursuance of hegemonic aspirations, in particular where regional power intervention is involved.

## 3.3 Ethical context

Military intervention cannot be separated from the ethics of world politics and confronts the decision maker with moral dilemmas.[79] It has always been regarded as an "enemy" of the ruling norms and principles of international relations — those of sovereignty, self-determination and territorial integrity in particular.[80] Since the ethical context of military intervention is integral to the discussion of the international law regime and just war principles that follows at a later stage,[81] suffice it to refer briefly to its dual significance. Firstly, with reference to intervention in general and humanitarian and peaceful intervention in particular, ethical concerns are a major cause, and therefore a primary source, of justification for the intervenient use of military force. In this respect the notion of legitimate or justifiable intervention relates to a rights-based approach to intervention — that is, the circumstances that justify and the rules that dictate and regulate forcible intervention. These include those pertaining to the protection of a state's citizens abroad, self-defence, self-determination, treaty obligations and humanitarian reasons. However, as Paskins implies, these ethical concerns also relate to a virtue-based approach to intervention that emphasises the virtues of humanity, justice, prudence and fortitude.[82]

Secondly, if linked to justifiable intervention as viewed from the South, and also considering the negative Cold War connotations of military intervention, the ethical context comes into play as a necessary condition for the reversal of negative perceptions regarding the usefulness of intervention in contemporary world politics. Since intervention is one way in which states can act collectively for the common good, views on intervention are highly dependent on the rationale, objective and actual mode of intervention. Hence a dialogue that explores commonalties and justifies intervention is required to promote the feeling that international norms do help regulate world affairs; the positive values in the international community, one of which might be intervention itself; and the elements such as democracy, law, information and education that underpin the emerging world society and the use of intervention.[83] As such the ethical context serves both as a constraint that limits the excesses usually associated with military intervention, and as a forum for a discourse that aims to remove distrust of the justified use of military intervention.

## 4. ANATOMY OF MILITARY INTERVENTION

Additional information concerning the what, why, who, how, where and when of its use is provided by the following anatomy of military intervention (Figure 1).[84] An exhaustive analysis is not intended and the main emphasis is on its fundamental nature and key features.

### 4.1 Categories

Military intervention, as previously indicated, is variform. Depending on the criteria used, different categories can be distinguished. Concerning the number of actors involved in the intervenient action, a basic distinction is made between the unilateral and multilateral forms of military intervention. Whereas unilateral intervention involves a single state as intervener, multilateral intervention involves more than one state or a group of states. In respect of its contemporary use the latter refers either to the involvement of two or more states, not necessarily acting in concert; or to what is commonly known as collective intervention — that is, intervention undertaken by, or in the name and under the auspices of, an intergovernmental organisation such as the UN. The significance of this distinction, however, extends beyond the mere number of actors involved and also relates to the justification of the intervention. In general, collective intervention possesses a legitimacy not normally accorded to unilateral intervention. Whereas the modern international

*Military intervention: nature and scope*

## FIGURE 1: ANATOMY OF MILITARY INTERVENTION

| LOCUS | FORM | LEVEL | DURATION | PEACEFUL MODE | | | | | CONFLICT COERCIVE MODE | | |
|---|---|---|---|---|---|---|---|---|---|---|---|
| | | | | SUPPORTIVE | COMBAT | SUPPORTIVE | PARACOMBAT | COMBAT | SUPPORTIVE | PARACOMBAT | COMBAT |
| Humanitarian | Multilateral | Massive | Protracted | Peace restoration strategies | Peace enforcement strategies | Military warning | Advisory | Invasion (regular) | | | |
| Internal | | Medium | | Peacekeeping | Peace enforcement | Transport | Arms supply | Specialist functions | | | |
| | | | | | | Base facilities | | | | | |
| | | | | **COLLABORATION** | | | | | | | |
| Regional | | Limited | Quick-decisive | Peace building strategies | Peace maintenance strategies | Food and medicine | Training | Invasion (irregular) | | | |
| | Unilateral | Non-intervention | | Pre- and post-conflict peace building | Preventive deployment | Storage facilities | Blockade | Strikes, bombing and shelling | | | |
| Extraregional | | | | | | Safe passage | Financial support | | | | |
| | | | | | | Arms sales | | | | | |

DIRECT / INDIRECT

**CATEGORIES OF MILITARY INTERVENTION**

**CATEGORIES OF WARFARE AND CONFLICT**

| Intrastate | Mixed conflict | Interstate |
|---|---|---|
| Civil conflict | | International conflict |

**POLICY, ETHICAL AND LEGAL CONTEXT**

| Morality (idealism) | | National interest (realism) |
|---|---|---|
| Justice | Permissible intervention | Order |
| Intervention by right | | Intervention by might |

27

community does not approve of intervention by a single state and considers it to be an undesirable and even illegal activity, collective intervention is widely seen as proper and desirable since it has been authorised by an international body having widespread legitimacy.[85]

In their description of combat-related military intervention, Jentleson and Levite distinguish between protracted and quick-decisive foreign military intervention. This distinction is based upon three descriptive factors namely the duration of the military intervention as measured from the "getting in" to the "getting out" or "drawn-down" (to pre-intervention levels of non-combatant stationed forces) stage; the severity of the intervention as measured by the casualties suffered by the intervener; and the resultant outcome in terms of objectives attained and costs incurred.[86] Protracted foreign military intervention is longer in duration, more severe regarding casualties, and more high risk in respect of the significance of objectives and costs than quick-decisive intervention. This distinction is less typological since it does not reside in the essential nature of military intervention, but in its duration, severity and significance.

Depending on the degree of major power involvement according to the scope and duration of the intervention, and the degree of willingness to use force, Miller distinguishes between four levels of intervention.[87] These are massive intervention, which refers to a large-scale deployment of forces in reaction to a regional crisis, and a willingness to resort to them unless demands and objectives are met within a finite time period (>100000 troops and the massive use of firepower); medium intervention, which refers to medium-scale involvement and a considerable willingness to use force and to maintain the deployment for a considerable period of time (>10000 troops and maximum use of firepower); limited intervention, which refers to low-level military engagement on a temporary basis, with a limited willingness to use force (>1000 troops and limited use of firepower); and non-intervention, which refers to no military intervention, with the exception of the occasional use of airpower, supported by diplomatic and economic involvement. Non-intervention, also known as negative intervention, paradoxically is an unorthodox form of intervention in terms of which abstention constitutes a premeditated and wide-ranging act of interference in the affairs of a state.[88] Since these criteria concern major power involvement, it would be appropriate to adjust the scale of intervention downward in the case of regional power intervention in the South.

More peculiar to the South, and based on the argument that the use of military force to further the national interest is not out of place in this particular part of the world, Croft and Treacher distinguish between regional power intervention and internal intervention as distinct from extraregional military intervention.[89] These categories are indicative of the geographical locus of the intervention relative to the intervener. They also denote a particular unit level of intervention typical of the South without implying a difference in the intrinsic nature of military intervention. Regional power intervention focuses on "the actions of the most powerful states in a particular region, or of those states which wish to attain that status".[90] This includes the pursuance of regional hegemony through the use of force or the forcible removal of actual or potential threats to existing regional hegemony. In this category the interests of the state are paramount and may be termed expansionist in power terms. Internal intervention "considers the use of the military instrument by governments not against their neighbours but, rather, against their own population. In such cases, military forces are used by political and military elites to intervene in political and security developments within the state, to prevent particular groups from obtaining, or maintaining, a particular position of military power".[91] Thus it refers to the use of violence in a state, by a ruling elite against others deemed to be enemies, as a major source of insecurity.

Finally, depending on the instruments and type of military action involved, several self-explanatory categories can be distinguished that include defensive and offensive military intervention; coercive (forcible) and non-coercive (non-forcible) military intervention; direct and indirect military intervention; overt and covert military intervention; and intermittent, competitive, collective, parallel and expansionist intervention.[92] These categories denote various subtypes of military intervention, and it suffices merely to only take note of them.

## 4.2 Justification, objectives and motives

Because the correlate principles of sovereignty and non-intervention form the basis of contemporary international relations, military intervention always requires justification. This justification is intimately linked to the legality of the objectives of armed intervention, as well as the principles of justice these objectives serve. As such the non-intervention and just war doctrines provide the most important legal and ethical foundations for the lawful, legitimate and justified use of military intervention, bearing in mind that the content and implementation of these doctrines are subject to change and varying interpretations. With the exception of a brief reference to their policy relevance, the legal and ethical complexities of these issues fall beyond the scope of this analysis. It is, however, necessary to comment briefly on the declared and attributed objectives and motives commonly used to justify intervention. These cover a wide spectrum ranging from intervention by right, through permissible or lawful intervention not based on right, to state practice guided by the national interest.[93] Geldenhuys provides a useful framework by distinguishing between three broad categories of objectives — namely, political, socio-economic and security objectives.[94]

Political objectives are highly diverse and include remedying intrastate injustices, the pursuance of national liberation or self-determination, democratisation, re-unification, political stability, policy change, changing existing authority structures and influencing the balance of intrastate political forces. Owing to specific demands of the time or prevailing causes such as historical, imperial and ideological destiny or responsibility, some of these political objectives are dictated by considerations of higher legitimacy and therefore become more salient. Although some Third World (South) countries have at times maintained that normally intervention is not justified at any time,[95] others have claimed the right to intervene to support those fighting racist or colonialist regimes.[96] Currently, African states also reserve the right to intervene in response to imminent or actual *coup d'états* that pose a threat to democratic reform and transformation.[97] Socio-economic objectives concerning the target state, irrespective of whether they are benign or malign, include humanitarian relief and assistance, the promotion of economic development, the enhancement of general welfare, structural adjustments, changing economic activities and undermining economic capabilities. The intervener can also pursue own economic gain. Security objectives include the protection of own nationals abroad, anticipatory or responsive self-defence, conflict termination, law and order, and improving or undermining the defensive capabilities of a state. However, in its post-Cold War context and indicative of the movement away from non-interventionism towards benign interventionism, collective intervention authorised and sanctioned by an international organisation tends to focus on a range of principal objectives that have acquired "new prominence" and "greater substance". These include humanitarian relief and assistance, the promotion of democracy and good governance, state (re)building, nation building, self-determination and peace promotion.[98]

Another way of addressing the issue of justification, objectives and motive is to consider situations that permit acts of multilateral coercive intervention. Haas lists the following – to prevent and punish aggression by one state against another; in a civil war, to re-impose peace terms that resulted from UN peacemaking on one party that has reneged; to enforce international agreements banning the possession or manufacture of, or trade in weapons of mass destruction; to enforce agreements banning or limiting trade in conventional arms, including trade in dual-use or forbidden technologies; to prevent an event certified by experts as an immediate, impending ecological catastrophe; to prevent genocide; to protect an established democratic polity from antidemocratic armed challenges, but not to protect a dubious or fictitious one; and to prevent famine and mass epidemics.[99] He also refers to situations that may make coercive acts justifiable, bearing in mind that governments differ on the extent to which intervention is allowed or disallowed in all or some of these situations. Apart from the above, these situations include preventing a dangerous crime from being committed; preventing international economic disasters; stopping persistent and gross violations of human rights; and ensuring the exercise of the right to self-determination.[100]

A major problem is that purpose and motive are usually equated with the proclaimed national interest of the interveners. Although the explicit use of military intervention as an instrument of statecraft serving foreign policy is a practice generally frowned upon in world politics, the fact cannot be ignored that national interest, but not necessarily the defence of national security or territorial integrity, is likely to remain paramount as motivation for military intervention. Admittedly, it would always be difficult to distinguish the (arguably disproportionate) exercise of military force for selfish or predatory reasons, or for a strategic advantage, from its use for lawful, justified or humanitarian purposes.[101] The dynamism, uncertainty, complexity and potential destructiveness of military intervention provide adequate scope, but also enhance its utility, for achieving some other and very different objective(s) than that purported or declared. Since military intervention cannot be completely delinked from national interest, and irrespective of the justification, it will always be questioned and deemed suspect by non-beneficiary actors.

## 4.3 Interveners and targets

Specifying the participants involved in military intervention is not as simple as it may appear. The range of actors is dependent on the definition of military intervention that applies. As a point of departure, a basic distinction is made between the intervener and the target — namely those who initiate and undertake the intervention, and those against whom intervention is directed, who are affected by it or who suffer from it. By definition both the intervener and the target would be a state (or independent political community)[102] and/or a group of states. This is based on the fact that the state, apart from being the dominant political entity or prevailing unit of the international system, still exercises a monopoly over the use of armed force. Since the state is a sovereignty-bound collectivity, intervenient action will as a matter of course be undertaken by a representative or agency of the state (such as the government, the defence force or even an intelligence agency). The foreign territory that constitutes the target would include all territory subject to the jurisdiction of the state, as well as non-self-governing territories such as colonies, protectorates, mandated and trust territories or occupied lands not fully integrated within the generally recognised boundaries of the state.[103]

Unless the perpetrator and victim of military intervention are clearly specified, the actors involved will merely be reduced to states.[104] This would create uncertainty about the involvement and status of "quasi-states" enjoying positive (juridical) sovereignty but lacking negative (substantive) sovereignty; "failed or imploded states" without an identifiable, legitimate and recognised government or authority; and a plethora of non-state actors. Similarly, the intervener could also be an intergovernmental organisation (such as the UN), either acting on behalf of member states as a single collectivity in its own right, or by mandating and sanctioning military actions to be undertaken by member states in its name or under its auspices. In the case of paramilitary and covert intervention, private organisations (such as multinational corporations or private/mercenary armies or exiled invasion forces) and other non-state actors (such as ethnic nations, religious groups, rebel forces, national liberation movements, terrorist organisations and even political parties) could also be regarded as interveners if backed by a state or if they act as agents on behalf of a state.[105] They are excluded if they act independently, also considering that their activities would then constitute something other than military intervention (that is, insurgency, mercenary involvement or terrorism). There is an equally broad category of targets. Although at a most general level the state, government, regime, political community, electorate, political leaders and even society would be included, the target could also assume a non-unit character.

For example the target could be internal developments, the actions or capabilities of a state, the structure of political authority and decision-making capabilities. In this respect the target can be described as the "identity of those who make the decisions that are binding for the entire society and/or to the processes through which such decisions are made".[106]

## 4.4 Instruments

Depending on the definition of military intervention, the military action that is undertaken can vary significantly Consequently the list of instruments becomes extremely lengthy. As a minimum the instruments have to be military or have to find a military application. Their use commences on the first day of military action in foreign territory and ceases through either the withdrawal of contingents from the foreign territory or subsequent inactivity among the armed forces remaining in the territory. In a combat-related context the instruments of overt foreign military intervention include, firstly, conventional deployments of ground combat units in alert patrols, offensive manoeuvres, riot quelling, armed occupation of territory, and battle; and, secondly, less intense combatant military actions such as commando or other small unit raids, aerial bombing, strafing and rocketry, ground-based artillery or rocketry, and naval gunnery and rocketry. This viewpoint specifically excludes two categories of instruments. Firstly, it excludes less blatant forms of military interference such as covert operations; military alerts; shows of force; garrison deployments; deployments of non-combat-ready contingents; cross-border incursions not involving territorial occupation or other overt military actions; and the activities of police units, irregular forces, multinational peace forces and international observer groups that do not involve overt military action. Secondly, it excludes sporadic incidents confined to small-arms border fire; engagements between vessels at sea; and encounters between aircraft in flight.[107]

If overt military intervention is extended from combat involvement to paracombat and supportive activities — also making provision for direct and indirect participation — a classification of military instruments is presented (Figure 1):[108] Firstly, direct combat involvement in the form of regular invasion and specialist functions. Regular invasion refers to combat troops sent to the foreign country as part of the intervener's regular forces; while specialist functions are undertaken by specialist military personnel who are incorporated in the weapon systems of a party to the conflict or in those of the intervener. Secondly, indirect combat involvement in the form of irregular invasion and shelling. Irregular invasion refers to the use of irregular forces under the intervener's command in the foreign territory; while shelling means continuous heavy bombardment of the foreign territory carried out by forces not stationed there — that is, from neighbouring territories or from the air. Thirdly, direct paracombat involvement in the form of advisory functions and arms supply. Advisory functions refer to the control of air traffic, airport and communication systems involving advisers dispatched by the intervener; while arms supply refers to the donation of weapons, including token weapon transactions or weapons on loan, to a party to the conflict. Fourthly, indirect paramilitary involvement in the form of military training, armed blockade and financial support. Military training refers to the instruction of the armed forces in a conflict; armed blockade, to military surveillance in order to control military passage to and from the foreign territory; and financial support to monetary assistance of a military nature to a party to the conflict. Fifthly, direct supporting activities in the form of military warning, transport and base functions. Military warning refers to a verbal threat, supported by military deployments, to enter an existing conflict as an intervener; transport, to assistance to a party to the conflict in moving the latter's personnel and weapons through own and/or foreign territory; and base functions, to a host country allowing the concentration of military personnel of a party to a conflict on its territory. Finally, indirect support activities involve further measures an intervener may take to support a party to a conflict — such as the provision of food, medicine and other necessities; arms sales; the use of its territory for storage, etc.

In a wider context, military intervention potentially includes some or all of the instruments specifically excluded from or not included in the above. These can range from covert instruments, such as the training and use of guerrilla insurgencies or organised exile invasion forces, the supply of military weaponry and the provision of transport through contracted airlines;[109] to peace support operations of either a combat or a supportive nature that include peacekeeping, peace building (pre- and post-conflict), preventive deployment and peace enforcement.[110] Although military intervention, particularly involving lethal military force, arguably remains the most important and obvious tool of intervention, it can be augmented by various other instruments. These alternatives include non-forcible coercion in the form of economic leverage, diplomacy and moral suasion, as well as the forcible and coercive use of non-lethal weapons (or less lethal technology) that incapacitate rather than kill personnel and that disable rather than destroy equipment.[111]

The very nature of these instruments and their use supports the idea that military intervention is primarily the prerogative of major powers, regional hegemons and intergovernmental organisations; that it is the prerogative of the more-developed, influential and rich actors in world politics. This corresponds with traditional thinking which has always regarded military intervention as a tool of the powerful against the weak; of older and established states against new states; and of the centre or "inner circle" of world politics against those marginalised or peripheral. A reversal of previous trends has been produced in the South by the proliferation of low-technology warfare; the access to surplus Cold War arms supplies; the availability of more basic but nonetheless lethal weapons; the supply of weapons through past and present proxy intervention; the contracting of mercenary forces or commercially based "security" assistance; and the emerging pattern of arms transfers involving legitimate governments, rogue forces, rebel factions, criminal syndicates and business enterprises. As a result post-Cold War military intervention, particularly in the South, has now also become an occupation of the poor in some of the world's most remote, resourceless and unproductive places.[112] While several less-developed countries of the South have been and still remain objects of intervention, they have themselves become interveners in civil and mixed conflicts, particularly at a regional and subregional level.

## 4.5 Stages

The success of military intervention is to a large extent dependent on the timing and effectiveness of its use. This can be equated with the different stages of actual involvement between the initial onset and the final outcome of military intervention – namely the "getting in stage", the "staying in stage" and the "getting out stage".[113]

The "getting in stage" is not a single decision but a process covering the initial stage of military intervention. As such it includes the setting that precipitates military intervention – namely the developments that threaten to alter fundamentally the political *status quo* in the target state or territory. This stage extends to the translation of the policy context (the goals, objectives, strategic assumptions and domestic factors of the intervener) into operational actions (overt military intervention). As such it involves the use of alternative strategies for exerting political influence prior to the commitment of armed forces; the reasons, decision-making process and timing of the actual decision to escalate to military intervention; and the extent to which military intervention is prompted by an inability to attain policy objectives through alternative strategies. Additional factors that impact on this stage are domestic and international considerations other than the civil strife that influences the decision to intervene; the key tenets of the intervention strategy that transform political goals into military objectives; risk assessments; and relationships with possible allies.

The "staying in stage" refers to the actual dynamics or "middle game" of military intervention. It involves dealing with the initial "fog of war"; the assessment of effectiveness considering various indigenous, domestic, regional and international factors that impact on military intervention; the gradual escalation or de-escalation of military commitments and expectations, and the corresponding recalibration of the size of the military commitment; attending to key organisational and institutional dilemmas; and the maintenance of a strategic balance based on an evaluation of how the military interventions are fought, what strategies and tactics work best, and what changes should be introduced.

The "getting out stage" pertains to the determinants and the act of disengagement. The determinants include the effect of superpower (or major power) relations and exogenous events; changes in enemy composition, resources and strategy, particularly those "gambling for resurrection" to salvage past losses; the financial, material and political cost of intervention; and the role of public opinion. The act of disengagement involves the exit strategy as well as factors associated with the termination of war, such as bargaining tactics and the escalation of military operations. Military intervention, however, differs from classical war since it provides for a unilateral withdrawal option as a viable alternative to "remaining in", an option not equated with winning (or losing) as in war. In addition, although direct combat-related actions may cease, other alternative strategies may be employed. These include "combatless" options such as paracombat and supportive actions; and maintaining a "step-down" or "drawn-down" military presence, even to pre-intervention levels of non-combatant stationed forces. Since disengagement means different things in different situations, the conditions that make it imperative should be taken into account. This requires an assessment of the (in)decisiveness, problems, effects, ramifications and lessons of military involvement.

## 5. POLITICAL-STRATEGIC CONSIDERATIONS OF MILITARY INTERVENTION

Apart from the informative-descriptive factors covered by the preceding overview, any discussion of military intervention is incomplete without reference to select political-strategic considerations of a more prescriptive nature. Although these considerations have a bearing on the success or failure of military intervention, they are not elevated to the level of a dogma that has to be propagated or rejected. They essentially indicate how intervention is to succeed in its goals and objectives (which may be ethically and legally justified or unjustified), if used as an instrument of statecraft (which, again, may be morally right or wrong).

## 5.1 Strategic policy

Irrespective of the seemingly inchoate appearance of post-Cold War military intervention, such intervention is usually selectively and sparingly used as informed by a coherent logic guided by (foreign) policy, doctrine and strategy. Since the use of military intervention is influenced by the vagaries of the actors, interests and issues involved, an exhaustive overview of the prescriptions or general conditions that direct its use is ruled out here. Nonetheless, the following principles, rules and guidelines form the basis of an ideal-type template and provide some semblance of coherence and consistency to military intervention.

As a point of departure it can be argued that in the anarchical society envisaged by realists, "self-help" would be the guiding principle. The application of this principle requires clarity as to what constitutes the national interest and a unifying threat to this national interest. In this respect the most appropriate threshold of military intervention is the degree to which action or inaction will impact on the whole spectrum of national interest narrowly defined.[114] Bearing the presumed rationality of this process in mind, any decision to intervene should also subscribe to the fundamental principle of foreign policy namely that new burdens be assumed as parsimoniously as possible.[115]

In a plural world characterised by complex interdependence, increasing globalisation and integrated societies, the functionality of military intervention cannot simply be equated with rational decision making in a realist or neo-realist mode. It is furthermore mitigated by several societal elements such as international law, international morality, structural imperatives and common interests. As a result the use of military intervention is circumspect and controlled.[116] At a practical level, considering recent developments and new technologies, an intervention policy of the future should recognise risks since intervention is easier to begin than to end; it should be selective about where and when to intervene, and it should preserve and expand the options and instruments for doing so effectively. This approach should be supported by a strategy that emphasises core competencies; uses scenario-based planning for alternative futures in an inherently uncertain world; and employs adaptive and time-orientated options. Challenging and contentious issues should also be addressed intellectually and organisationally. These include the need for adequate intelligence gathering and analysis; the need for a research and development agenda covering doctrine, strategies, operational tactics, instruments and weapon systems; prioritising and deciding on the core values, interests, goals and objectives that should be upheld; deciding on when and where to intervene; organising the international community for intervention; and ensuring compliance with ethical and legal prescriptions.[117]

At a policy level, provision should be made for a variety of considerations that have serious implications for decision making and the execution of military intervention.[118] As a first step a decision is required on when and where to intervene. This should start from the presumption of non-intervention, followed by a consideration of the unacceptability of inaction. If a decision is made to intervene, it should satisfy the following practical considerations — the existence of conditions that necessitate and justify intervention; the legality of intervention; and the advancement of own and common interests. In respect of the latter, the magnitude of the burden should correlate with the interests at stake. Furthermore, since the intervention should have a high probability of success, there should be sufficient resources and the political will and commitment to guarantee a decisive outcome. The intervener should also create a sense of urgency, particularly in the mind of the target, for complete compliance. Although asymmetry of military power and motivation is required, the means of intervention should nonetheless be proportional to the objectives sought, and collateral damage and innocent casualties should be minimised at all costs. Although difficult to determine in advance, intervention should be on the "right" side. If it is on the "wrong" side, acceptable policy alternatives should be considered.

In addition, objectives should be clearly understood and the mission clearly defined in terms of scope and duration, with criteria for determining goal attainment and measuring success. It is also extremely important that consideration be given to what should follow the intervention. Hence the need for a strategic plan that integrates political and military goals. There should also be realistic criteria for ending the operation, a termination or exit strategy, as well as alternatives if unacceptable levels of "mission creep" develop, or if the intervention becomes protracted on account of the inability to achieve quick and decisive results. It is therefore essential to continuously assess ongoing intervention in the light of changing circumstances. Further prerequisites include sustained domestic and legislative support for the duration of the intervention; preserving the capability to intervene in higher priority contingencies; and securing multilateral consensus, support and participation amongst the "willing" others, most notably regional and global organisations.

At a strategic level the mode of intervention – peaceful or coercive – has to be determined. In respect of the former, a choice must be made between multilateral peace operations and unilateral (or even multilateral) intervention in the form of a policing model.[119] If peaceful intervention roles are anticipated, the military should be adapted accordingly. This requires doctrine rationalisation; organising and equipping units for these tasks; integrating civil-military planning and co-ordination at a strategic and operational level; and sufficient training and education. Coercive intervention roles require adequate intelligence; maintaining the technological edge; ensuring force flexibility and mobility; and balancing the peaceful and coercive roles.[120] A choice must also be made between available strategies that include unilateralism; selective coalitions, regionally based, with existing or emerging powers; a global major power coalition; or a broad international collective security system under the auspices of the UN or a regional organisation.[121]

Also to be considered is the extension of military involvement to include police involvement. A need may develop to make police forces available for international peace support missions if military intervention and diplomacy prove inadequate to deal with complex, multifaceted crises. If law and order is not re-established or created, it is likely to remain a source of political instability. In these situations peace operations are likely to face difficulties and may even fail. Military intervention may therefore only be the beginning of what may become long-standing involvement in international crisis areas that also require the use of police forces.[122]

Due consideration should be given to weaknesses that affect military responses. Apart from obvious shortcomings relating to the aforesaid, particular reference can be made to the lack of an agreed strategic doctrine within government for military intervention; the lack of a strategic plan that integrates political and military goals; the lack of a clear conception of preferred military and, more specifically, political outcomes of intervention; inadequate capabilities for unilateral or multilateral operations; the absence of a doctrine for peace operations; insufficient language capabilities for areas of operation; and the slow procurement and integration of high-technology capabilities that enhance military effectiveness and reduce casualties (especially civilian casualties) during military interventions.[123]

Finally, these policy formulations should conform to certain general criteria of a legal and ethical nature. Although inextricably linked to international law that regulates intervention and the use of force, these prescriptions exhibit a distinct political nature that makes them relevant in a policy context. Most importantly, intervention should be specifically requested of the potential intervener by the government of the country under attack; the requesting government should have the clear support of the majority of its population; the requesting government should itself act with intelligence and humanity and be demonstrably more responsive to the needs of the people than any opposition grouping; the decision to intervene should have the acquiescence of the majority of the intervener's electorate and serve the interests of the intervener; and the intervention should be directed or controlled by an external power.[124]

Interveners should also adhere to the first principles of "just war". These are just cause, that is using force only to correct a grave, public evil; comparative justice, meaning that where there are rights and wrongs on all sides of a conflict, the injustice suffered by one party should significantly outweigh that suffered by the other; legitimate authority, that is force used by a duly constituted authority; right intention, that is using force for a just purpose and only for that purpose; a probability of success, that is not using arms for a futile cause requiring disproportionate measures; last resort, using force only after peaceful alternatives had been earnestly tried and exhausted; proportionality, meaning that the good achieved should outweigh the overall destruction expected from the use of force; and non-combatant immunity, that is excluding civilians as the object of direct attack and minimising indirect harm to civilians.[125]

## 5.2 Policy doctrine

Strategic policy often finds expression in explicit policy doctrine on the use of armed force and military intervention. Similar to foreign policy, policy on intervention is confronted with the persistent problem of balancing morality and interest. This is a consequence of the constant tension between idealism and realism, with idealism being used to morally justify actions and realism to calculate interests.[126] Although not representative of all possibilities, the policy positions of the US, Europe and Africa provide an indication of current thinking.

In respect of the US, bearing their Indochina experience in mind, the US Secretary of Defence, Casper Weinberger, argued in 1984 that US forces should be sent into combat (also for the purposes of military intervention) only if the stakes were "vital". Furthermore, troops should be sent in "with the clear intention of winning"; they should serve "clearly defined military and political objectives", and their actions should be limited to the levels "needed to do just that".[127] During the 1990s, and irrespective of its conferred (but not self-imposed) policing role as the sole remaining superpower in pursuance of a "new world order", the US maintained this position. In 1993 President George Bush stated that "(u)sing military force makes sense as a policy where the stakes warrant, where and when force can be effective, where no other policies are likely to prove effective, where applications can be limited in scope and time, and where the potential benefits justify the potential costs and sacrifice".[128] This position still applies. In 1999 the National Security Adviser, Sandy Berger, listed three specific sets of circumstances as preconditions for US military intervention in Africa. The first condition pertains to "humanitarian intervention" as a just cause, in respect of which it was declared that the "US and its allies will not stand by and fail to act when... there is a systematic effort by a nation, by a government, to eliminate an entire people". The second and third conditions are more specifically related to the previous guidelines. The second condition is that "we have a national interest engaged – as we clearly did in Kosovo because of what would have followed in Europe had we not ended ethnic cleansing of Kosovar Albanians". The third condition is that US military intervention will be an option "where we have the capacity to act..."[129]

Within the post-Cold War European context the situation regarding the involvement of the Western European Union (WEU) and NATO in particular is more complex. Except in the unlikely event of a major war involving them, the member states of the European Union (EU) and NATO are not expected to intervene militarily and on a large scale in any local conflict in former Soviet bloc countries or in the periphery or so-called "Near Abroad" of Russia. Except where their territorial integrity or vital interests are at stake, European states are not prepared to commit vast resources and the lives of their troops to military intervention. The exception is the defence of human rights and alleviation of humanitarian suffering in the Balkans, which is by no means unproblematic or unrelated to core European interests. With the exception of the aforesaid, European security is sought through economic partnership and social reconstruction, and not through military intervention. Extra-European military intervention is an even more remote possibility, again with the exception of collective humanitarian intervention mandated by and undertaken under the auspices of the UN or a regional organisation.[130] More recently this position was also adopted by France, the former *gendarme* of Francophone Africa.[131]

The African position is more ambivalent and open to varying interpretation. It started out in the 1960s with the assumption, which still applies, that non-intervention in the internal affairs of states and the unreserved condemnation of subversive activities on the part of states should be the guiding precepts of international relations.[132] The position on intervention in interstate war was, however, not made abundantly clear. During the 1970s, in accordance with resolutions passed at Organisation of African Unity (OAU) summits, non-African interference was again condemned, but African states were also accorded the right to call on outside assistance when their security and sovereignty were threatened.[133] During the late 1970s and early 1980s the Economic Community of West African States (ECOWAS), for example, adopted two sets of protocols that, among other things, relate to direct military intervention. The first applied to non-aggression and prohibited assistance to dissident groups and foreigners who intervened. The latter involved mutual assistance and defence and provided for counteraggression intervention in the form of interposition in an interstate war, but excluded intervention in internal conflicts.[134] Hence the 1970s and 1980s saw several instances of extra- and intracontinental military intervention, all of which did not comply with the prescriptions of the time and which were not necessarily condemned.

During the 1990s the African focus shifted towards the prevention, management and resolution of conflict, the provision of humanitarian assistance and active support of democratisation. Subsequently, several initiatives were launched at a regional and subregional level that either directly or indirectly implicated military intervention. Although the non-intervention principle is still emphasised, the proviso is that it should be interpreted and applied in a manner supportive of conflict prevention and resolution. Not only is humanitarian intervention regarded as justifiable, but provision is also made, under the general terms of the UN Charter and with UN assistance where necessary, for peace support operations, punitive measures and collective international intervention where conflicts escalate. Military intervention, of whatever nature, is decided upon only after all other possible political alternatives have been exhausted in accordance with the UN and OAU Charters.[135] Although no specific reference was made to the use of military intervention as such, decisions taken at the OAU Heads of State and Government Summit at Algiers (Algeria) in 1999, by implication opened new possibilities for intervention. These decisions were encapsulated in the Algiers Declaration (highlighting Africa's priorities in the new millennium). In its encouragement of democracy on the continent, the OAU summit resolved unconditionally to condemn and isolate any government that came to power by force of arms through a *coup d'état*.[136]

## 6. RISK AND MILITARY INTERVENTION

Risk and risk analysis have always been integral to the practice and theory of military intervention. By nature, such intervention is an extremely risky undertaking accompanied by uncertainty. This observation holds true not only for the actual execution and outcome of military intervention, but also for foreign military intervention decisions. Although the analysis of risk and military intervention is an imprecise science of recent origin,[137] cognisance should be taken of the following theoretical and practical factors involved.

## 6.1 Theory

Although the relationship between risk taking and decision making is multifaceted and complex, due mainly to the ill-defined nature of political-military problems involving military intervention, the nature, texture and context of risk provide some indication of the dynamics involved.[138]

With reference to military intervention, Vertzberger defines risks as "the likelihood of the materialization of validly predictable direct and indirect consequences with potentially adverse values, arising from events, self-behaviour, environmental constraints, or the reaction of an opponent or third party".[139] In a generic sense, three types of risk can be identified, namely real risk, or the actual risk resulting from a situation or behaviour; perceived risk, or the level of risk decision makers attribute to a situation or behaviour; and acceptable risk, or the level of risk representing the costs that decision makers perceive as sustainable and bearable. The assessment of these risks depends on the confidence with which decision makers estimate the probability of positive or negative outcomes, and results in risk seeking or risk averse policies.

The texture of risk refers to various attributes that define the nature and salience of risk. These attributes of risk are transparency, or the clarity and understanding of risky consequences; severity, or its seriousness and damaging nature; certainty, or the (un)certainty of the risk actually materialising; horizon, or its closeness in time; complexity, as determined by the measurability, variability, multiplicity and interactivity of risk dimensions; reversibility, or whether the risk can be reversed and at what cost; controllability and containability, or the extent to which it can be contained to manageable proportions; and accountability, or whether decision makers will be held responsible for it. The (non-) recognition of these attributes influences the ability of decision makers to deal with information and understand the situation and risks involved; to adopt an open-minded and imaginative approach to managing risk; and to deal with awkward or unpleasant aspects of the situation. Also to be considered is the taste for risk, that is the preference of decision makers for a particular type or combination of risks and risk attributes.

The context of risk is determined by three variables: the vividness and salience of risk, prior planning and existing commitments. Vividness is associated with the inherent nature of the risk and salience with the context of the situation involving the risk. More severe adverse consequences and concrete or manifest outcomes will increase the vividness. Risks will become more salient if more information is available; if the time horizon decreases and the risk draws closer; if events are intrinsically risky; if outcomes are irreversible; if decision makers are personally held accountable for their decisions; if risks involve core values, interests and objectives; and if risks emerge in a comprehensive rather than a piecemeal fashion.

Planning, according to Vertzberger, is the "formalized premises, beliefs, action directives, and expectations that organize and structure present and future realities so as to remove much of the inherent uncertainty and allow for the framing of operational guidelines towards goal-orientated outcomes".[140] Since risky policies should be preceded by planning, the planning process has to anticipate and manage the risks. Therefore, meticulous planning is essential if military intervention is to be used as a policy instrument. Paradoxically, (over-)planning can be counterproductive if it leads to overconfidence which enhances the inclination to incur higher risks; to the incorrect estimation of the time required to attain the goal of military intervention, since decision makers often overestimate what can be achieved within the available time; and to a greater involvement of high-level political decision makers who lack knowledge and experience of the military *modus operandi*.

Commitment and entrapment relate to prior events and expectations that prevent or constrain decision makers from considering alternative courses of action or exercising options other than military intervention. This could arise from a contractual agreement obligating a party to intervene if a particular state of affairs exists, through a premeditated single choice with a clear predetermined goal; or from a series of decisions and actions that culminate in a commitment to military intervention. The dynamics of the situation can furthermore lead to commitment escalation and entrapment. Commitment escalation is the result of success that tempts the intervener to extend and increase its objectives, involvement and expectations, or of entrapment whereby the decision makers escalate their commitment to a previously chosen, but failing course of action. The latter usually results from uncertainty about the possibilities and consequences of either persistence or withdrawal, caused by the belief that prior setbacks or failures were only situational or temporary, and by shifting the responsibility to prevent escalation to the rival party.

## 6.2 Practice

Without referring to specific examples, an indication is given of the most common risks that accompany military intervention. These risks in the form of costs and detrimental consequences mainly concern the intervener, but they can also apply to the target. The risks can be grouped together in three interrelated categories, namely political, military and socio-economic risks.

Political risks, at an external level, pertain primarily to the extent to which the intervener's military intervention is justified and complies with ethical, legal and constitutional prescriptions. By defaulting on these counts, the intervener's action runs the risk of being labelled as aggression, a violation of the sovereignty and territorial integrity of the target state, and a breach of the norms and principles that regulate and provide normality to international relations. Countermeasures of an individual or collective nature taken in response, ranging from diplomatic condemnation to military action, constitute negative outcomes for the intervener. As a rogue actor the intervener also runs the risk of becoming an isolated pariah in world politics. Another risk with similar consequences is supporting the "wrong" side (in an ethical or legal sense) or the "losing" side (in a military sense). Since military intervention is a form of political investment, the intervener might also be faced with negative dividends in the form of "losing face and good will". This may impact on future relations with the target state or elements within the target state, particularly where animosity or a residue of dissatisfaction remains after the intervention.

At an internal level, existing authority structures and decision makers in the intervening and in the target state may have to contend with a range of consequences that include loss of face, lack of public support, hostile public opinion, declining legitimacy, legislative censure, bureaucratic competition, electoral defeat, a change of administration or government, or even a *coup*. Policy will also come under scrutiny, particularly where bureaucratic incompetence, failure or suboptimal performance, or a lack of policy alternatives and exit strategies had increased the risks of military intervention.

In respect of the target state, if there is a failure to attain the goals and objectives of intervention, the initial causes of intervention may well persist, increase in severity and even extend to other areas. This will not only increase internal instability, but may spill over into the region as a whole. There is also the risk that once having completed the military intervention and having disengaged, the need for intervention may again arise.

The major (and self-explanatory) military risks are, firstly, the escalation of the conflict from peaceful (or non-combatant) intervention to coercive (combatant) intervention or from military intervention to limited and even major war; and, secondly, actually "losing" the military confrontation. By implication the former will increase the level of military commitment, force levels, rates of attrition of human resources and equipment, the duration of the conflict, etc. The latter translates not only into a military but also into a political defeat. At a lower level of risk, "mission creep" may develop, that is the gradual expansion of involvement due to the acceptance of additional commitments. The scope of military intervention may also expand, particularly if counter-intervention and regional "spill-over" involve new conflicting parties.

The socio-economic risks of military intervention, for the intervener and the target state, often appear to be residual but are in fact more fundamental in nature. Military intervention always incurs financial and economic costs. A major issue is the extent to which the intervener (and also the target) can sustain these costs and are willing to bear them. By crossing a threshold, irreversible damage may be done to economic systems, sectoral concerns and investor confidence. Since the economy of a country is intimately linked to its social system, the latter may suffer similar consequences. In addition to the destruction of infrastructure as a result of military action, military intervention usually produces a range of residual outcomes that include population displacement, refugee problems, human rights violations, humanitarian suffering and resource scarcity. Apart from their obvious detrimental effect, these consequences are aggravated by and also compound the impact of other risk categories. In the present era where the definition and agenda of security include non-political and non-military issues, economic decline will impact negatively on sociocultural conditions, particularly if intensified by the corollary effects of detrimental political-military developments. A similar negative "spill-over" to the political sphere will also compound real socio-economic risks.

## 7. CONCLUSION

Since the ending of the Cold War the world has experienced the re-emergence and resurgence of military intervention, particularly in the South. In what is deemed an "era of intervention", Africa in general and sub-Saharan Africa in particular have been the focus of military intervention of a benign and humanitarian nature supportive of peace. The continent has, however, also been afflicted by military intervention of a more malign, self-centred and geopolitical nature. This overview stems from the need to provide a framework for the analysis and assessment of military intervention in sub-Saharan Africa, and from the desire to contextualise and describe the contemporary nature and risk of military intervention. Since a summary would be superfluous, suffice it to conclude with these general comments.

Firstly, the "puzzle of intervention" or "problem of definition" remains unresolved. The provision of a nominal or stipulative definition is a function of analytical considerations and personal predisposition. A basic choice exists between more limited, exclusive and combat-related conceptualisations, and those of a more comprehensive and inclusive nature that extend into the domain of the peaceful role of military instruments in peace support operations. This is not a discriminatory distinction, but one of degree. Intervention, more specifically military intervention, occupies a particular segment of a continuum of possible actions by international actors. Since different categories and subcategories overlap, intermingle and fuse, the dividing lines between them are indistinct. It should, however, be borne in mind that the definitions and typology primarily serve an analytical purpose. Neither is a definitive and unambiguous definition of military intervention intended, nor is a particular conceptualisation advanced or prescribed.

Secondly, the conceptual problem extends into the operational sphere where the difference between action and inaction, between intervention and non-intervention, between the politics of engagement and intervention, between coercive diplomacy, military involvement, military intervention and limited war, between combat, paracombat and combat-related support, and between the peaceful and coercive use of military instruments becomes equally opaque. From the point of view of policy, strategy and tactics, this has serious implications for the decision maker and strategic planner. Again it is advisable to regard these various activities as policy alternatives on a continuum ranging from peace to war and from co-operation to conflict.

Thirdly, whereas an overview was presented of select theoretical aspects of military intervention, these aspects are ideal-types and abstract in nature. Although the theoretical aspects find tangible expression in practical examples, they remain abstract constructs that neither accurately represent reality in its totality, nor comprehensively cover all facets of the phenomenon. As an introduction to military intervention in sub-Saharan Africa their purpose is primarily descriptive, rather than explanatory and analytical.

Fourthly, military intervention constitutes a factual situation and a (policy) problem. As a result the translation of the conceptual and contextual dimensions of military intervention into situational and operational outcomes, also involves normative preferences. These not only include moral principles and legal rules, but also prescriptions governing the prudent and parsimonious use of military intervention as an instrument of statecraft. Hence the normative dimensions of military intervention should be accorded recognition, without reducing them to dogma.

Fifthly, the preceding discussion is clearly based on ideal-type assumptions of a predominantly realist and neo-realist nature. Admittedly, it reflects a more orthodox, Western-centric approach to military intervention — embedded in positivist and explanatory theorising — that is open to post-positivist, reflectivist criticism. It also tends to (over)emphasise a predominantly major power or most developed country predisposition, representative of a "top-down" or "centre-towards-periphery" approach.

Finally, it may also create the impression that all military interventions exhibit high levels of sophistication in respect of policy doctrine, decision making, military execution, risk assessment and compliance with legal and ethical prescriptions. In practice this is not the case. Admittedly, military intervention has more shades to it and it is differently conceptualised, utilised and justified by different states or groups of states. The states of the South and Africa are no exception.

Rather than prejudging the African experience, an inductive, empirical approach is adopted. Against the background of this theoretical introduction, an analysis and assessment is subsequently made of military intervention in sub-Saharan Africa. The emphasis is, however, specifically placed on overt foreign military intervention of a combatative and coercive nature in interstate conflicts and mixed conflicts (arising from intrastate conflicts), thereby excluding peaceful intervention and internal intervention in intrastate conflict. Hence a platform is provided for the comparison of various African examples and the drawing of general conclusions on the (a)typical features and use of military intervention in Africa.

## ENDNOTES

1. Bull, H, "Introduction", in Bull, H (ed), *Intervention in World Politics*, Clarendon Press, Oxford, 1984, p 2; Little, R, "Recent literature on intervention and non-intervention", in Forbes, I and M Hoffman (eds), *Political theory, International Relations, and the ethics of intervention*, Macmillan Press, Houndmills, 1993, p 14; Mayall, J, "Introduction", in Mayall, J (ed), *The new interventionism 1991-1994: United Nations experience in Cambodia, former Yugoslavia and Somalia*, Cambridge University Press, Cambridge, 1996, p 3; and Otte, T G, "On intervention: Some introductory remarks", in Dorman, A M and T G Otte (eds), *Military intervention: From gunboat diplomacy to humanitarian intervention*, Dartmouth Publishing Company, Aldershot, 1995, p 3.

2. A conventional distinction is made between the empirical and normative dimensions (and analyses) of intervention. For a discussion, see Little, R, *op cit*, pp 14-26.

3. Geldenhuys, D, *Foreign political engagement: Remaking states in the post-Cold War world*, Macmillan Press, Houndmills, 1998, pp 28-37; and Richardson, J, "Strategic thinking in an era of intervention: Thinking out of a box with no sides", *Comparative Strategy*, Vol 18, No 1, January-March 1999, p 31.

4. Beadham, B, "Sword and pen: Journalists and the wars of the future", in Williamson, R (ed), *Some corner of a foreign field: Intervention and world order*, Macmillan Press, Houndmills, 1998, p 231; and Freedman, L, "The changing forms of military conflict",

5. paper presented at the 40th Annual Conference of The International Institute for Strategic Studies (IISS) on *The changing shape of international relations and wars of the future*, Oxford, 3-6 September 1998, p 1.

5. This is to a large extent encapsulated by the version of a "new world order" proclaimed by President George Bush of the United States of America (US) in 1990 and 1991, and by doctrinal components of foreign policy respectively labeled liberal internationalism, liberal institutionalism, liberal interventionism, (aggressive or assertive) multilateralism, democratic globalism and neo-Wilsonian idealism. For a detailed discussion of these aspects, see: Geldenhuys, D, *op cit*, pp 18-19 and 28-35; and Dunne, T, "Liberalism", in Baylis, J and S Smith (eds), *The globalization of World Politics: An introduction to International Relations*, Oxford University Press, Oxford, 1997, pp 147-163.

6. See, *inter alia*: Richardson, J, op cit, p 46; and Rosenau, J N, *Turbulence in World Politics: A theory of change and continuity*, Princeton University Press, Princeton, 1990, pp 5-7.

7. Mason, R A (Air Vice-Marshall), "Foreword", in Dorman, A M and T G Otte (eds), *op cit*, p x.

8. Rosenau, J, "Intervention as a scientific concept", *Journal of Conflict Resolution*, Vol 13, No 1, April 1969, p 155.

9. Vattel, E de, *Le Droit des Gens ou Principe de la Loi Naturelle*, London, 1758, I para.31f, in Otte, T G, *op cit*, p 3n.

10. Otte, T G, *op cit*, p 5; and Roper, J, "The foreign policy of Western countries: The problem of intervention", in Williamson, R, *op cit*, p 205.

11. Rosenau, J, "The concept of intervention", *Journal of International Affairs*, Vol 22, No 2, 1968, p 167.

12. Freedman, L, "Introduction", in Freedman, L (ed), *Military intervention in European conflicts*, Blackwell Publishers, Oxford, 1994, p 1.

13. "When we speak of intervening in a conflict we are speaking of intervening in an existing intervention." Millar, T B, "Conflict and intervention", in Ayoob, M (ed), *Conflict and intervention in the Third World*, Croom Helm, London, 1980, p 1. See also Vertzberger, Y Y I, *Risk taking and decisionmaking: Foreign military intervention decisions*, Stanford University Press, Stanford, 1998, p 114.

14. Oppenheim, L. *International Law: A treatise, Vol I - Peace*, edited by H Lauterpacht, 6th edition, Longman, Green & Co, London, 1947, p 272; and Tillema, H K, "Foreign overt military intervention in the Nuclear Age", *Journal of Peace Research*, Vol 26, No 2, 1989, pp 179 and 181.

15. Luard, E, "Collective intervention", in Bull, H (ed), *op cit*, p 157.

16. Geldenhuys, D, *op cit*, p 70; and Brooks, L F and A Kanter, "Introduction", in Kanter, A and LF Brooks (eds), *U.S. intervention policy for the post-Cold War: New challenges and new responses*, W W Norton & Company, New York, 1994, p 15.

17. Schwarz, U, "Great power intervention in the modern world", in Buchan, A (ed), *Problems of modern strategy*, Chatto & Windus, London, 1970, p 176; and Otte, T G, *op cit*, p 3.

18. For a discussion of this "problem of definition" or "intervention puzzle" see, *inter alia*: Bull, H, *op cit*, pp 1-6; Geldenhuys, D, *op cit*, pp 4-7; Haas, E B, "Beware of the slippery slope: Notes toward the definition of justifiable intervention", in Reed, L W and C Kaysen (eds), *Emerging norms of justified intervention: A collection of essays from a project of the American Academy of Arts and Sciences*, American Academy of Arts and Sciences, Cambridge, 1993, pp 65-68; Otte, T G, *op cit*, pp 3-10; Rosenau, J, "Intervention as a scientific concept", *op cit*; Rosenau, J, "The concept of intervention", *op cit*; and Thomas, C, *New states, sovereignty and intervention*, Gower Publishing Company, Aldershot, 1985, pp 9-21. Based on the definitions by various international law and international relations scholars, Geldenhuys provides the following stipulative definition of intervention: "It is the calculated action of a state, a group of states, an international organization or some other international actor(s) to influence the political system of another state (including its structure of authority, its domestic policies and its political leaders) against its will by using various means of coercion (forcible or non-forcible) in pursuit of particular political objectives". Geldenhuys, D, *op cit*, p 6.

19. Little, R, *Intervention: External involvement in civil wars*, Martin Robertson, London, 1975, p 11; and Tillema, H K, op cit, p 181. A notable exception is Haas who in a more circumspect manner qualifies (justified) intervention by noting that it should not include "acts of aggression". "To count them would be tantamount to making the concept of intervention coterminous with the ideas of war and conflict management... Put differently, in order to

count as intervention the act must be so uncommon as to be subject to elimination from the repertoire of state behavior if shown to be unjustified". Haas, E B, *op cit*, p66.

20. Otte, T G, *op cit*, pp 4-5.

21. Keohane, R O and J S Nye, *Power and interdependence*, 2$^{nd}$ edition, HarperCollins Publishers, 1989, pp 27-29; Otte, T G, op cit, p 3; and Sewall, J O B, "Adapting conventional military forces to a new environment", in Kanter, A and L F Brooks, *op cit*, pp 85cf.

22. Jentleson, B W and A E Levite, "The analysis of protracted foreign military intervention", in Levite, A E, Jentleson, B W and L Berman (eds), *Foreign military intervention: The dynamics of protracted conflict*, Columbia University Press, New York, 1992, pp 6-9.

23. *Ibid*, pp 4-6. This distinction is more problematic than may appear at first glance. For example, depending on the definition that is used, military interventions can include divergent events such as the Korean War (1949-1953) and the Gulf War (1990-1991); various intervening actions in Central and West Africa during the 1990s and the South Africa-Botswana / Southern African Development Community (SADC) intervention in Lesotho (1998-1999); internal Russian military action against secessionist factions in the Chechen Republic (1998-1999) and the Republic of Dagestan (1999); and United Nations (UN) peace support operations. Furthermore, military intervention can occur in the event of a spectrum of conflict ranging from major interstate war, through intrastate or civil war, to internal conflict, and can include the coercive (forcible or non-forcible) or peaceful military use of armed forces in these instances.

24. Otte, T G, *op cit*, p 10.

25. Otte, T G, "Military intervention: Conclusions and reflections", in Dorman, A M and T G Otte, *op cit*, p 195.

26. Tillema, H K, *op cit*, p 181.

27. See section 4.3 for a description of the foreign territory (target) involved.

28. Tillema, H K, *op cit*, p 181.

29. Quoted from the Overt Military Intervention File in *Ibid*, p 181. See also pp 179 and 183. Based on this conceptualisation, 97 states were found to have initiated 591 foreign overt military interventions within 269 international armed conflicts between

*Anton du Plessis*

      1945 and 1985. Well-known African examples range from the Algerian war (1954-1962), through the Congolese civil war (1959-1965), the Angolan war (1960-1978), the Anya Nya war (1964, 1966, 1968 and 1971), the Namibian conflict (1975-1989), the Polisario war (1973-1991), Shaba (1977 and 1978-1979), the Ogaden war (1977-1985), the Kagara war (1978-1981), to the Chadian civil war (1978-1982 and 1983-1985). Also included are lesser interventions ranging from the Mau-Mau violence (1952-1956), through the East African mutinies (1964), the Entebbe Airport raid (1976), Bokassa's overthrow in the Central African Republic (1979), to South Africa's anti-ANC raids on Maputo (1981 and 1983), Maseru (1982) and Gaborone (1985).

30. Vertzberger, Y Y I, *op cit*, p 114.
31. *Ibid.*
32. *Ibid*, pp 114-115.
33. Schraeder, P J, "Paramilitary intervention", in Schraeder, P J (ed), *Intervention in the 1980s: US foreign policy in the Third World*, Lynne Rienner Publications, Boulder, 1989, p 115. In the case of the US, examples of paramilitary or covert intervention during the 1950s to 1970s include Guatemala (1954), Indonesia (1956-1958), Tibet (1956-1973), Cuba (1959-1961), Laos (1960-1973), Iraq (1972-1975) and Angola (1975); and during the 1980s, Angola (1976-1989), Cambodia / Kampuchea (1978-1989), Afghanistan (1979-1989) and Nicaragua (1979-1989).
34. *Ibid.*
35. Freedman, L, "Introduction", *op cit*, p 3.
36. *Ibid.*
37. Dunér, B, "The many-pronged spear: External military intervention in civil wars in the 1970s", *Journal of Peace Research*, Vol 20, No 1, 1983, p 60.
38. Based on a survey of research reports and publications covering the period from 1945 to the early-1980s, Dunér concludes that external intervention was fairly common in internal or civil conflicts, the bulk of which was related to Third World states, but far from occurring in every case. He estimated that external intervention was involved in between one third and two thirds of the cases. *Ibid*, pp 60 and 65.
39. Defined as "the deliberate involvement ... in the affairs of another state or transnational organization in order to change its behavior or character, using techniques that run the gamut from targeted

information activities to economic sanctions to military force". The American Assembly (Columbia University), "Final report of the Eighty-Fifth American Assembly", in Kanter, A and L F Brooks, *op cit*, pp 227-228.

40. Sewall, J O B, *op cit*, pp 84-85 and 96. Some of the better-known examples of peaceful intervention include the peace support operations undertaken by or under the auspices of intergovernmental organisations in the form of preventive deployment, such as the UN and North Atlantic Treaty Organisation (NATO) contingents in the Former Yugoslav Republic of Macedonia; peacekeeping, such as the UN Truce Supervision Organization (UNTSO) in Palestine (1948), the UN Operation in the Congo (ONUC) (1960-1964) and the UN Peace-Keeping Force in Cyprus (UNFICYP) (1964 to present), as well as the NATO Stabilisation Force (SFOR) in Bosnia and the NATO-force Kosovo (both of which include an element of peace enforcement); peace enforcement, such as the UN Operation in Somalia (UNISOM II) (1993 to present) and the enforcement of "no-fly zones" in Iraq (by Allied powers such as the US and the United Kingdom) and Bosnia (by the NATO Implementation Force [IFOR]) during the 1990s; and peace building, such as the UN Advance Mission in Cambodia (UNAMIC) (1991-1992), the UN Transitional Authority in Cambodia (UNTAC) (1992-1993), the UN Operation in Somalia (UNISOM II) (1993 to present) and the UN Mission for Rwanda (UNAMIR) (1993 to present).

41. With reference to the British Army. Freedman, L, "Introduction", *op cit*, p 3.

42. United Nations, Department of Public Information, *An Agenda for Peace*, published in the name of the Secretary-General, Boutros Boutros-Ghali, United Nations Publications, New York, 1992.

43. For a more detailed discussion, see *inter alia: Ibid*; Evans, G, *Cooperating for peace: The global agenda for the 1990s and beyond*, Allen & Unwin, St Leonards, 1993, pp 8-13; Ramsbotham, D, "The changing nature of intervention: The role of UN peacekeeping", *Conflict Studies*, No 282, August 1995, pp 1-24; and Sewall, J O B, op cit, pp 85-90. In their discussion of developments in modern warfare, Snyder and Malik also include this type of intervention. Snyder, C A and J M Malik, "Developments in modern warfare", in Snyder, C A (ed), Contemporary security and strategy, Macmillan, London, 1999, pp 205-207.

44. Arend, A C and R J Beck, *International Law and the use of force: Beyond the UN Charter paradigm*, Routledge, London, 1993, p 112.

45. Ramsbotham, O, "Humanitarian intervention: The contemporary debate", in Williamson, R, *op cit*, pp 64-65.

46. For a detailed discussion of humanitarian intervention, in particular the body of rules that apply, criteria to be met and examples, see: Arend, A C and R J Beck, op cit, pp 112-137; Akehurst, M, "Humanitarian intervention", in Bull, H (ed), *op cit*, pp 95-112; Ero, C and S Long, "Humanitarian intervention: A new role for the United Nations?", in Williamson, R, *op cit*, pp 121-130; and Croft, S and A Treacher, "Aspects of intervention in the South", in Dorman, A M and T G Otte, *op cit*, pp 145-148.

47. Arend, A C and R J Beck, *op cit*, p 114; and O'Halloran, P J, "Humanitarian intervention and the genocide in Rwanda", *Conflict Studies*, No 277, January 1995, pp 18-19.

48. Roper, J, *op cit*, p 208.

49. Ero, C and S Long, *op cit*, p 122. Apart from the multilateral peace support operations that involve an element of humanitarian intervention (see *supra* 40), the most frequently cited examples of purported or possible humanitarian intervention during the Cold War era include intervention by various states in the Palestine conflict (1948), the Congo (1960 and 1964), the Dominican Republic (1965), East Pakistan (1971), East Timor (1975), Angola (1975), Cambodia / Kampuchea (1978), Uganda (1979), Central African Republic (1979) and Grenada (1983). Recent post-Cold War examples include the Economic Community of West African States (ECOWAS) force in Liberia (1990), the Allied Operations Provide Comfort and Southern Watch in Iraq (1991), the UN Protection Force (UNPROFOR) in Bosnia (1992), the US Operation Restore Hope and UNISOM I in Somalia (1992), Operation Turquoise in Rwanda (1994) and Operation Uphold Democracy in Haiti (1994).

50. Glennon, M J, "The new interventionism: The search for a just International Law", *Foreign Affairs*, Vol 78, May/June 1999, p 7; and Stockholm International Peace Research Institute (SIPRI), *SIPRI Yearbook 1999: Armaments, disarmament and international security*, Oxford University Press, Oxford, 1999, p 4.

51. For example UNISOM I and II in Somalia.

52. SIPRI, *op cit*, p 4.

53. Jentleson, B W, Levite, A E and L Berman, "Foreign military intervention in perspective", in Levite, A E (*et al*), *op cit*, p 320.
54. Otte, T H, "Of congresses and gunboats: Military intervention in the Nineteenth Century", in Dorman, A M and T G Otte, op cit, pp 36-38; and Pagedas, C A, "Continuity and change: The United States, Great Britain and military intervention in the Cold War", in Dorman, A M and T G Otte, *op cit*, p 53.
55. Du Plessis, A, "The geopolitical context: A sea change from old to new geopolitics", in Carlsnaes, W & M Muller (eds), *Change and South African external relations*, International Thomson Publishing, Johannesburg, 1997, pp 19-20.
56. Otte, T H, "Of congresses and gunboats ...", *op cit*, pp 54-57; and Pagedas, C A, op cit, p 53.
57. Mayall, J, *op cit*, pp 5-6; and Zakaria, F, "A framework for interventionism in the post-Cold War era", in Kanter, A and L F Brooks, *op cit*, p 183.
58. Bull, H, "Intervention in the Third World", in Bull, H (ed), *op cit*, pp 135-156.
59. Otte, T H, "Military intervention ", *op cit*, p 200.
60. Falk, R, *op cit*, p 150.
61. Du Plessis, A, *op cit*, pp 24-25; and Geldenhuys, D, *op cit*, p 38.
62. "Final report of the Eighty-Fifth American Assembly", in Kanter, A and L F Brooks, *op cit*, pp 227-228; and Richardson, J, *op cit*, p 43.
63. Malik, S P and A M Dorman, "United Nations and military intervention: A study in the politics of contradiction", in Dorman, A M and T G Otte, *op cit*, pp 181-182.
64. Amongst others, by the former editor of the *The Times* (London), Simon Jenkins, who has castigated the new doctrine of military intervention in humanitarian crises as immoral and ineffective since it tends to replace one undoubted wrong by another undoubted wrong, at great cost to lives and infrastructure. *The Star* (Johannesburg), 23 February 2000.
65. Falk, R, *op cit*, p 150.
66. In this respect Falk contends that "neither international relations nor practice lends much support to such a benevolent role for Great Powers, nor, it should be added, does the evidence support the opposite view that geopolitically motivated action will never confer humanitarian benefits". Falk, R, "Post-Cold War illusions

and daunting realities", in Williamson, R, *op cit*, p 143. See also p 144.

67. Otte, T H, "Military intervention ...", *op cit*, pp 197-198.
68. Malik, S P and A M Dorman, *op cit*, pp 181-182.
69. Otte, T H, "Military intervention ...", *op cit*, pp 197-198.
70. Falk, R, *op cit*, p 150.
71. Dorman, A M, "Western Europe and military intervention: Unity in diversity", in Dorman, A M and T G Otte, *op cit*, pp 109 and 126; and Otte, T H, "Military intervention ...", *op cit*, pp 196 and 200.
72. Freedman, L, "The changing forms of military conflict", *op cit*, p 3.
73. Freedman regards militia-based warfare as an alternative to the "Western way" and labels it as a "non-Western strategy". *Ibid*, pp 1-17.
74. *Ibid*, pp 44-45.
75. Although different scholars propose different categorise of civil conflict, the formulation as indicated is preferred. Arend, A C and R J Beck, *op cit*, pp 81-82.
76. *Ibid*, pp 87-88.
77. The first tier being "Western states" and the second tier those states on the periphery of the first tier that experience periodic crises or have pockets of ungovernability within their territory. Metz, S, "Deterring conflict short of war", *Strategic Review*, Vol 22, No 4, 1994, pp 9-13; and Snyder, C A and J M Malik, *op cit*, p 205.
78. Blacker, C D. "A typology of post-Cold War conflicts", in Kanter, A and L F Brooks, *op cit*, pp 46-49 and 50-54.
79. For a discussion of these moral dilemmas, see Johnson, P, "Intervention and moral dilemmas", in Forbes, I and M Hoffman, *op cit*, pp 62-64.
80. Rengger, J, "Contextuality, interdependence and the ethics of intervention", in Forbes, I and M Hoffman, (eds), *Political theory, International Relations and the ethics of intervention*, Macmillan Press, Houndmills, 1993, pp 179-180.
81. Among others, just cause, comparative justice, legitimate authority, right intention, last resort, proportionality and non-combatant immunity. Beach, H, "Second thoughts on first principles", in Williamson, R, *op cit*, pp 73-83.

82. Paskins, B, "Intervention and virtue", in Forbes, I and M Hoffman, *op cit*, pp 113-114.
83. Gamba, V, "Emerging norms", in Reed, L W and C Kaysen, *op cit*, pp 116-124.
84. As an extension of the previous discussion of the definitions and typology of military intervention, this anatomy is based on the two-dimensional matrix produced by the continuums of direct-indirect military intervention and peaceful-coercive military intervention. The instruments of military intervention are positioned within this matrix. The categories of military intervention, namely the locus, form, level and duration thereof, represent additional ($3^{rd}$) dimensions. This anatomy is situationally contextualised with reference to the categories of warfare and the political, ethical and legal framework of intervention.
85. Luard, E, "Collective intervention", in Bull, H (ed), *op cit*, pp 157-158. Typical examples of unilateral and multilateral intervention are respectively US intervention in Panama (1989) and India in Sri Lanka (1987-1990); and the US, Australia and others in Indochina (Vietnam) (1960s-1970s) and the Allied powers in the Gulf (1990-1991). For examples of collective intervention, see *supra* 40.
86. Jentleson, B W and A E Levite, *op cit*, pp 9-10. Examples of quick-decisive intervention are the intervention of the US in Lebanon (1958), the Dominican Republic (1965), Grenada (1983) and Panama (1989) and the Soviet Union (Warschau Pact) in Hungary (1956) and Czechoslovakia (1968); and of protracted intervention, intervention by the US in Indochina (1962-1975), South Africa and Cuba in Angola (1975-1989), the Soviet Union in Afghanistan (1979-1989), Syria and Israel in Lebanon (1982-1985) and India in Sri Lanka (1987-1990).
87. Miller, B, "The logic of US military intervention in the post-Cold War era", *Contemporary Security Policy*, Vol 19, No 3, December 1998, p 75. For example, during the post-Cold War era, massive intervention in the Gulf (1990-1991); medium intervention in Panama (1989), Haiti (1994), Bosnia (1995) and the Gulf deployments (1994 and 1997-1998); limited intervention in Somalia (1992-1993), Rwanda (1994) and Liberia (1996); and non-intervention in Bosnia (1992-1995)
88. Geldenhuys, D, *op cit*, p 15.
89. Croft, S and A Treacher, *op cit*, pp 135-138. They also include humanitarian intervention as a distinctive Southern variation of

intervention, but conclude that it is "a theory without practice in the South". *Ibid*, p 154. Examples of regional power intervention are the People's Republic of China in Vietnam (1978), the Soviet Union in Afghanistan (1979-1989), Syria and Israel in Lebanon (1982-1985), India in Sri Lanka (1987-1990) and South Africa in Angola (1975-1989); and of internal intervention, ongoing intervention by both India and Pakistan in their respective sections of Kashmir; by Sri Lanka against Tamil secessionists; by Burma (Myanmar) against various ethnic groups; by Indonesia in East Timor; by both Turkey and Iraq against the Kurds; and by several Latin American countries such as Colombia and Guatemala against rebel factions. Extraregional intervention would include most of the examples previously cited, most notable of which are US intervention in Southeast Asia, the Middle East and Africa, and Cuban intervention in Angola.

90. *Ibid*, p 136.

91. *Ibid*, p 148. They also argue that to "ignore Internal Intervention in examining relations in the South would be to pose an ethnocentric perspective on the politics of much of the world." *Ibid*, p 154.

92. See, among others: Carpenter, T G, Direct military intervention", in Schraeder, P J (ed), *op cit*, p 130; Dunér, B, *op cit*, p 60; Geldenhuys, D, *op cit*, p 14; Kaw, M, "Predicting Soviet military intervention", *Journal of Conflict Resolution*, Vol 33, No 3, September 1989, pp 419-420; Matheson, N, *The 'rules of the game' of superpower military intervention in the Third World 1975-1989*, University Press of America, Washington, 1982, pp 9-10; Schraeder, P J, *op cit*, p 115; and Tillema, H K, *op cit*, pp 179cf.

93. This basic distinction was made by Von Glahn, G, *Law among nations: An introduction to Public International Law*, Macmillan, London, 1971, pp 164-172. Intervention by right includes intervention in terms of treaty stipulations, at the explicit invitation of a lawful government or to support or protect own citizens mistreated in another country. Permissible intervention includes humanitarian intervention and intervention to end chronic disorder in a neighbouring state. See also: Geldenhuys, D, *op cit*, pp 7-9.

94. Geldenhuys, D, *op cit*, pp 11-13 and p 251.

95. Haas, E B, *op cit*, p 71.

96. Arend, A C and R J Beck, *op cit*, p 92.

97. See for example the policy position of African countries on this issue in the context of democratisation. British Broadcasting Corporation (BBC), "World: Africa leaders promise new era", in *BBC News*, BBC Online Network, 14 July 1999. In 1998 the aim of the military intervention by the Combined Task Force of South Africa and Botswana under SADC auspices in Lesotho was "to restore stability to the Kingdom of Lesotho...", fearing a possible *coup d'état* by dissident elements. Department of Defence: South Africa, "Military assistance to Lesotho: Operation Boleas", *Bulletin*, No 57/98, 22 September 1998, p 1. See also: Department of Defence: South Africa, *The SADC intervention in Lesotho: A military perspective*, Internet http://www.mil.za/SANDF, 22 May 1999. In this respect the Deputy Minister of Defence, Mr Ronnie Kasrils, stated: "Let us be reminded that our assistance was urgently requested by an elected government on the basis of a SADC agreement to prevent military coups in our region". Department of Defence: South Africa, "The SANDF's baptism of fire - Article by Mr Ronnie Kasrils - Deputy Minister of Defence", *Bulletin*, No 57/98, 22 September 1998, p 1.

98. Geldenhuys, D, *op cit*, pp 40-49. See also Beach, H, "Causes, aims and motivation of intervention", in Williamson, R, *op cit*, pp 191-204.

99. Haas, E B, *op cit*, p 81.

100. *Ibid*, pp 71-74.

101. Bull, H, "Conclusion", *op cit*, pp 191-192; Mason, R A, *op cit*, p xi; and Millar, T B, *op cit*, p 7.

102. Bull, H, "Intervention in the Third World", in Bull, H (ed), *op cit*, p 135.

103. Tillema, H K, *op cit*, p 187n.

104. Haas, E B, *op cit*, p 65.

105. Hoffman, S, "The problem of intervention", in Bull, H (ed), *op cit*, p 10; and Schraeder, P J, *op cit*, p 115.

106. Vincent, R J, *Non-intervention and International Law*, pp 5-6 as quoted in Geldenhuys, D, *op cit*, p 16.

107. Tillema, H K, *op cit*, pp 187-188n.

108. Dunér, B, *op cit*, pp 60-62. A statistical indication is also provided of the minimum force levels and extent of the involvement required for the use of each instrument to be considered an act of intervention.

109. Schraeder, P J, *op cit*, p 114.

110. Beach H, "Causes, aims and motivation of intervention", *op cit*, pp 199-203; and Evans, G, *op cit*, pp 8-13.
111. Brooks, L F and A Kanter, *op cit*, pp 26-30.
112. A paraphrasing of John Keegans' comment on war from a lecture at Southampton University, Fall 1994, as quoted in Beach, H, "Causes, aims and motivation of intervention", *op cit*, p 191.
113. For a more detailed discussion of these stages, see the sources on which this summary is based, namely: Cohen, E A, "The dynamics of military intervention", in Levite, A E (*et al*), *op cit*, pp 263-284; Downs, G W, "The lessons of disengagement", in Levite, AE (*et al*), *op cit*, pp 287-299; Jentleson, B W and A E Levite, *op cit*, pp 16-19; and Kupchan, C A, "Getting in: The initial stage of military intervention", in Levite, A E (et al), *op cit*, pp 243-259.
114. Blacker, C D, *op cit*, p 61.
115. Lewis, W, "Challenge and response: Coercive intervention issues", in Kanter, A and LF Brooks, *op cit*, p 78.
116. See, for example, the discussion in Otte, T G, "Military intervention", *op cit*, pp 193-195. Although both "push-pull" factors contribute to a policy decision to intervene, it has to be borne in mind that "(i)t is not simply an action/inaction decision or choice, but rather which type of action to choose from among a number of alternatives... as a preferred course of action". Jentleson, B W, Levite, A E and L Berman, *op cit*, p 320.
117. Brooks, L F and A Kanter, *op cit*, pp 35-40.
118. This discussion is based on: The American Assembly, *op cit*, pp 236-238; Beach, H, "Causes, aims and means of intervention", *op cit*, pp 198 and 200; Lewis, W, *op cit*, p 81; Otte, T G, "Military intervention", *op cit*, p 202; and Roper, J, *op cit*, pp 211-214.
119. Beach, H, "Causes, aims and means of intervention", *op cit*, pp 194-195.
120. Sewall, J O B, *op cit*, pp 90-104.
121. Lewis, W, *op cit*, p 70.
122. An appeal of this nature has, for example, already been made by Javier Solana, the European Union's security and foreign affairs representative, in respect of KFOR in Kosovo. *Financial Times* (London), 4-5 March 2000.
123. The American Assembly, *op cit*, p 232.
124. Millar, T B, *op cit*, p 10.

125. Beach, H, "Second thoughts ...", *op cit*, pp 75-82.
126. Vasquez, J A, "Morality and politics", in Vasquez, J A (ed), *Classics of International Relations*, 3rd edition, Prentice Hall, Upper Saddle River, 1996, p 7.
127. As quoted in Carpenter, T G, *op cit*, p 134.
128. Speech to the US Military Academy, West Point, 5 January 1993, quoted in Roper, J, *op cit*, pp 213-214.
129. *The East African* (Nairobi), 17 August 1999.
130. Hirst, P, "Security challenges in post-Communist Europe", in Freedman, L, "Introduction", *op cit*, pp 179-182 and 186-189.
131. *Beeld* (Johannesburg), 29 August 1997; and *The Star* (Johannesburg), 9 October 1997.
132. *Charter of the Organization of African Unity, 1963*, Article III(2) and (5).
133. Sesay, A, *Africa and Europe: From partition to interdependence or dependence?*, Croom Helm, London, 1986, p 170.
134. Economic Community of West African States (ECOWAS), *Protocols annexed to the Treaty of ECOWAS*, undated, pp 130-139. This includes the *Protocol on Non-Aggression, 1973* and the *Protocol on Mutual Assistance and Defence, 1981*.
135. See, *inter alia*: *Kampala Document for a proposed Conference on Security, Stability, Development and Cooperation in Africa (CSSDCA)*, 23 May 1991, Section II.A.(I) and B; Organisation of African Unity (OAU), *Resolving conflict in Africa*, 1992, p 17; OAU, *Declaration of the Assembly of Heads of State and Government on the Establishment within the OAU of a Mechanism for Conflict Prevention, Management and Resolution*, 30 June 1993, par 14, 15 and 16; and Southern African Development Community (SADC), *The Southern African Development Community (SADC) Organ for Politics, Defence and Security*, 28 June 1996, Principles (a), (d) and (g), and Objectives (d), (g) and (l).
136. British Broadcasting Corporation (BBC), *op cit*, 14 July 1999.
137. See, *inter alia*: Brands, H W, "Decisions on American armed intervention: Lebanon, Dominican Republic, and Grenada", *Political Studies Quarterly*, No 102, 1987-88; Levite, A E (*et al*), *op cit*; Little, R, *Intervention: External involvement in civil wars*, Rowman and Littlefield, Totowa, 1975; Vertzberger, Y Y I, "Rethinking and reconceptualizing risk in foreign policy decision-making: A sociocognitive approach", *Political Psychology*, Vol 16, 1995; Vertzberger, Y Y I, "Making and taking risky

decisions", *Cooperation and Conflict*, Vol 33, No 1, 1998; and Vertzberger, Y Y I, *Risk taking and decisionmaking...*, *op cit*. The latter is the most comprehensive work on this topic.

138. Except where otherwise indicated, the discussion of the theory of risk and military intervention is based on and summarises: Vertzberger, Y Y I, "Making and taking risky decisions", op cit, pp 5-29; and Vertzberger, Y Y I, *Risk taking and decisionmaking...*, *op cit*, pp 17-42.

139. Vertzberger, Y Y I, "Rethinking and reconceptualizing risk...", *op cit*, p 351.

140. Vertzberger, Y Y I, "Making and taking risky decisions", *op cit*, p 12.

# Chapter 2

## INTERNATIONAL LAW AND FORCIBLE INTERVENTION: A MILLENNIUM ASSESSMENT

### George Barrie

### 1. INTRODUCTION

Intervention is a term loosely used to refer to interference by a state in the affairs of another state which can be calculated to have certain consequences on that other state. Such interference can be in the external or internal affairs of another state. It is not a new phenomenon and has been a significant characteristic of international politics. Intervention has been political, economic and military. There is consequently a lack of consensus on a definition of intervention and the phrase has become a portmanteau term covering a wide spectrum of scenarios. International political scientists approach intervention from a different perspective to the international law practitioner focusing more on the whys and wherefores of the interference. The international lawyer again is more interested in the legalities of the intervention and approaches the issue from the premise that state sovereignty is a supreme principle of international law. This chapter will concentrate on intervention from an international law perspective, moving from the legal principle of non-intervention to legal justifications allowing intervention.

## 2. THE PRINCIPLE OF INTERNATIONAL NON-INTERVENTION

The leading nations of the world have at various times gathered to fill in the cracks appearing in the international order. At Westphalia 1648, Vienna 1814-1815, Versailles 1919 and San Francisco 1945 they attempted to set out the contours of a new order and lay down rules governing the world of future generations. One basic rule that the leading nations could always agree on was the equality of states which impliedly guaranteed state sovereignty and prohibited aggression except if used defensively. The principle of sovereignty of states has as its basic premise the norm of non-intervention in domestic affairs, be it forcible or non-forcible.

The norm of non-intervention is proclaimed widely and is seen to be a legal obligation and not a practice of comity. The norm of non-intervention has a long history and has found expression in numerous international instruments of a universal, regional and bilateral kind aptly illustrated in the 1933 *Montevideo Convention on the Rights and Duties of States* which declared that "no state has the right to intervene in the internal or external affairs of another".[1]

The same principle is expressed in the Charter of the Organisation of American States.[2]

> No State or group of States has the right to intervene, directly or indirectly, for any reason whatever, in the internal or external affairs of any other State. The foregoing principle prohibits not only armed force but also any other form of interference or attempted threat against the personality of the State or against its political, economic, and cultural elements.

The United Nations Charter did not adopt the formulation of the *Montevideo Convention* or other early instruments. Its prohibition in Article 2(7) of intervention in domestic jurisdiction is addressed to the United Nations Organisation (UN) and not to states. Several key articles of the charter however clearly indicate that the framers of the charter did not intend to see intervention by states as being acceptable. Charter provisions clearly set out non-intervention as a norm and see non-intervention as a legal obligation.

Article 1(2) for example affirms the principles of equal rights and self-determination. Article 2(1) states that the United Nations is based on the principle of sovereign equality of all member states. Article 2(4) specifically requires states to refrain in their international relations from the threat or use of force against the territorial integrity or political independence of any state.

These skeletal norms have been given flesh by the UN General Assembly through various declarations. In 1965 it adopted the *Declaration on the Inadmissibility of Intervention in the Domestic Affairs of States and the Protection of their Independence and Sovereignty* (known as the Declaration on Intervention).[3] Nineteen seventy saw the same terms embodied in the *Declaration on Principles of International Law concerning Friendly Relations and Cooperation among States in Accordance with the United Nations* (known as the Friendly Relations Declaration).[4]

This Friendly Relations Declaration has a more legalistic tone and refers to "violations of international law". Key passages state:

> No State or group of States has the right to intervene, directly or indirectly, for any reason whatever, in the internal or external affairs of any other State. Consequently, armed intervention and all other forms of interference or attempted threat against the personality

of the State or against its political, economic, and cultural elements, are [condemned] in violation of international law.

No State may use or encourage the use of economic, political or any other type of measures to coerce another State in order to obtain from it the subordination of the exercise of its sovereign rights [or] and to secure from it advantages of any kind. Also, no State shall organize, assist, foment, finance, incite or tolerate subversive, terrorist or armed activities directed towards the violent overthrow of the régime of another State, or interfere in civil strife in another State.

The use of force to deprive peoples of their national identity constitutes a violation of their inalienable rights and of the principle of non-intervention.

Every State has an inalienable right to choose its political, economic, social and cultural systems, without interference in any form by another State.

Noteworthy more recent texts embodying the principle of non-intervention are the 1981 *Algiers Accord* where the United States pledged that it would not intervene in Iran's internal affairs.[5] In 1987 five Central American presidents signed an agreement that affirmed the right of all nations to determine freely and without outside interference of any kind their economic, political and social models.[6] In 1988 Afghanistan and Pakistan signed accords (guaranteed by the United States and the Soviet Union) with several references to non-intervention forcible and non-forcible.[7]

The Cold War ended with a whimper in the 1990s but this major and dramatic development did not lead to a modern Westphalia, Vienna, Versailles or San Francisco to clarify the contours of the new world order. This was a major lapse as history may still point out. The 1990s saw the old rules of interstate relationships changing and saw erosions of national sovereignty. New phenomena presented themselves. An example is states without governments such as Somalia. The UN Security Council became a more active promoter of democracy and humanitarian values and its actions caused a reappraisal of the state sovereignty principle. The Security Council started authorising force where breaches of the peace or threats to the peace emerged. In these instances the use of force became less attributable to governments and more *collectively* organised.

The time was ripe for the international community to re-examine the principles regarding the use of force. The questions that immediately came to the fore were: Are the principles of state sovereignty still paramount or are the interests of the international community not more important at the turn of the millennium? Can these two approaches (sovereignty and international community interests) not be reconciled?

There has been no Westphalia, Vienna, Versailles or San Francisco to rethink these important issues and one is thus left with state practice to determine what modern international law has to say on the issue of intervention.

Intervention as referred to above has implied the use of the term as generally understood to encompass either non-forcible intervention or forcible intervention. This chapter will consider the position of forcible intervention in the sense of military or allied types of intervention.[8]

It will therefore not discuss non-forcible intervention such as the recalling of diplomats, economic sanctions, refusal to grant credit, transnational funding to influence a political contest, financial assistance to electoral campaigns, and so on.

## 3. DEFINING INTERVENTION

The term intervention[9] was known and practised widely in the ancient states system and was also prevalent in the sixteenth and seventeenth centuries and in the Napoleonic era.[10] The twentieth century saw frequent intervention. So much so that in the late 1960s it was regarded as a core problem of world politics. In the 1970s intervention was described as a ubiquitous feature of modern international relations and "perhaps an inherent feature of it."[11] The 1970s saw numerous case studies of foreign military intervention.[12]

Because the term intervention has been used in so many contexts from interference to meddling to forcible intervention there is confusion as to its meaning or definition. Intervention can be seen as the recalling of diplomats, trade sanctions and refusal to grant credit, or it can be seen to be interference by a state (or group of states) associated with the use of force in an attempt to impose its will on another state or to restore law and order on request.

Intervention thus can have various meanings. The meaning can differ if the term is used by a political scientist, an international affairs analyst or an international lawyer.

Geldenhuys,[13] after an exhaustive study of the various definitions ascribed to intervention by international relations scholars and international lawyers, sees the following definition as representative:

> It is the calculated action of a state, a group of states, an international organization or some other international actor(s) to influence the political system of another state (including its structure of authority, its domestic policies and its political leaders) against its will by using various means of coercion (forcible or non-forcible) in pursuit of particular political objectives.

To this definition may be added the scenario where forcible intervention is requested — as an exercise in restoring law and order.

Forcible intervention is well documented, ranging from armed invasion to blockades to the supplying of palace guards. Recent examples are the United States (US) in Vietnam in the 1960s, the Dominican Republic (1965), Grenada (1983) and Panama (1989). The Soviet Union intervened in Hungary (1956), Czechoslovakia (1968) and Afghanistan (1979). Other examples are military interventions by the United Kingdom, France, Belgium, Israel, Cuba, Libya, Syria, Tanzania, Morocco and South Africa.

## 4. MILITARY INTERVENTION

International lawyers, being interested in the legalities of all international state pursuits, are particularly concerned with the legality of forcible intervention. Intervention is, as a rule, prohibited by international law.[14] This prohibition is the corollary of every state's right to sovereignty, territorial integrity and political independence.

Where intervention involves the use of armed force it also violates Article 2(4) of the UN Charter which prohibits the threat or use of force against the territorial integrity or political independence of any state or in any other matter inconsistent with the principles of the United Nations.

Article 2(4) is also reflected in customary international law. This was found in the *Military and Paramilitary Activities Case* (Nicaragua v United States).[15]

The prohibition of intervention *is embodied in several treaties. Examples are Article 8 of the Montevideo Convention on the Rights and Duties of States 1933,*[16] *Article 15 of the Charter of the Organisation of American States 1948;*[17] Article 8 of the

*Charter of the League of Arab States* 1945;[18] Article 3 of the *Charter of the Organisation of African Unity* 1963.[19] Article 3 of the *International Law Commission's Draft Declaration on Rights and Duties of States* emphatically states that every state has the duty to refrain from intervention in the internal or external affairs of any other state.[20]

In 1965 the General Assembly adopted the *Declaration on the Inadmissibility of Intervention*[21] by 109 votes in favour, none against, and one abstention. This resolution declared that no state has the right to intervene directly or indirectly, *for any reason whatsoever*, in the internal or external affairs of any other state and that, consequently, armed intervention and all other forms of interference are condemned. It was declared that strict observance of these obligations was essential for international peace – a breach would violate the letter and principle of the UN Charter.

Similar provisions can be found in the *Declaration on Principles of International Law concerning Friendly Relations and Cooperation among States*[22] and in Principle VI of the *Declaration on Principles Guiding Relations between Participating States*, which forms part of the *Final Act of the Helsinki Conference on Security and Co-operation in Europe* 1975.[23]

What is the effect of consent to such resolutions of the General Assembly and more particularly the Friendly Relations Declaration? The International Court of Justice has regarded the effect of consent to such resolutions as not merely a reiteration or elucidation of the treaty commitment undertaken in the UN Charter, but as an acceptance of the validity of the rules declared by the resolutions by themselves, and as an expression of the *opinio iuris*.[24]

Besides the above, Article 2(7) of the UN Charter prohibits intervention in essentially domestic matters.

Despite international legal principles forbidding states to intervene directly or indirectly in the internal and external affairs of other states, history has seen various instances of intervention with statesmen and international lawyers differing only in their judgement as to which circumstances *justify* intervention and which do not. Geldenhuys refers to intervention "by right" and intervention "not based on right".[25] The former would include intervention in terms of a treaty at the explicit invitation of a lawful government, in support of a state's own citizens mistreated in another country[26] and collective action undertaken by an international organ. A controversial issue has been so-called humanitarian intervention and intervention to bring chronic disorder in a neighbouring state to an end lest it threaten the interests of the intervening state.

Humanitarian intervention will be discussed in greater detail later. Those who defend humanitarian intervention, see it as a right that comes into being when a state renders itself guilty of cruelties against and persecution of its nationals in such a way as to deny their fundamental human rights and to shock the conscience of mankind[27]. It has been argued that the interests of humanity in these circumstances outweigh the prohibition on intervention.

There have been various instances of humanitarian interventions during the past two centuries. In 1827 England, France and Russia intervened in the struggle between revolutionary Greece and Turkey to prevent the extermination of the Greeks. Christian powers regularly intervened on behalf of Christian minorities in the Muslim Middle East. In 1860 the French occupied parts of Syria. In 1898 the United States intervened militarily in Cuba to put an end to the barbarities attributed to Spanish colonial rule.

Since 1945 supposedly humanitarian interventions have included Belgian military action in the Congo in 1960 and 1964; US intervention in the Dominican Republic in 1965; and the 1975 Indonesian intervention in East Timor.[28]

Justification for the despatch of United States military forces to Mexico in 1916 was allegedly based on the need to end chronic disorder in a neighbouring state. US intervention in the Dominican Republic in 1965 was justified in terms of preventing communists seizing power in that country.

Assisting a "people" to achieve self-determination has often been used to justify intervention.[29] It is widely argued, for example, that intervention is permissible in support of indigenous pro-democracy forces engaged in conflict with a repressive regime.

Whereas international lawyers have tended to find legal justifications for the types of interventions sketched above, international relationists have not placed so much emphasis on the legalities. They see the practical value of intervention and focus on the historical roots of intervention. International relations scholars argue that in modern times strategic, political, economic and social considerations make the involvement of nations in one another's affairs imperative and therefore proper[30]. Politically justified objectives for intervention that have been put forward include remedying injustices in other states; bringing about national liberation (self-determination), promoting democracy; reuniting divided populations and stabilising unstable societies.

This approach is epitomised to Roosevelt's latter day (1904) application of the Monroe Doctrine where the United States arrogated to itself the duty to intervene in the Western hemisphere where chronic wrongdoing or impotence resulted in the undermining of civilised society. This led to the United

States seeing itself as an international policing power. This approach, on "doctrine", was used in the previous century to justify 31 interventions in Latin America before the United States in 1935 formally accepted the principle of non-intervention.[31]

The era of the Cold War saw the Truman Doctrine which maintained that where the will of the minority was forcibly imposed on the majority and maintained through oppression, it would be the policy of the United States to support people resisting such subjugation by armed minorities and outside pressures.[32]

This "watchman on the walls of freedom" approach was upheld by President John F Kennedy and Lyndon B Johnson and used to justify several US interventions. A corollary to this was the Brezhnev Doctrine claiming a right to intervene in socialist countries, an example of which was the Soviet Union intervention in Czechoslovakia in 1968.[33]

Nowadays the distinction between unilateral and collective intervention has a direct bearing on the acceptable justification for intervention. Single-state intervention has become "socially" unacceptable in the modern world and has become tainted with "illegality". Collective intervention is enjoying greater "legitimacy" especially with the Cold War divisions disappearing and the state of paralysis between permanent members of the Security Council becoming a thing of the past. The recent NATO incursion into Yugoslavia precipitated by the Kosovo crisis is an example of this. The UN Security Council however still sees itself under Chapter VII of the charter as being the ultimate legitimator of coercive intervention.

## 5. COERCIVE INTERFERENCE VERSUS NON-INTERFERENCE: THE CASE OF NICARAGUA VERSUS THE USA

As stated above, intervention can mean different things and one's view of it is influenced by one's point of departure – international lawyer or international relationist. From an international lawyer's perspective intervention has a stricter meaning than that ascribed to it by the international relationist. For the international lawyer intervention is a forcible or dictatorial interference by a state in the affairs of another state, calculated to impose certain conduct or consequences on that other state[34]. According to the International Court of Justice[35] an intervention is prohibited if (a) it impinges on matters regarding which each state is permitted to make decisions by itself freely (eg choice of its own political or economic system or adoption of its own foreign policy); and (b) it involves interference in regard to this freedom by methods of coercion, especially force. Anything that falls short of this is strictly speaking not intervention within the meaning of the prohibition under international law.

Intervention is thus a form of interference by one state in the affairs (internal or external) of another state affecting those affairs directly or indirectly. Such interference infringes a state's sovereignty and is not legally permitted.

Support for the opposition in another state was the central issue in the *Military and Paramilitary Activities Case*.[36] Here the International Court of Justice held that the support given by the United States of America to the opposition forces within Nicaragua was unlawful.

It may be an opportune moment to look at the *Military and Paramilitary Activities Case* in more detail.

In April 1984 the United States heard that the Government of Nicaragua was about to file a claim against it in the International Court of Justice concerning its role in the ongoing Nicaraguan civil war. In response, the United States filed a statement with the court in which it suspended its acceptance of the court's jurisdiction regarding disputes with any Central American state.

In November 1984 the court ruled that it retained jurisdiction over the claim filed by Nicaragua despite the US action and decided to consider the merits of the case. The United States then announced that it was withdrawing from further participation in the case on the grounds that the controversy involved an inherently political problem that was not appropriate for judicial resolution. On 7 October 1985 the United States took a further step by terminating its acceptance of the court's compulsory jurisdiction under Article 36(2) of the Statute of the International Court of Justice. Meanwhile, proceedings in the court continued without further participation by the United States, and on 27 June 1986 the court handed down its decision.

In essence the court decided by twelve votes to three that the United States of America, by training, arming, equipping, financing and supplying the Contra forces or otherwise encouraging, supporting and aiding military and paramilitary activities in and against Nicaragua, had acted against the Republic of Nicaragua, in breach of its obligation under customary international law not to intervene in the affairs of another state.

The court also found that the United States had violated the rules of customary international law prohibiting the use of force against another state; that by directing and authorising overflights of Nicaraguan territory and by other acts the

United States was in breach of its obligation under customary international law not to violate the sovereignty of another state; that by laying mines and failing to make known their location (by fourteen votes to one) the United States had violated its obligations under customary international law not to use force, not to intervene and not to violate the sovereignty of another state.

The court gave its judgement on the principles of customary international law, the rules of non-intervention, the use of force and respect for territorial integrity and sovereignty.

The attitude adopted by the United States was unexpected. After participating fully in the proceedings on provisional measures, the jurisdiction of the court and the admissibility of the Nicaraguan Application — and losing them all — the United States on 18 January 1985 petulantly withdrew from participation in any further proceedings in the case; and, in flagrant disregard of its obligations under Articles 59 and 60 of the Statute and Article 94 of the UN Charter, it denounced the court's judgement of 26 November 1984 as manifestly erroneous and resolved to reserve its rights as to any future decision by the court.

Such a "reservation of rights" the court found to have no bearing on the validity of its decision.

The court devoted much attention to the argument of the United States that it had acted in asserting its rights of self-defence. The court found that the right of self-defence — whether individual or collective — was recognised and firmly established in international law. The court saw the legal basis for self-defence the fact that the state concerned had been the victim of an armed attack.

With regard to "armed attack" the court observed:

> [T]he Court does not believe that the concept of 'armed attack' includes only acts by armed bands where such acts occur on a significant scale but also assistance to rebels in the form of the provision of weapons or logistical or other support. Such assistance may be regarded as a threat or use of force, or amount to intervention in the internal or external affairs of other States.[37]

Regarding the relationship between armed attack and collective self-defence the court held:

> It is also clear that it is the State which is the victim of an armed attack which must form and declare the view that it has been so attacked. There is no rule in customary international law permitting another State to exercise the right of collective self-defence on the basis of its own assessment of the situation.[38]

On the customary rule of non-intervention the court held that the principle forbids all states or groups of states to intervene directly or indirectly in the internal or external affairs of other states. A prohibited intervention should accordingly be one bearing on matters in which each state is permitted, by the principle of state sovereignty, to decide freely. One of these is the choice of a political, economic, social and cultural system, and the formulation of foreign policy. Intervention is wrongful when it uses methods of coercion in regard to such choices, which should remain free ones. The element of coercion, which defines and indeed forms the very essence of prohibited intervention, is particularly obvious in the case of an intervention that uses force, either in the direct form of military action, or in the indirect form of support for subversive or terrorist activities within another state.[39]

This judgement of the International Court of Justice represents a fascinating attempt to assess the relevance of international law to forcible intervention. The court ultimately adjudicated mainly in favour of a small, beleaguered Third World country that was confronted by a pattern of escalating military intervention being planned and financed by the government of a superpower. This judgement was rendered under difficult circumstances. The United States government signalled its bitter opposition in advance to any recourse to judicial procedures, refused to appear during the merits phase of the proceedings, and scornfully repudiated the authority of the court to pronounce upon the issues in question. Never in its history had the court been, at once, so prominent and so embattled. At the moment of genuine jurisprudential triumph, the court's institutional authority was attacked as never before, and from a source previously supportive of it.

The International Court of Justice ruled in favour of state equality and sovereign rights and placed the weight of international law behind weaker states without being influenced by ideological overtones and without favouring the imperial and privileged state actors.

To constitute prohibited intervention in a legal sense, the interference must be coercive and it must deprive the state intervened against of control over the issues involved. Severance of diplomatic relations, economic boycotts and other types of sanctions fall short of being coercive and do not constitute unlawful intervention.

Coercive intervention may involve the use of armed force directly through military action or it may be done indirectly by giving support to subversive or terrorist activities in another state. In the *Military and Paramilitary Case* the International Court of Justice specifically held that the support given by the United States of America to forces in Nicaragua fighting against the established government constituted unlawful intervention. This support consisted of financial support, training, supply of weapons, intelligence and logistical support. The International Court of Justice declared that the *Declaration on the Inadmissibility of Intervention in the Domestic Affairs of State and the Protection of their Independence and Sovereignty* (*supra*) was a *law-making* resolution. Such a finding by the International Court of Justice is important as it authoritatively recognises that declaration (expressed in General Assembly Resolution 2131 (XX)) as being *legally binding*.[40]

Where economic or political support for subversive or terrorist activities in another state has a coercive effect, such actions could also constitute illegal intervention.[41]

## 6. CIRCUMSTANCES JUSTIFYING INTERVENTION

Are there circumstances that justify intervention from an international law perspective? Are there limitations as to the manner and circumstances of the intervention which comply with the prohibition against the use or threat of force laid down by the UN Charter? Must the actions be proportional to the circumstances giving rise to the intervention? Must all other alternatives first be exhausted (such as diplomatic representations) before resorting to intervention? Six reasons have been put forward to justify a state intervening in the affairs of another state. These are (i) intervention at request; (ii) a state's right to protect its citizens abroad; (iii) self-defence; (iv) self-determination; (v) as result of a treaty, and (vi) for humanitarian reasons. These six averred justifications will be considered in the next sections.

### 6.1 Intervention at request

The UN Security Council has accepted that it is the inherent and lawful right of every state, in the exercise of its sovereignty, to request assistance from another state or group of states.[42] This principle was also accepted by the International Court of Justice.[43] An intervention consisting of assistance rendered by one state to another at the request and with the consent of the latter is therefore excluded from the general prohibition against intervention.

Such consent can be given on an *ad hoc* basis or by treaty. Such requests in many instances are requests for assistance by means of armed forces or the supply of military equipment. There are various examples of such requests. In 1957 British forces at the request of the Sultan went to the aid of Muscat and Oman. Jordan and Lebanon in 1958 requested the intervention of US forces; British forces assisted Uganda, Tanganyika and Kenya in 1964 and Zambia in 1965, at their request. During the Vietnam conflict US forces assisted the Republic of Vietnam at the request of the latter; in 1968, 1969 and 1983 French forces responded to requests for assistance from Chad and in 1978 responded to a request from Zaire. In 1977 military forces from the Federal Republic of Germany freed a hijacked aircraft at Mogadishu airport at the request of Somalia. In 1982 United States, Italian and French forces landed in Beirut following an agreement with Lebanon. In 1987 Sri Lanka allowed Indian forces to assist in the restoration of order. In 1988 Indian troops were requested to help the Maldives restore order in that country after an attempted *coup*.

When the Soviet Union sent its forces into Hungary in 1956 questions were asked about the possible abuse of the exception of intervention by request. Questions arose as to the abuse of the exception by for example fabricating requests or the request for assistance coming from a government with only limited or temporary authority.

Such abuse is a real problem and consequently the issue as to whether a request for assistance should be regarded as genuine — or not, will have to be determined in the light of all the relevant circumstances.

The entry of Soviet forces into Afghanistan in 1979 preceded by an alleged request from Afghanistan — was contemporaneous with the execution of the previous president and his replacement by a new president who was not even in Afghanistan at the time.[44] Questions were asked about the landing of US forces in Grenada in 1983 and in Panama in 1989. The Panama landing was aimed at securing the arrest of General Noriega, the military leader and effective ruler of Panama. The United States justified its action by submitting that the landing had taken place with the consent of the constitutional authority of Panama. It further justified its actions on grounds such as self-defence, the need to restore democracy in Panama, the need to defend the Panama Canal and the refusal of Noriega to honour election results which showed Estrada to be the winner. The United States said it was acting with the tacit consent of Estrada who was sworn in as president within hours of the landing of the US forces.

This was followed by a proposed Security Council resolution condemning the United States for flagrantly violating international law[45]. This resolution was not adopted because of three veto votes.[46] An equivalent resolution was however adopted by the General Assembly by 75 votes to 20 with 40 abstentions.[47]

While it is accepted that a lawfully established government is entitled to seek assistance from other states in preserving internal law and order or to defend itself against unlawful attacks, what are the limits to this lawfulness when a civil war is raging? According to Jennings and Watts it depends on whether the government is in overall control of the state and the internal disturbances are essentially limited to matters of local law and order or isolated guerrilla or terrorist activities. If so, it may seek assistance from other states.[48]

But if a civil war exists where the control of the state is divided between the warring factions, intervention or assistance could be contrary to international law. States are obligated to refrain from action encouraging any activity that would promote the civil strife.

Various major and regional powers have used civil wars as a pretext to advance their own ideological interests. Many of these interventions were based on shaky legal foundations.[49] The evidence of foreign support for the rebels in the cases of Hungary, Afghanistan and Grenada was never substantiated. To many the US argument that Vietnam comprised two separate states instead of one unit in which a civil war was being fought between North and South, was highly suspect.[50]

The *Declaration on the Inadmissibility of Intervention in the Domestic Affairs of States and the Protection of their Independence and Sovereignty* 1965[51] succinctly declares in section 2 that no state shall organise, assist, foment, finance, incite or tolerate subversive, terrorist or armed activities directed towards the violent overthrow of the regime of another state, or interfere in civil strife in another state.

South Africa's intervention in Angola in 1975-1976 was therefore of doubtful legality. South Africa's defence of its actions was that the MPLA government was supported by Cuba and the Soviet Union who were attempting to subvert the whole of Angola.[52] South Africa's defence was condemned by the UN Security Council[53] on the ground that the evidence supported the MLPA's claim that it had invited Cuba to send troops to Angola to assist it against South African aggression.

South Africa's subsequent intervention and active support for UNITA was justified as self-defence against Angolan-supported SWAPO bases.[54] This defence was also rejected by the Security Council.[55]

The only form of intervention allowed where a civil war is being fought, and the control of the state is divided between warring factions, would probably be intervention of a humanitarian nature.[56]

According to Shearer[57] since the coming into force of the UN Charter it can no longer be asserted that in a civil war there is a right of intervention in support of the government unless forces opposed to the government are being supported by another state. He is supported by Wright[58] who is of the opinion that international law does not permit the use of force in the territory of another state on invitation either of the recognised or insurgent government in times of rebellion, insurrection or civil war. Harris[59] declares that internal conflicts are the concern of the state alone.

If one keeps in mind that the underlying premise of the *Military and Paramilitary Activities Case*[60] was based on the view that the internationalisation of conflict must be minimalised, the premise is in line with modern international law views that states must stay out of civil wars in other states. It should also be borne in mind that both the *1965 Declaration on the Inadmissibility of Intervention*[61] and the *Declaration of Principles of International Law concerning Friendly Relations and Co-operation Among States*[62] both declare that the internal conflicts within states are the concern of those states alone.

The United Kingdom supports the non-intervention principle but does not consider that this rule is in any way prejudiced by the right of a legally constituted and internationally recognised government to seek and receive assistance from a friendly state to preserve law and order. The only condition would be that the government that responds to such a request for assistance would have to satisfy itself that its response is proper and will have to expect that its actions will come under close scrutiny by the international community.[63]

## 6.2 A state's right to protect its citizens abroad

It appears that where a state's citizens are being wrongfully treated abroad it is justifiable for that state to intervene in order to secure their proper treatment. This justification has been put forward frequently.

The United Kingdom and France in 1956 landed forces in Egypt ostensibly to protect British nationals who were in danger after Israel attached Egypt. Belgian forces landed in the Congo in 1960 to protect Belgian nationals when civil disturbances broke out. In 1964 Belgian and US forces landed in the Congo to rescue hostages. In 1965 US forces landed in the Dominican Republic at the time of political upheavals. In 1976 Israeli commandos landed in Entebbe, Uganda, to free the passengers of a hijacked aircraft. In 1978 Egyptian forces landed in Cyprus to rescue Egyptian hostages held in a hijacked aircraft. In 1978 French and Belgian forces landed in Zaire to protect Belgian and other European nationals after serious rebel activities. In 1983 US forces landed in Grenada allegedly to protect US nationals.

This type of intervention is held to be justified where the nationals are in immediate danger of losing their lives or are threatened with serious injury.

The need to protect property is also advanced to justify intervention in another state. This argument was put forward when the United Kingdom landed forces in Egypt in 1956. It was also advanced by South Africa in 1976 when it sent forces into Angola to protect the Calueque Dam and construction site which was regarded as being vital to the economy of Namibia (then under control of South Africa.)

The rationale for US intervention in Grenada was ostensibly to protect 11,000 US nationals resident there. It should not be overlooked that US participation in the invasion was in response to an urgent request by six Caribbean states for the United States to help restore political order in Grenada. Such help would at the same time contribute to halting Marxist influence throughout the region. There was also US concern about a 9 000-metres airport runway being constructed by Cubans at Point Salives. It was believed that this airport facility would be used as a fuelling stop for Soviet planes carrying military equipment to Nicaragua. It was also believed that the airport might be employed as a Cuban base for supplying troops in Angola, as well as a strategic springboard for launching subversive operations throughout the lower Caribbean basin and into Latin America.

Did the United States have the lawful right to intervene militarily, alone or in concert, in the domestic political affairs of Grenada? Upon close inspection, says Joyner, one would have to look hard to find acceptable justification under international law for the US action.[64]

## 6.3 Individual or collective self-defence

The International Court of Justice accepted in the *Military and Paramilitary Activities Case*[65] that collective self-defence could justify action that would otherwise constitute unlawful intervention.[66]

The right to self-defence or collective self-defence has been asserted on various occasions. In 1956 Israel invoked self-defence when launching an attack on Egypt and also in 1967 when invading Arab territories. In 1962 US and South Vietnamese forces entered Cambodia in order to attack North Vietnamese forces who were using Cambodian territory to wage war against South Vietnam. In 1981 Israel attacked nuclear installations in Iraq, justifying the action on the grounds of self-defence. In 1982 the United Kingdom used armed force in self-defence in response to Argentina's seizure of the Falkland Islands. In the 1980s the United States attempted to justify its actions against Nicaragua on the grounds of collective self-defence. The International Court of Justice rejected these claims.[67] In 1986 the United States attacked terrorist installations in Libya, basing their action on self-defence. In 1987 United States warships and aircraft attacked Iranian vessels that were allegedly laying mines in the Persian Gulf during the Iran-Iraq conflict. These mines had damaged neutral and US shipping. Kuwait in 1990, together with a number of other states acting in collective self-defence, responded to Iraq's occupation of Kuwait.[68]

The assessment as to whether circumstances justify the exercise of self-defence is fraught with danger. Examples are the shooting down of a Korean civilian airlines in 1981 by the Soviet Union; in 1987 the commander of the USS Stark, a neutral United States warship in the Persian Gulf, took no action against approaching aircraft, which then fired missiles causing serious loss of life on the ship; in 1988 during the same Iraq-Iran hostilities the USS Vincennes shot down an Iranian civil airliner; in 1989 US aircraft over the Mediterranean high seas shot down two Libyan military aircraft which appeared to be hostile.

## 6.4  Intervention in support of self-determination

While the principle of self-determination is generally accepted, the parent state retains its sovereignty and the lawfulness of such intervention remains open to doubt. This is so despite numerous General Assembly resolutions requesting states to give assistance to national liberation movements.[69]

These resolutions are generously phrased and call upon states to provide the necessary moral, political and material assistance to national liberation movements. Such resolutions can be interpreted as being authorisation for military support. It is submitted however that these resolutions make it lawful for a state to give people struggling for self-determination moral, political and humanitarian assistance but not to intervene in the struggle with force or to provide arms and logistical support for armed rebellion.

The parent state retains the rights and responsibilities of sovereignty and must maintain law and order. Article 2(4) of the UN Charter should also be kept in mind as it obligates states to refrain from the threat or use of force against the territorial integrity or political independence of any state.

## 6.5  A right of intervention resulting from a treaty

A state can by virtue of a treaty consent to intervention. Great Britain, France and Russia guaranteed the independence of Greece and consequently intervened during the First World War to re-establish constitutional government in conformity with the *Treaty of London* of 1863.[70] A similar treaty is the 1960 *Treaty of Guarantee*[71] relating to Cyprus whereby Greece, Turkey and the United Kingdom reserve the right to take action with the sole aim of re-establishing the state affairs created by the treaty.

In 1974 after a *coup* in Cyprus a pro-Greek regime was established. Turkey, acting under the *Treaty of Guarantee*, invaded Cyprus and occupied part of the island. This part of the island then purported to establish itself as the Turkish Federated State of Cyprus.

In 1963 the three guarantor states provided joint armed forces to assist the government of Cyprus, at its request, to restore order after disturbances between the two communities.

## 7. HUMANITARIAN INTERVENTION

Elias sees a state forcibly intervening at the request of another state, and intervention for humanitarian purposes as being "dubious exceptions" to Article 2(4) of the UN Charter which forbids the use or threat of force against the political independence or integrity of any state.[72]

Humanitarian intervention has however become a serious option for states and is an obvious product of the international human rights movement. Because of its modern relevance it may be opportune to trace briefly the origins of humanitarian intervention so as to determine more accurately its international legality and sustainability. The idea of humanitarian intervention has grown not only with the international human rights movement but also with the idea of international criminal law.[73]

### 7.1 Earlier legal approaches

Nowhere does it appear from the writers of the pre-twentieth century that there was consensus that a state has a *right* to act against another state for breaches of international law. The consensus rather was that no state may sit in judgement over the acts of another state. This appeared to be the view at the time the European state system had become well established after the *Treaty of Westphalia* in 1648 and the Concert established by the *Treaty of Vienna* in 1815. There were rare occasions when states were prepared to move against other states which were thought to be treating their subjects in an unacceptable manner. The general state practice at the end of the nineteenth century was that *prima facie* intervention in the affairs of another state could never be legal — whatever the conditions that might agitate the world community to take humanitarian action. If such action were undertaken, it was generally held, it should never take place other than in the name of the international society at large.

Westlake early in the twentieth century revived the idea that a right to intervene in the name of humanity did exist and could even be undertaken by a state acting on its own.[74] In 1904 president Theodore Roosevelt revealed similar sentiments:

> There are occasional crimes committed on so vast a scale and of such peculiar horror as to make us doubt whether it is not our manifest duty to endeavour at least to show our disapproval of the deed and our sympathy with those who have suffered by it. The cases must be extreme in which such a course is justifiable ... [and] in extreme cases action may be justifiable and proper. What form the action shall take must depend upon the circumstances of the case; that is, upon the degree of the atrocity and upon our power to remedy it. The cases in which we would interfere by force of arms ... are necessarily very few. Yet it is to be expected that a people like ours ... which shows by its consistent practice its belief in the principles of civil and religious liberty and of orderly freedom ... that such a nation should desire eagerly to give expression to its horror on an occasion like that of the massacre of the Jews in Kishine, or when it witnesses such systematic and long-extended cruelty and oppression as the cruelty and oppression of which the Armenians have been the victims,

and which have won for them the indignant pity of the civilised world.[75]

This commitment to a humanitarian world-view prompted Stowell to assert that humanitarian intervention can be defined as the justifiable use of force for the purpose of protecting the inhabitants of another state from treatment so arbitrary and persistently abusive as to exceed the limits within which the sovereign state is presumed to act with reason and justice.[76]

However, Stowell's view did not carry much weight if one looks at state practice prior to the Second World War. The priorities of states at this time appeared to be a desire to defend the balance of power and preserve the independence of states. Toynbee correctly saw the reaction of states to the atrocities being perpetrated by the German government as "plainly platonic".[77]

If one looks at the world in the late 1930s one discerns a situation where there was no international insistence on common standards of justice or religious toleration in respect of internal government. Atrocities committed by foreign countries were seen to be of no concern. Conduct that should have placed governments outside the pale of civilised society was deemed to be no obstacle to diplomatic relations. At most, verbal condemnation and diplomatic protest was the norm.

## 7.2 Contemporary legal approach

According to a strict interpretation of territorial sovereignty, a state can treat its nationals as it sees fit. Are there no limits to this discretion? A substantial body of international political and legal opinion appears to be developing which supports the view that there are limits to such discretion. Where a state persecutes its nationals in such a way as to deny their fundamental human rights and to shock the conscience of mankind, such matters cease to be of sole concern to that state and intervention in the interests of humanity may be legally permissible.[78]

What do the contemporary highly respected authorities on international law say to the question: Is intervention by a state (or states) for humanitarian purposes a legally justified intervention in international law?

The answer is clouded in uncertainty. Shearer[79] declares that humanitarian intervention as an exception to the rule of non-intervention must remain of dubious legality. Jennings and Watts are[80] of the opinion that humanitarian intervention when resorted to by *individual* states has weak standing as a lawful practice because it has been abused in the past. When the humanitarian intervention *is applied by states collectively*, however, it is acceptable as being a basic rule of organised society. Dugard[81] supports the above opinions by declaring that the weight of authority is against the recognition of a right of humanitarian intervention. It is prohibited by Article 2(4) of the UN Charter, there is little state practice to support it, and the danger of abuse of such "right" outweighs its benefit to humanity. Like euthanasia, it is unlawful but tolerated by the law in genuine cases. Harris[82] sees the reluctance of states to support humanitarian intervention as proof that if such a right to intervention did ever exist, it has not survived Article 2(4) of the UN Charter.

The UN Security Council however is not bound by the prohibition contained in Article 2(4) of the Charter. When it acts under Chapter VII of the charter it may recommend intervention on humanitarian grounds by UN forces as in Yugoslavia[83] or by individual states as in the case of the protection of the Kurds in Northern Iraq.[84]

## 7.3 State practice

A substantial body of opinion and practice appears to be emerging that when a state persecutes its nationals in such a way as to deny them their fundamental human rights and to shock the conscience of mankind, the matter ceases to be the sole concern of that state and that intervention in the interests of humanity may be legally permissible.

Examples of humanitarian intervention are the following: In 1827 Great Britain, France and Russia intervened in the struggle between revolutionary Greece and Turkey after public opinion was horrified by the cruelties committed in that struggle. India justified its military intervention in Bangladesh in 1971 on humanitarian grounds. Humanitarian action was the motivation in 1991 for certain states, primarily the United States, with units from several other states, providing emergency aid to large numbers of Kurdish refugees in the border areas of northern Iraq. This led to Security Council Resolution 668 of 1991[85] insisting that Iraq allow immediate humanitarian access. This was followed by overflights by British and US military aircraft delivering supplies and the entry of military units from various states into northern Iraq.

The declaration issued at the end of the London Economic Summit 1991[86] states:

> We note that the urgent and overwhelming nature of the humanitarian problem in Iraq caused by violent repression by the Government required exceptional action by the international community, following UNSCR 688. We urge the UN and its affiliated agencies to be ready to consider similar action in the future if circumstances require it. The international community cannot stand idly by in cases where widespread human suffering from famine, war,

oppression, refugee flows, disease or flood reaches urgent and overwhelming proportions.

## 7.4 Is there such a "right" in international law?

Before protagonists of humanitarian intervention being a "right" get carried away by the legal significance of Security Council Resolution 668 (1991), the resolution should be assessed objectively. It found that the consequences of the repression in Iraq *threatened the international peace and security of the region*. This is a precedent for the view that for humanitarian intervention to be lawful it must be linked to a crisis with international repercussions. Resolution 668 did not authorise the Security Council to use force to protect human rights in these circumstances. The resolution contained no reference to Chapter VII of the charter which permits the Security Council to use or sanction the use of force. The resolution, important as it was in the context of humanitarian intervention, clearly had a very narrow scope. The question can be asked: Did it sanction humanitarian intervention at all, since humanitarian intervention by definition entails the use of force?

It would appear in hindsight that with Resolution 668 the Security Council sought to avoid a precedent for future action. Even those states supporting the resolution struggled during the debate to accept the conflict with the principle of non-intervention in a state's internal affairs as at that stage Iraq had a single, sovereign and functioning government. It should also be noted that the resolution ordered Iraq to permit humanitarian assistance.

Whereas Iraq had a government, Somalia had no functioning central government. The Security Council reacted to the Somalia situation with Resolution 794 (1992).[87] Here too the Security Council found that the human rights crisis in

Somalia constituted a threat to international peace and security. It authorised all necessary means to establish a secure environment for relief efforts.[88] The Security Council also invoked the use of force under Chapter VII of the UN Charter.

This authorisation to use force was based on the above aim to create a secure environment for international agencies to deliver humanitarian assistance. The use of force was *limited to this purpose only*. The consent of the sovereign state to such assistance was problematic (as there was no entity from which to obtain consent). This void made the Security Council action more acceptable and possible, but it does make the impact of Resolution 794 (1992) difficult to assess as this was a unique situation.

Security Council Resolution 940 (1994)[89] with regard to Haiti differed from that with regard to Iraq or Somalia in that in Haiti there were two competing governments with the *de facto* military government committing human rights abuses. Resolution 940 expressed grave concern about Haiti's deteriorating social order, the systematic violations of civil liberties and the plight of the Haitian refugees. In authorising the use of force under Chapter VII of the UN Charter the express purpose of the UN intervention was to facilitate the departure of the military government and the return of the elected president as the legitimate authority. Resolution 940 did not authorise the specific use of force to deal with the humanitarian aspects of the crisis (as was the case in Iraq). Resolution 940 intended to restore a democratically elected government. Could this be termed humanitarian intervention?[90]

Where does the above exposition of recent state practice bring us? It would appear that unilateral intervention for humanitarian reasons is not favoured by most states. This is as a result of the principles of sovereignty, non-intervention and the prohibition on the use of force. The emerging international law of human rights has modified this traditional approach however and these matters have become the subject of intense international scrutiny and concern. The notion of collective action in the general interest of states has become palatable and an exception to the prohibition on intervention. Examples of action taken under the auspices of regional organisations include the military force established by the Organisation for African Unity (OAU) which undertook peacekeeping functions in Chad in 1981, and the action taken by primarily military forces of the United States (with contingents from Barbados and Jamaica) in Grenada in 1983 at the request of the Organisation of Eastern Caribbean States.

In respect of forcible humanitarian intervention the acceptable lawful avenue to follow would be to request the Security Council, acting under Chapter VII of the charter, to recommend humanitarian intervention by UN forces or by individual states (or a collection of states) where appropriate.

This is the furthest international law can take it at present. Besides the above scenarios there is virtually no evidence that states have accepted a right of forcible humanitarian intervention. This is because the possibilities for abuse are manifest. Such a cynical conclusion undermines the late twentieth century emphasis on human rights. Harsh as this conclusion may seem, states still value their independence and political sovereignty more highly than they prize the protection of human rights. This unfortunately is the realistic position and there is no moralistic magic that can manufacture a "right" simply because it ought to exist.[91]

Besides having sincere humanitarian motives, the leading participants in the mentioned Iraq and Haitian scenarios all had some additional stakes in the situation. The United States, France and the United Kingdom, who played leading roles in the humanitarian intervention in Iraq were also the principal powers in the war against Iraq. The Haitian intervention was carried out by the United States leading a unified task force to restore a democratically elected president who would symbolise democracy in Latin America. The United States had a clear regional interest in ensuring stability in Haiti.

## 7.5 Rwanda

The weakness in the international legal (and political) system in respect of humanitarian intervention was dramatically exemplified in Rwanda. Here was a classic case for international humanitarian intervention. There was well-publicised genocide on a massive scale. The carnage was covered extensively by the international media. Yet the United Nations did not authorise the use of force to halt it. In fairness to the United Nations it should be said that Security Council passed a resolution[92] establishing a commission to investigate violations of humanitarian law in Rwanda. Pursuant to this the Security Council[93] set up an international tribunal to prosecute persons for genocide and other violations of humanitarian law in Rwanda. Was this international inaction because the major powers had no specific stake in the situation? The only state prepared to get involved in Rwanda was France who had historical, political and economic connections with that country.

## 7.6 What is the *opinio iuris*?

It would appear that forcible humanitarian intervention under multilateral (mainly UN) auspices is at present viewed as permissible. The principle of state sovereignty has however not yet disintegrated to such an extent as to make unilateral forcible intervention for humanitarian reasons permissible under international law. Such action is not yet accepted state practice supported by adequate *opinio iuris*.

Jennings and Watts[94] maintained that if humanitarian intervention is ever to be justified, it will only be in extreme and very particular circumstances. Crucial considerations are likely to include extreme and large-scale humanitarian distress demanding immediate relief, whether the territorial state is itself incapable of meeting the needs of the situation or is unwilling to do so or is perhaps itself the cause of the situation; whether competent organs of the international community are unable to respond effectively or speedily enough to meet the demands of the situation; whether there is any practicable alternative to the action to be taken; whether there is likely to be any active resistance on the part of the territorial state; and whether the action taken is limited both in time and scope to the needs of the emergency.

To sum up, it would have to be action (which does not preclude it from being carried out by military forces) in a compelling emergency situation. The transgression of the territorial state's territory will have to be clearly outweighed by overwhelming and immediate humanitarian considerations, and the general support of the international community must be evident.[95]

The recent action of the North Atlantic Treaty Organisation (NATO) in Yugoslavia may be an example of precisely such a situation. This action of NATO may be a litmus test for the argument that humanitarian needs, the principles of international humanitarian law and the general support of the international community make forcible intervention acceptable. Proponents of above argument also maintain that a large-scale human tragedy in Kosovo was averted by the intervention.

A more conservative approach would be that according to Article 53 of the UN Charter a Security Council mandate is required for each peace enforcement mission undertaken by subregional organisations, including NATO.

A more liberal approach again would be that the humanitarian needs of Kosovo required a circumvention of the Security Council as a veto was likely and decision paralysis under the circumstances was unacceptable to the international community.

Quite clearly NATO's actions effectively bypassed the United Nations. Was such bypassing not a result of the inability of the United Nations to act? Was the international community not prepared to reach consensus and act speedily in situations such as the humanitarian crisis in Kosovo?

History and state practice will determine whether NATO's action in Kosovo becomes a norm of customary international law or not. It is too early to make any judgement at this stage.

What is clear, however, is that the eleven-week NATO air war on Yugoslavia to end President Milosevic's crackdown in Kosovo, a province with an ethnic Albanian majority, should be judged in the context of forcible humanitarian intervention. The legality of the action will have to be determined by developments in international law in the near and medium future. A rule of customary international law may be in the making.

The Kosovo precedent could well influence humanitarian forcible intervention in Africa in the future. The lack of international action during the genocide in Rwanda and the catastrophic events in Burundi are cases in point. An African force that could forcibly intervene in African humanitarian crises could conceivably reduce the call for intervention by the Security Council of the United Nations. As recently stated by a South African commentator, there is no difference between Kosovo, in NATO's backyard, and Sierra Leone, in ECOWAS's (Economic Community of West African States) backyard.[96]

## 8. CONCLUSION

The right of states to use force is a perennially sensitive issue. Articles 2(4) and 51 of the UN Charter restrict the right of states to use force — other than under UN auspices except in self-defence. There has however been a trend to expand the scope of self-defence beyond the literal limits of Article 51. In April 1986, when US aircraft bombed targets in Libya in response to terrorist attacks on US citizens overseas, it was claimed that the United States was acting in self-defence in conformity with the UN Charter. There have been uses of force in anticipation of possible attacks or to stop unwanted political developments within a so-called "sphere of influence", or by way of reprisal, or to rescue victims of aircraft hijackings.

The security arrangements of the post-1945 world have been reconciled with the principles of the UN Charter and with the idea that defence is the only legitimate basis for the use of force. This is evident in Article 5 of the 1949 *North Atlantic Treaty*[97] and Article 4 of the 1955 *Warsaw Treaty*.[98] Both treaties begin with the acceptance of the peaceful settlement of disputes and the non-use of force contained in Articles 2(3) and 2(4) of the UN Charter. Both treaties also echo the provisions of Articles 51 and 52 on self-defence.

While the United Nations has been reasonably consistent in condemning the use of armed force, it has not developed a consistent set of principles governing some of the more ambiguous uses of force. This applies particularly to the most disputed use of force in the modern world: intervention by outside powers in the *domestic conflicts* of other states. No clear doctrine has been formulated to facilitate the judgements in such cases, or on the justifications widely used in defence of such actions (for example, the need to protect nationals of the intervening state, the maintenance of law and order, the defence of a constitutional government or the overthrow of a tyrannical one).

Although many writers identify Article 2(4) of the UN Charter as the most important in the charter, different views are expressed concerning its proper scope and meaning. The question is still being asked: What is the permissible limit for a state to use force or the threat of force in its international relations with other states?[99]

What the founding fathers of the UN Charter in San Francisco had in mind when drawing up Article 2(4) was probably transborder transgression committed by uniformed military forces of a state. Since 1945, however, new considerations have arisen regarding the possible threat or use of force between states. Examples are wars of national liberation; unstable regimes set up after a process of decolonisation; unstable regimes in states where a quasi civil war is taking place; and the "two dubious exceptions"[100] to the prohibition of the use of force: intervention for humanitarian purposes or intervention with the consent of the state which is the victim of the intervention.

Customary international law has always been opposed to the threat or use of force in international relations. Article 2(4) of the UN Charter makes this clear. In the *Corfu Channel Case*[101] the International Court of Justice stated:

> The Court can only regard the alleged right of intervention as the manifestation of a policy of force, such as has, in the

past, given rise to most serious abuses and such as cannot, whatever be the present defects in international organisation, find a place in international law.

In the *Military and Paramilitary Activities Case*[102] the International Court of Justice ruled by 14 votes to one that two principles of international law were paramount: that states should refrain in their international relations from the threat or use of force against the territorial integrity or the political independence of any state, and that states should not intervene in matters within the domestic jurisdiction of another.

The norm of non-intervention remains a key tenet in international law. States are obligated in their international dealings to refrain from intervening militarily in the internal or external affairs of others states except in certain specified cases: (a) for legitimate self-defence; (b) to avenge maltreatment of their citizens after all available peaceful remedies have been exhausted; (c) in accordance with an existing treaty permitting such intervention; (d) ostensibly to promote self-determination; (e) ostensibly for humanitarian reasons, and (f) ostensibly at the request of another state. Such a request should be an explicit and genuine invitation by the lawful government of the requesting state.[103]

Where collective action is taken by an international organisation, such actions must be taken on behalf of the community of nations and for the enforcement of the principles and rules of international law.

Notwithstanding the above exceptions, which may be expedient, desirable, feasible or based on morality, the fact remains that under international law, armed intervention *per se* violates accepted rights. Armed intervention is a hostile act under international law.

Unilateral and group-sanctioned armed intervention cannot enhance the respect for international law in a world consisting of sovereign states. International law best serves those states who make it work over the long term. Governments who compromise international law for short-term policy gains will eventually rue the political and legal implications of their actions. Regional trust and goodwill may turn into pervasive suspicion and political resentment. This may be a high price to pay for what sometimes in effect boils down to temporarily occupying what is nothing more than a flyspeck of territory on a vast continent or a minute piece of land in a vast ocean.

## ENDNOTES

1. 165 League of Nations Treaty Series (LNTS) 19, Art 8.
2. 119 United Nations Treaty Series (UNTS) 3, Art 8.
3. General Assembly Resolution 2131 (XX) Dec 21, 1965.
4. General Assembly Resolution 2625 (XXV) Oct 24, 1970.
5. *American Journal of International Law*, Vol 75, 1981, p 418.
6. *International Legal Materials* Vol 26, 1987, p 1164.
7. *International Legal Materials*, Vol 27, 1988, p 577.
8. For non-forcible intervention see Damrosch, L F, "Politics Across Borders: Nonintervention and Nonforcible Influence over Domestic Affairs", *American Journal of International Law*, Vol 83, 1989, p 1.
9. For an extensive exposition of intervention through history see Geldenhuys, D, *Foreign Political Engagement*, Macmillan Press, London, 1998.
10. Young, O R, "Intervention and international systems" *Journal of International Affairs* Vol 22, 1986, p 179.
11. Roseneau, J N, "Intervention as a scientific concept", *Journal of Conflict Resolution* Vol 13, 1969, p 160.
12. Bull, H, in Bull, H (ed), *Intervention in World Politics*, Clarendon Press, Oxford, 1986, p2.
13. Geldenhuys, D, *op cit*, p 6.

14. Jennings, R and A Watts (eds), *Oppenheim's International Law*, Vol I, Ninth edition, Longman, Harlow, 1992, p 428.
15. International Court of Justice Reports, 1986, p 14.
16. League of Nations Treaty Series, 165, p 19.
17. United Nations Treaty Series, 119, p 49.
18. United Nations Treaty Series, 70, p 237.
19. *International Legal Materials*, Vol 2, 1963, p 766.
20. *Yearbook of the International Law Commission*, 1949, p 286.
21. General Assembly Resolution 2131 (XX) 1965.
22. General Assembly Resolution 2625 (XXV) 1970.
23. *International Legal Materials*, Vol 14, 1975, p 1292.
24. *Military and Paramilitaries Case, op cit*, p 99, where it was held that *opinio iuris* may, though with due caution be deducted from, *inter alia*, the attitude of states towards certain General Assembly resolutions: "The effect of consent to the text of such resolutions may be understood as an acceptance of the validity of the rule or set of rules declared by the resolution". For the legal effect of General Assembly Resolutions see Dugard, J, *International Law*, Juta, Kenwyn, 1994, p 298.
25. Geldenhuys, D, *op cit*, p 8.
26. Henkin, L, *Right v Might: International Law and the Use of Force*, Council of Foreign Relations Press, New York, 1991, p 41.
27. Stowell, E C, *Intervention In International Law*, John Byrne & Co, Washington DC, 1921, p 53.
28. Arend, A C and R J Beck, *International Law and the Use of Force Beyond the UN Charter Paradigm*, Routledge, London, 1993, p 113, conclude that genuine instances of humanitarian intervention have been rare if they have occurred at all.
29. Reisman, W M, "Coercion and Self-Determination: Construing Charter Article 2(4)", *American Journal of International Law*, Vol 78, 1984, p 612.
30. Scott, A M, "Non-intervention and conditional intervention", *Journal of International Affairs*, Vol 22, 1968, p 208.
31. Hinsley, F H, *Power and the Pursuit of Peace*, Cambridge University Press, Cambridge, 1967, p 359.
32. Barnett, R J, *Intervention and Revolution: The United States in the Third World*, MacGibbon and Gee, London, 1970, p 258; Renning, C N, *Intervention in Latin America*, Alfred A Knopf, New York,

1970, p 8; Gaddis, J L, *The United States and Origins of the Cold War*, Columbia University Press, New York 1972, p 351.

33. Moore, J N and R F Turner, *International Law and the Brezhnev Doctrine*, University Press of America, Lanham, 1987.
34. Jennings, R and A Watts, *op cit*, p 430.
35. *Military and Paramilitary Activities Case, op cit*.
36. *Ibid*.
37. *Ibid*, p 103.
38. *Ibid*, p 104.
39. *Ibid*, p 108.
40. *Ibid*. Roberts, A and B Kingsbury (ed), *United Nations, Divided World*, Clarendon Press, Oxford 1989, p 172.
41. Jennings, R and A Watts, *op cit*, p 434.
42. Security Council Resolution 387 (1976).
43. *Military and Paramilitary Activities Case, op cit*, p 126.
44. Jennings, R and A Watts, *op cit*, p 435.
45. General Assembly Resolution ES – 6/2 14 January 1980.
46. Dugard, J, *op cit*, p 306.
47. General Assembly Resolution 44/240 29 December 1989.
48. Jennings, R and A Watts, *op cit*, p 438; Dugard, J, *op cit*, p 326; Shearer, I, *Starke's International Law*, 11$^{th}$ edition, Butterworths, Durban, 1994, pp 96 and 139.
49. For examples see Harris, D J, *Cases and Materials on International Law*, 4$^{th}$ edition, Sweet and Maxwell, London, 1991, p 842.
50. See Falk, R A (ed), *The Vietnam War and International Law*, Princeton University Press, 1968, where it emerges clearly that the legal situation relating to the American presence in Vietnam was sufficiently unclear to allow reasonable men of professional competence to arrive at diametrically opposed conclusions on the legal issues.
51. General Assembly Resolution 2131 (XX), 21 December 1965. For the legal effect of resolutions of the political organs of the United Nations see Dugard, J, *op cit*, p29.
52. House of Assembly Debates, Vol 60, col 368, 30 January 1976; *South African Yearbook of International Law*, Vol 2, 1976, p 279.
53. Security Council Resolution 387 (1977); Security Council Resolution 428 (1978).

54. *South African Yearbook of International Law*, Vol 8, 1982, p 263.
55. Security Council Resolution 567 (1985).
56. Harris, D J, op cit, p 843. Humanitarian intervention is discussed *infra*.
57. Shearer, I, *op cit*, p 96.
58. Wright, Q, "Subversive Intervention", *American Journal of International Law*, Vol 54, 1960, p 521.
59. Harris, D J, *op cit*, p 842.
60. *Military and Paramilitary Activities Case, op cit.*
61. General Assembly Resolution 2131 (XX) 1965.
62. General Assembly Resolution 2625 (XXV) 1970.
63. United Kingdom representative in the UN Special Committee on Principles of International Law, United Nations Document A/AC 125/SR 5; 1986, Foreign Office Policy Document No 148, paras II, 6-9 reprinted in *British Yearbook of International Law*, Vol 59, 1986, p 614.
64. Joyner, C J, "The United States Action in Grenada", *American Journal of International Law*, Vol 78, 1984, p 131.
65. *Military and Paramilitary Activities Case, op cit.*
66. States have attempted to justify the pursuit of fugitives across a frontier (hot pursuit) as being action in self-defence. There has however been no disposition on the part of other states to accept that such a right exists. Examples are South Africa's pursuit of armed guerrillas into Zambia and into Angola.
67. *Military and Paramilitary Activities Case, op cit.*
68. This was after the adoption by the United Nations Security Council of Resolution 678 in November 1990 authorising the use of force.
69. General Assembly Resolution 2625 (XXV) 1970; General Assembly Resolution 2918 (XXVII) 1972; General Assembly Resolution 3034 (XXVII) 1972; General Assembly Resolution 3314 (XXIV) 1974.
70. Text in *American Journal of International Law*, Vol 12, 1918, p 312.
71. United Kingdom Treaty Series No 5 (1961).
72. Elias, T O, "Scope and Meaning of Art 2(4) of the UN Charter", in *Contemporary Problems of International Law*, B Cheng and E D Brown (eds), Stevens and Sons, London, 1988, p 72.

73. Green, L C, "International Criminal Law and the Protection of Human Rights", in *Contemporary Problems of International Law*, *op cit*, p 116.

74. Westlake, J, *International Law: Part I Peace*, 1910, p 318, quoted in B Cheng and E D Brown, *op cit*, p 129.

75. Adler, C and A M Margalith, *With Firmness in the Right: American Diplomatic Action Affecting Jews 1840-1945*, (1946), p 261, quoted in Bin Cheng and Brown, E D, *op cit*, p 130.

76. Stowell, E C, International Law, (1931), p 349 quoted by B Cheng and E D Brown, op cit, p 130.

77. Toynbee, A, *Survey of International Affairs* 1933, 1934, p 371 quoted by B Cheng and E D Brown, *op cit*, p 131.

78. Jennings, R and A Watts, A, *op cit*, p 442, n17 for authorities.

79. Shearer, I, *op cit*, p 98.

80. Jennings, R and A Watts, *op cit*, p 443.

81. Dugard, J, *op cit*, p 323.

82. Harris, D J, *op cit*, p 873.

83. Security Council Resolution 752 (1992).

84. Security Council Resolution 688 (1991).

85. *Ibid*.

86. Quoted in Jennings, R and A Watts, *op cit*, p 443.

87. Security Council Resolution 794 (1992).

88. Lyons, T and A I Samatar, *Somalia: State Collapse, Multilateral Intervention, and Strategies for Political Reconstruction*, The Brookings Institution, Washington DC, 1995. Geldenhuys, D, *op cit*, pp 124-150 for an in-depth account of the United Nations action towards Somalia. The United States provided the bulk of UNITAF's (Unified Task Force) 37000 troops with 23 other countries also sending military units. UNITAF was eventually taken over by UNOSOM (United Nations Mission in Somalia). At full strength UNOSOM – under the command of General Cevil Bir of Turkey – consisted of 28000 military personnel drawn form 29 countries. It was the largest peacekeeping force the United Nations had deployed to date. The operation however was a failure leaving Somalia in the same state of collapse that it had been in before UN forces landed.

89. Security Council Resolution 940 (1994).

90. Gordon, R E, "Humanitarian Intervention by the United Nations: Iraq, Somalia and Haiti", *Texas International Law Journal*, 1996, p 43. Twenty thousand troops landed in Haiti. Although 28 states were members of the MNR (Multinational Force) it was led by and comprised almost entirely of United States forces.
91. Dixon, M, *Textbook of International Law*, Blackstone Press Ltd, 1990, p 262.
92. Security Council Resolution 935 (1994).
93. Security Council Resolution 955 (1994).
94. Jennings, R and A Watts, *op cit*, p 443, n 20.
95. Franck, T and N Rodley, "After Bangladesh: The Law of Humanitarian Intervention by Military Force", *American Journal of International Law*, Vol 67, 1973, p 275.
96. *Business Day* (Johannesburg), 10 July 1999.
97. United Nations Treaties Series Vol 34, p 243.
98. United Nations Treaties Series Vol 219, p 3.
99. Elias, T O, "Scope and Meaning of Article 2(4) of the United Nations Charter", in B Cheng and E D Brown, *op cit*, p 70; Franck, T M, "Who Killed Article 2(4)?", *American Journal of International Law*, Vol 64, 1970, p 809; Reisman, M, "Coercion and Self-Determination: Constructing Charter Article 2(4)", *American Journal of International Law*, Vol 78, 1984, p 642.
100. Elias, T A, *op cit*, p 72.
101. *Corfu Channel Case* (Merits), 1949, International Court of Justice Reports, 4 at 35.
102. *Military and Paramilitary Case, op cit*, p 187.
103. Joyner, C J, *op cit*, p 133.

## Chapter 3

# AFRICAN CONFLICT AT THE TURN OF THE CENTURY: MANIFESTATIONS, PROPENSITY AND MANAGEMENT

## Louis du Plessis

### 1. INTRODUCTION: SECURITY AND CONFLICT

At the turn of the century the initial high expectations for Africa's postcolonial development appear to have been unfounded. Although some societies are relatively satisfied with their living conditions, several are in the grip of extreme violence while many have virtually disintegrated. Economically, most sub-Saharan communities are in deep trouble.[1] While some experiences, which fill the daily lives of sub-Saharan Africans, promote security, other experiences impose grave insecurity, often related to conflict. To explore these, a few introductory comments will be made on the nature of security and conflict.

One way of viewing security is as a condition of freedom from actual or perceived threats. As a condition it is most often defined in terms of the reaction to possible threats and, more specifically, to external and internal threats of the state or its interests.[2] Physical violence is generally perceived to be the ultimate threat against a modern state. The real and tangible threat is thus to the survival of the state and its structures.

However, a multidimensional interpretation of security includes economic and ideological threats, as well as the wellbeing (particularly freedom from threats) of ordinary citizens in society.[3] According to this perspective, "the security of people is as important as the security of states".[4] Baynham argues that the security of people in most Third World societies is collectively being "threatened" by an enormous range of internal and regional problems.[5] This collective threat is especially true of the security issues facing sub-Saharan Africa.[6]

Levels of individual insecurity are often directly related to the experience of collective threats to safety, family and property. Moreover, some of the most serious collective threats flow directly from vulnerability during intergroup and interstate conflict, especially where armed forces become involved as a result of irreconcilable or incompatible interests. In this respect intrasocietal (often politically motivated) armed conflict may be distinguished from intersocietal (normally interstate) armed conflict. Viewed from a slightly different angle, some analysts make a distinction between two types of "incompatible positions". The first type is related mainly to government and includes struggles to replace the political system. The second type is related mainly to territory and includes interstate conflict to control territory or ensure secession.[7]

Furthermore, intrasocietal armed conflicts may be complicated by external support. When an internal conflict involves forces from other states on the side of either of the internal parties, it is treated as an internal conflict with foreign intervention.[8] A distinction can thus also be made between

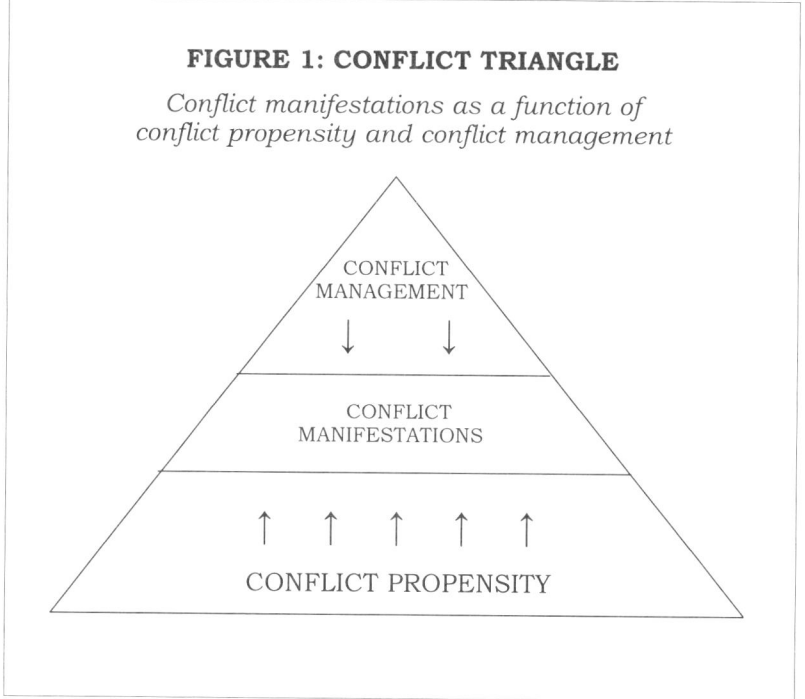

**FIGURE 1: CONFLICT TRIANGLE**

*Conflict manifestations as a function of conflict propensity and conflict management*

"mainly internal conflicts" and "internal conflicts with foreign intervention". Such intervention, especially with armed forces, is related directly to the degree to which the internal conflict involves (promotes or threatens) the national interests of the intervening state.

Another classification flows from the level of violence used in (either intrasocietal or intersocietal) armed conflict, ranges from mild deeds of terror to full-scale war, and is inevitably manifested in the magnitude of casualties. A "major armed conflict" can be defined as prolonged combat between the military forces of two or more governments, or of one government and at least one organised armed group, incurring the battle-related deaths of at least a thousand people during the entire conflict.[9]

According to the conflict triangle model (Figure 1) the manifestations of conflict in Africa, of which many examples will be mentioned, can be interpreted as a function of two opposing forces. The first force is the propensity for conflict, determined by societal structures and changes, and the second is the opposing inclination of leading role players to curb the specific conflicts and to manage the outcome.

Applying these conceptual distinctions, this chapter will explore conflict in sub-Saharan societies by characterising the manifestations of the hostilities and the regions where they took place or are taking place. To ensure deeper insight into the resilience of many of the conflicts, some underlying demographic, political, geographical and ethnic realities will be interpreted. These factors may indeed clarify the conflict propensity of many sub-Saharan societies. Equally relevant are the responses of non-African and African actors to conflict. Consequently, questions on the changing approaches to conflict resolution will be explored.

## 2. MANIFESTATIONS OF SUB-SAHARAN ARMED CONFLICT

Hostilities and strife undermine not only safety, but also the fibre and quality of virtually every aspect of collective and individual security. This is especially so when armed conflict occurs. To bring the legacy of armed conflict in sub-Saharan Africa into focus, the general nature of the conflicts will be outlined, followed by a discussion of typical intrastate and cross-border hostilities and the destructive effects of these.

### 2.1 Nature of the conflicts

Intrastate and interstate conflict became endemic in the first four decades following the political independence of most sub-

Saharan societies. Since many of the independent "states" were often largely fictitious entities sustained as diplomatic or judicial units,[10] sub-Saharan societies were faced with a string of insurgencies, separatist movements and full-blown civil wars.[11] These problems impeded most long-term planning for development.

Armed campaigns to take control of states contributed to the overthrow of repressive regimes, but often also contributed to political violence - and even to civil war - and a collapse of state authority. The reasons for the internal and cross-border wars were often associated with ethnic divisions. Despite political leaders' ideological emphasis on nation building, tribal tensions from the colonial period became more articulated, and ethnic cleavages and clashes became a major disruptive factor.[12]

Several African governments were confronted with wars of secession, such as those in southern Sudan, in eastern Nigeria (Biafra) and in Katanga (now Shaba in the Congo). Some of the wars that have been fought to liberate countries from repressive regimes, such as in Uganda (1971) and more recently in Liberia, Rwanda and Congo Brazzaville, have resulted in intensified, violent conflicts and the massacre of civilians.[13] During the first decades of independence internal and cross-border conflicts erupted in every region.

Oyebade and Alao maintain that African conflicts have always had their own peculiar causes, independent of Cold War politics. What the Cold War did was to exacerbate existing conflicts, especially where a superpower had strategic interests, such as in the Horn of Africa or Southern Africa. Consequently, the end of the Cold War has not translated into a reduction of local conflicts.[14] Conflicts in Angola, Burundi, Somalia and Sudan continued, while the Liberian civil war started, and Rwanda soon went up in flames. Internal strife occurred in South Africa, Ghana, Mauritania, Senegal, Zaire, Kenya, Nigeria, Cameroon and Mozambique and a civil war started in Sierra Leone.[15]

A temporary trend of declining numbers of conflicts in Africa ended by 1997, when all the new conflicts were located on the African continent. In fact, there were more conflicts in Africa in 1997 than in any year since 1991.[16] There were spillover effects as in previous years, but there was also a change in the conflict patterns in which states increasingly became involved in disputes in neighbouring countries. Such involvement often included economic or political support for either of the warring parties. This was particularly obvious in the region stretching from Angola and Congo Brazzaville in the west to Kenya, Sudan and Tanzania in the east, where complex links emerged which had an effect on the development of three of the new conflicts, that is, in Burundi, Congo Brazzaville and Zaire.[17]

## 2.2 Typical intrastate hostilities

After a brief view of the typical intrastate conflicts in the various subregions of Southern Africa, West Africa, the Horn of Africa and Central Africa, a few remarks will be made on interstate hostilities and the general result of military struggles. (See Figure 4 on the main intrastate and interstate armed conflicts in Africa, 1998.)

In the last decades of the twentieth century different patterns emerged in the various regions of Southern Africa. While the predominantly white governments in South West Africa (later Namibia), Rhodesia (later Zimbabwe) and South Africa resisted the onslaught of the black nationalist political and guerrilla forces for a while, they eventually accepted multi-racial and multi-ethnic power sharing within a democratic political structure. The demographic composition and level of cultural development of the populations promoted such development. Angola and Mozambique were less fortunate, having suffered long civil wars. Only in the 1990s were these two countries able to start on the road to recovery.[18] However, Angola soon resumed its destructive war, which has plagued the war-torn country since 1975.[19]

Since independence West Africa has been characterised by internal conflict in several countries. In Togo the "ethnic cleansing" of non-Kabye personnel from the army caused soldiers to flee to Ghana.[20] Even in the more prosperous Nigeria, the First Republic collapsed largely as the result of ethnic tension in the army's officer corps. Heavy-handed attempts to correct the overrepresented Ibo people by promoting less well-educated northerners helped spur a *coup* in 1966. Since the civil war, successive regimes have striven to avoid the impression that one group is being favoured over another in the officer corps.[21]

The relative calm in West Africa was shattered by the civil war in Liberia where three international organisations, namely the Economic Community of West African States (ECOWAS), the Organisation of African Unity (OAU) and the United Nations (UN), attempted to secure peace. In the 1990s, while the number of armed wings increased, warring factions signed more than thirty peace agreements without success. As the economic situation deteriorated, more people took almost exclusively to banditry for their livelihood.[22]

In March 1991 conflict erupted in neighbouring Sierra Leone between the government and a rebel force, the Revolutionary United Front (RUF). The RUF attacked the mining industry, the mainstay of its economy, as well as foreigners. The fighting and chaos resulted in the withdrawal of foreign investment, the death of thousands of inhabitants and the incarceration of many others in refugee camps.[23]

In the Horn of Africa the Ethiopian government and the Eritrean secessionists have waged war against each other for almost two decades.[24] In Somalia, one of the very few culturally homogenous African countries, a civil war between clan warlords broke out in 1992. With no organised government, Somalia was soon engulfed in chaos and mass starvation. The small, underfunded and ill-prepared UN peacekeeping force (UNOSOM I) was incapable of engaging in any effective military or humanitarian operation.[25]

The protracted war in Sudan has deep historical roots in ethnic, cultural and religious differences. Moreover, in the colonial era the British imperial rulers reinforced the gulf between the predominantly Muslim north and the Christian south. Soon after independence in 1955 the tensions exploded in violent conflict. After the governing radical National Islamic Front (NIF) ended a decade of local autonomy for the south, a devastating war has been raging between the NIF and the southern Sudan People's Liberation Movement (SPLM). The rise of factions in the north and south complicated the struggles. Despite peace talks organised by a number of African countries, the war remains unresolved at the turn of the century.[26]

Over the past decades internal and cross-border clashes have torn the Central African states on both sides of the Congo River apart, not only in Congo Kinshasa (previously Zaire) but also in Congo Brazzaville, and since the 1970s the struggles between the Tutsi and Hutu peoples have given rise to successive military regimes, *coups* and massacres in Rwanda and Burundi.

When the ethnic war erupted in Rwanda in Central Africa in 1994, Hutu soldiers and their civilian collaborators murdered close to a million Tutsis within four months.[27] The deep-seated animosity between the Tutsi and the Hutu has its roots in Rwanda's colonial history. The colonial powers in Africa often adopted a sectional policy that tended to favour one group over another. Rwanda may be regarded as such a case, as there is evidence that Belgium favoured the Tutsi in education and placed its élite in the colonial bureaucracy. This promoted ethnic animosity, which the power-hungry Õlite exacerbated after independence.[28]

Since independence in 1962, Burundi, like its northern neighbour, Rwanda, experienced a series of violent conflicts between the politically subservient Hutu majority and the power-wielding Tutsi minority. In a clash with Tutsis in 1972 an estimated 200 000 Hutus were killed. In another clash in 1993 approximately 100 000 people died, the majority Tutsis, while another 200 000 fled to neighbouring countries.[29]

In the last years of the twentieth century savage battles between government and rebel forces tore the DRC (the former Zaire) apart, with both sides militarily supported by neighbouring states. Hostilities such as these did not normally deteriorate into full-fledged cross-border wars.

## 2.3 Nature and effects of interstate fighting

Since the 1980s a few regional powers succeeded in dominating their neighbours to such an extent that they could reap the economic benefits of those states without incorporating them. At the same time, weaker states became beset by uncontrollable insurgent groups, some externally supported, who used their territories as sanctuaries for incursions into neighbouring territories, while the host country paid a heavy price. Internal instability became contagious: this was especially true of the belligerent Central African subregion, stretching from northern Angola and Congo Brazzaville through Congo Kinshasa, Burundi, Rwanda and Uganda to Somalia, Ethiopia, Sudan and Eritrea (Figure 4).

The internal hostilities in one country often spilled over to its neighbours. Events in Rwanda can hardly be separated from those in Burundi. These events, in turn, spilled over to Uganda and the DRC. Similarly, for many years the problems of Zaire (now the DRC) in the Shaba province have routinely spilled over to Zambia. Kenya has also experienced banditry across its borders with Somalia and Sudan, and Kenya's vessels have been seized by Somali pirates.[30]

Albeit without the same determination and assertiveness as some Middle East or Southeast Asian states, several developing sub-Saharan powers, during the 1970s and 1980s, violated the territorial integrity and threatened the survival of neighbouring regimes. However, this did not entail the destruction, conquest or indefinite occupation of a neighbouring state. Invasions were (and are) usually limited to cross-border incursions and retaliatory strikes.[31] In addition, more so than elsewhere, Central and East Africa became the subregion in which some governments developed the practice (and ability) of supporting dissident ethnic groups in bordering states.[32]

Cross-border incursions often combined conventional and unconventional tactics. Although the most frequent type of warfare witnessed in sub-Sahara was based on guerrilla and counterguerrilla operations, the availability of sophisticated weapons and training has tended to accelerate the progression from the hit-and-run tactics of irregular operations to the fire-and-movement tactics of conventional mobile operations.[33]

The problem with military violence is that it hinders the creation of infrastructures, the establishment of stable security structures and the development of civil societies. At the same time it creates a cycle of increased conflict. Once the boundaries of peaceful political opposition have been crossed, the possibility of resorting to further violence increases enormously.[34]

The lack of political stability and the cycles of sub-Saharan strife had serious effects on human and animal life and on living standards.[35] In addition to the loss of life as a direct result of military action, the mentioned and other examples of sub-Saharan hostilities often destroyed food supplies and livestock. Since veterinary services proved impossible to maintain, animal diseases spread rapidly and resulted in massive stock losses. Disease ravaged infrastructures, such as village wells, roads and bridges, and disrupted the fragile sub-Saharan social welfare and security services. Schools and clinics were closed, ransacked or destroyed; immunisation programmes were discontinued and hospitals placed under immense strain.

Similar to internal conflicts, cross-border battles caused massive disturbances in the settlement of whole communities, often displacing them into vast squatter settlements on the edges of towns and giving rise to international refugee problems. The wars also destroyed religious and other normative or value systems, undermined faith in family, social or organisational codes and sometimes caused whole societies to succumb to fatalism.

Many students of security conclude that the inhabitants of the continent are irrevocably inclined to endemic and violent conflict. To challenge this perception and to explain the apparent sub-Saharan propensity for conflict, some universal characteristics of sub-Saharan societies will have to be identified and interpreted. If not, the exploration of conflict resolution measures will be superficial.

## 3. THE CONFLICT PROPENSITY IN PERSPECTIVE

During the following analysis of demographic, political, geographic and ethnic factors, it will be argued that the propensity for conflict can, among other things, be linked to the pressures of an uncontrolled population explosion, the suppressive nature of political authoritarianism, the rigidity of state boundaries and a growing ethnic consciousness. Before identifying the problematic political environment, a few comments on the demographics will be made.

### 3.1 The expanding African population

While only about 142 million people lived in Africa in 1920, 680 million people inhabited the 48 societies of sub-Saharan Africa at the end of the twentieth century and about 830 million the entire continent.[36] Africa is expected to pass the one billion mark early in the 21$^{st}$ century. Since about 1965 Africa has experienced the highest population growth in the world.

Compared with the prevailing population growth rates of approximately 1,8 per cent in Asia and Latin America and 0,4 per cent in Europe, Africa's growth rate is the highest in the world.[37] (See Figure 2, on fertility in Africa, 1997.) The population is expanding at an average rate of 2,8 per cent a year, that is 20 million extra people a year — roughly equal to the combined present population of Zambia and Zimbabwe.[38] While Africa is still the least urbanised of the world's continents, its urban populations are growing faster than anywhere else.[39]

# FIGURE 2:
# FERTILITY AS INDICATOR OF POPULATION GROWTH AND THE RESULTANT COMPETITION FOR SCARCE RESOURCES: AFRICA 1997

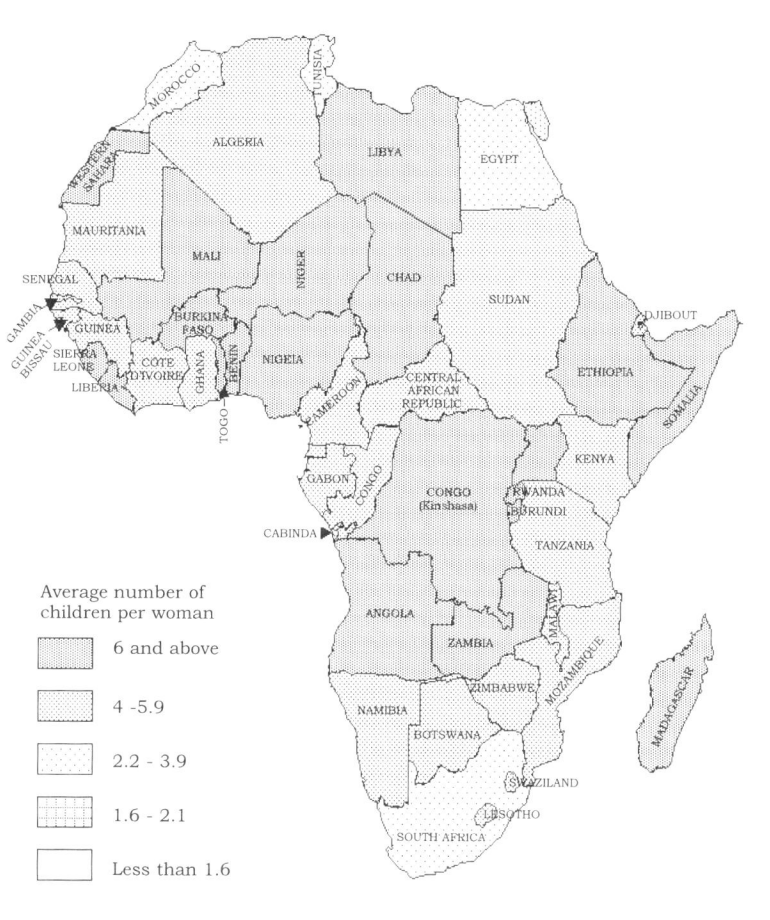

Source: "Population and resources", *National Geographic*, October 1998.

Such explosive growth — which may bolster expanding economies — strains and shatters declining ones, affects every aspect of living standards, exerts tremendous pressure on stability, and increases the conflict for scarce resources.

Another security and conflict-related question is: In what kinds of social, political and economic environments are the members of this expanding population finding themselves? In attempting to provide a few tentative answers, the establishment, development and nature of postcolonial African societies will be outlined.

## 3.2 The establishment of authoritarian societies

Prior to its colonisation, Africa was occupied by thousands of sovereign political entities varying in size. Colonisation replaced the innumerable clan groups, city-states, kingdoms and empires (many without fixed boundaries) with about fifty new states.[40] In many parts of Africa, for most of their known history and until only a century or so ago, people contrived to live together in sociopolitical communities but without powerful bureaucracies and standing armies. In addition, the communities normally lived in rural areas, without (the Western sense of) literacy and modern industries.[41]

Traditional communities lacked that degree of centralised government which most Western academics regard as necessary for the definition of a state. However, a Eurocentric historiography of Africa has sought to fit events into an understandable conceptual framework, while it may be argued that many of the political entities of precolonial Africa, which some historians have called "states" (like old Mali or old Congo) were hardly "states" at all. Imprecise concepts often obscure our capacity to understand Africa as it really was and, hence, as it really is.[42] It would be an oversimplification to believe that this prehistory of African societies was completely effaced by the creation and development of colonial states under independent African governments.[43]

The colonial powers created an élite class, which took over the new states, of which most became independent in the 1960s. These new élites often became more committed to perpetuating themselves in office than to advancing the interests of their new nations.[44] Laakso and Olukoshi point out that since unity was deemed desirable and diversity dangerous, a chasm soon developed between state and society, and the ruling élite became less and less accountable to the ruled masses. "Armed with the rhetoric of unity, the post-colonial African state, instead of enhancing its capacity to provide new economic and professional opportunities to all segments of the society, increasingly resorted to protecting itself against the populace."[45]

The concepts of authority and accountability are central to sociological, political and military studies. Accountability is the manifold and complex practice by which the ruled seek to hold the rulers to account. It defines the principle by which social, national and political communities remain together and integrated. While the threat of force is part of the calculus of power, its actual and repeated use manifests failed accountability.[46] In Africa, as elsewhere, the absence of the phenomenon of political accountability gave rise to the abuse of power.

Most rulers have been able to flout the constitutional mechanisms created upon independence: it has been difficult to call life-tenure presidencies, regime change through military *coups* and single-party states to account for their errors.[47] A dominant feature of the political systems since independence is that, over time, rulers appear to have become less, rather than more, accountable. Chabal describes this feature as the "dereliction of political accountability" in postcolonial Africa.[48]

It was naïve to assume that the hurried erection of parliamentary democracy – in colonies without serious experience of such a system and in a continent without historical experience of either the nation-state or of liberal representative politics – would result in a functioning political accountability. The parliamentary systems were mostly artificial constructs having neither depth nor roots in Africa. Most of the main conditions for democracy, namely high levels of literacy and education, high living standards and social homogeneity, are absent in Africa.[49] Consequently, the hastily carpentered institutions of liberal democracy quickly faded and disappeared in the face of growing authoritarianism and illegitimate coercion by both civilian and military regimes.[50] The long-term consequence of such a state of affairs was the decay of the postcolonial order – which peaked in countries like Uganda under Amin, Equatorial Guinea, Rwanda and Zaire.[51] These authoritarian practices may be linked to the serious problem of underdevelopment faced by contemporary Africa.

### 3.3 Authoritarianism, underdevelopment and conflict

While natural disasters and competitive international markets have much to do with problems of development, security and conflict, the authoritarianism and centralisation of domestic political institutions may be a critical factor.[52]

- Over four decades judicial and legislative power in almost all African countries was made subservient to an executive presidency and became part of, what is called, "a parasitical élite class supported by the state apparatus".[53] Power literally moved with experienced officials from the provinces to the capital.

- The centralisation of power facilitated the exploitation of the powerless by the powerful. In extreme cases the state usurped not only all the political roles and local governments but also all economic roles beyond the most simple enterprises.[54] In many states African socialist bureaucracies took the state regulation of the economy to the extreme.[55]

- Private organisations, such as co-operatives, labour unions, churches and universities have almost everywhere come under tight governmental control and, in some cases, have even been eradicated.

A critical difference between African states and most others across the world lies in the allocation not only of authority but also of available resources to the central versus local governments. Even in those Western societies where local governments are extensions of national governments, these institutions are major partners in delivering public services, and the percentage of total budgetary resources allocated to them is far greater than in Africa. The allocation of budgetary resources to local governments extends, for example, from France in the lower ranges with 17 per cent, to Sweden in the higher ranges with 66 per cent. Equivalent African figures are as low as 2 per cent.[56]

With the continuing centralisation of political and material assets in the hands of African state structures, it soon became evident that the closer to the centre of the political apparatus, the greater the chances of material reward.[57] Public service departments and public enterprises were soon regarded as virtually bottomless financial reservoirs for those who managed them and for the political authorities that headed them.[58] Spending the bulk of the funds at national level rendered treasuries giant common pools of resources. According to some observers: "All raid it as quickly as they can for the most personal use they can make of it before others do so first."[59] These practices have grave consequences when linked to the level of development and population growth.

The level of development in a country can be measured with the United Nations Human Development Index. This index takes into account life expectancy, adult literacy and living standards based on GDP (gross domestic product) per capita and ranks the countries as high, medium and low. With the exception of the islands Mauritius and Seychelles, no sub-Saharan country qualifies as being high level. The seven countries that fall in the medium category include South Africa, Botswana, Swaziland, Namibia and Zimbabwe in Southern Africa, plus Congo Brazzaville and Gabon. All other sub-Saharan countries fall in the low category.[60]

Even though agricultural output has increased over time, food production has consistently lagged behind population growth since 1970. As a result, food has had to be imported.[61] Sub-Saharan Africa has the lowest per capita GDP and per capita growth rate in the world, together with the world's highest population growth rates. Although sub-Saharan Africa's real GDP was growing by about 1,9 per cent in the mid-1990s, it was still 1 per cent lower than the population increase of 2,9 per cent. This considerable difference shows that, even though economic growth did take place, the inhabitants of the region had become poorer.[62] (See Figure 3, on per capita income in Africa, 1997.)

The consensus of many of those who have conducted analyses of the African development effort is that the authoritarian models imposed on much of Africa (either of the military or civil variety) have hindered, rather than fostered, development.[63] In fact, many of Africa's genuine successes have occurred despite the centralised state strategy. In their work on the failure of the African state, Wunsch and Olowu, point out how "extremely weak" centralised African governments have been.[64] Instead of fulfilling the needs of the urban and rural populations, governments mismanaged available assets and thus contributed to conflict over scarce resources. "Centralization has tended to increase, rather than to ease, the continent's underdevelopment."[65]

According to Sollenberg and Wallensteen, a striking feature of conflict in Africa and, to some extent, in Asia and South America is exactly this link between armed conflict and a weak state. All the conflicts in Africa at the end on the 1990s occurred in severely underdeveloped, weakened states. While the existence of a weakened state is not a guarantee that conflict will occur (just as strong states also experience conflict), the correlation is noticeable and raises difficult issues for the international community. In an immediate sense the most crucial challenge is whether that community is prepared to commit the necessary resources to disarm warlords and criminal elements that arise to fill the power vacuum left behind by collapsing states before any effective rebuilding can occur.[66]

In addition to the nearly unbearable pressures exerted by population expansion, political authoritarianism, economic underdevelopment and weakness of states, the conflict potential of sub-Saharan societies is continuously being heightened by the inherited geographical boundaries.

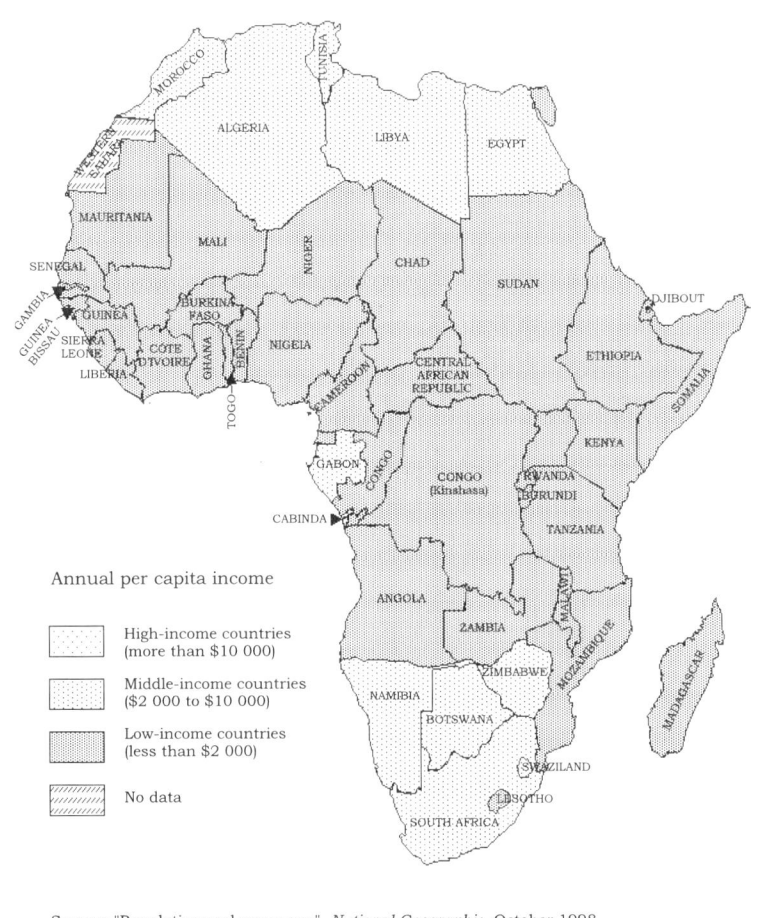

**FIGURE 3:**

**PER CAPITA INCOME AS INDICATOR OF COMPETITION FOR SCARCE RESOURCES**

PER CAPITA INCOME: AFRICA 1997

Annual per capita income

- High-income countries (more than $10 000)
- Middle-income countries ($2 000 to $10 000)
- Low-income countries (less than $2 000)
- No data

Source: "Population and resources", *National Geographic*, October 1998.

## 3.4 The rigidity of state boundaries

To establish the relationship between security and the history and nature of the boundaries of sub-Saharan states, three main features will be addressed: the artificiality, the legality and the conflict potential of African state boundaries.

### 3.4.1 The artificiality of boundaries

Over a period of less than eighty years of colonial rule the imperial powers incorporated the innumerable former communities in Africa into about fifty states. This process replaced traditional structures of authority (based on immediate blood relationships) with the new structures of the colonial state. These were based on impersonal borders and abstract doctrines quite alien to most African cultures.[67] Consequently, the colonial state has formed little more than a thin web around living social organisms.

At the Congress of Berlin in 1885, European colonial powers partitioned Africa into territorial units. Kingdoms, states and communities in Africa were arbitrarily divided; unrelated regions and peoples were just as arbitrarily joined together.[68] Since the Congress of Berlin delineated spheres of influence and laid down the ground rules for imperial expansion, the political frontiers of Africa have undergone only minor adjustments. In the 1960s the newly independent states inherited these boundaries.

Consequently, a profound characteristic of sub-Saharan Africa became the artificiality of its interstate boundaries. These boundaries do not reflect sub-Saharan geographical or ethnic realities.[69] Many of the lines drawn in Europe across the map of Africa bore little relation to any local political or social reality. In the largely unknown interior, lines of longitude and latitude were chosen in European chanceries to serve as borders in Africa.[70]

As Lonsdale maintains in his often-quoted view:[71] "Most Africans did not actually live in states until colonial rule fastened Leviathan's yoke upon them. Indeed the most distinctively African contribution to human history could be said to have been precisely the civilised art of living fairly peacefully together *not* in states." According to the decolonisation specialist, John Hargreaves, the nineteenth-century partition had left colonial rulers controlling "blocks of land and peoples which, if not wholly arbitrary, rarely shared any common and distinctive historical identity". For want of any evident alternative, the colonial boundaries soon hardened into state frontiers.[72]

### 3.4.2 The legality of boundaries

During decolonisation African political leaders decided to protect their newly won independence by respecting the inherited colonial boundaries. At the maiden summit conference in Addis Ababa in May 1963 the OAU Charter formulated as a main aim "to safeguard and consolidate the hard-won independence, as well as the sovereignty and territorial integrity of our states, and to fight against neo-colonialism in all its forms".[73] Apart from this emphasis on "territorial integrity" in the Charter, the sanctity of these boundaries was endorsed by the resolution of the 1964 OAU summit conference held in Cairo, Egypt.

The reason for this aim should be understood. Although many countries acknowledged the irrationality of the inherited colonial division, they decided to accept these boundaries because they felt that any attempt to redraw them would create more problems than it would solve.[74] The irony is that the black African leaders who led the successful revolts against colonial rule did not dismantle the alien Western political frameworks, but sought to preserve legally the arbitrarily demarcated artificial boundaries — virtually at all costs.[75] The African leaders ensured that the borders would be rigid, inflexible and permanent.

In addition, the new artificial African "states" were welcomed into the international legal system. The paradox was that, even when entire regions had successfully defied central governments by exercising *de facto* control over large areas, their claims failed to win international recognition.[76] This state of affairs inevitably had negative consequences for the cohesion of the new societies.

### 3.4.3 The conflict potential of boundaries

One of the most controversial legacies of colonialism is precisely this creation of artificial boundaries, which had lasting effects on African security. Almost immediately after the clause accepting existing borders was put into the OAU Charter, many ethnic groups started clamouring for secession from the states they were locked into, while some states saw the need to redraw their boundaries with neighbours. This soon resulted in civil wars or in border clashes with neighbours.[77]

The creation of artificial national boundaries around or right through the historical territories of different ethnic and religious groups, inevitably sowed the seeds of ethnically-based resistance movements.[78] Ngari refers to the wars between neighbouring countries - often inhabited by the same peoples - as a "pernicious threat as they are a sequel of colonialism", because the conflicts were often directly related to the drawing of these borders by foreign powers.[79]

The haphazard demarcation of African boundaries without regard for ethnic or religious differences thus created two intertwined problems. First, several ethnic groups who felt uncomfortable, even suppressed, within a state dominated by another group, became involved in *intra*state struggles, often demanding secession. Second, several political leaders became involved in interstate disputes with neighbouring African states as regards their boundaries.[80]

The potential for bloody interstate conflict arising from border disputes increases when the environment of the artificial border is also rich in natural assets. According to Oyebade and Alao: "The tendency of border disputes to create deep conflict becomes even more marked if the disputed territory is potentially rich in natural or mineral resources."[81] The dispute between Nigeria and Cameroon over the Bakassi Peninsula is still a cause of deep animosity between the two countries.

In contrast to the European model of the nation-state, the borders of most sub-Saharan states did not include one ethnic group, but many. In various ways ethnicity became a significant link to the African experiences of security, insecurity and conflict.

## 3.5 The power of ethnicity

The ethnic diversity of sub-Saharan countries has an immediate effect on the structure of their societies, as well as on the scope of security issues. The fact is that, because the more than forty sub-Saharan countries are home to several hundreds of identifiable ethnic communities, nearly all countries are ethnically heterogeneous.[82] A few comments on the nature of ethnicity and its implications for conflict, are crucial.

## 3.5.1 The nature of African ethnicity

The ethnic links of individuals are related to a common culture. Although it is possible that several ethnic groups may share a common language or dialect, members from one ethnic group normally speak only one language and normally also share the consciousness of a common history. However, common characteristics are not permanent. The time factor is important. Throughout the history of Africa many separate ethnic groups have been formed, while others have been integrated with one another. Cultures have blended. This has happened and is still happening voluntarily or forcibly through conquest.[83]

Since their demarcation by colonial powers, few African countries have had culturally homogeneous societies where virtually all the people share the same mother tongue.[84] It has been pointed out that most colonial states "lumped together disparate groups within the confines of culturally irrelevant boundaries".[85] In a few countries, such as Lesotho, Swaziland and Somalia, virtually all the people speak the same mother tongue. In some countries a single ethnic group outnumbers the combined total of all the others, such as Zimbabwe and Benin. However, most societies are multi-ethnic.[86] Moreover, the ethnic groups forced to co-exist within many of the newly independent states have fairly long precolonial histories of rivalry.[87] Although the power of colonial authorities often suppressed these rivalries, they surfaced after independence.

For several reasons compromises are difficult to reach in ethnic conflicts. First, opponents are seen as belonging to a group with different, often nearly unalterable characteristics, such as race, language or religion. Second, existing state structures often discriminate in favour of and against certain groups. Some ethnic movements are then regarded as legal and some as illegal, and competitors thus perceive their rivals as threats to their economic and political survival. This is why, as Gurr and Harf have indicated, many ethnic conflicts are manifestations of the hostilities within states, where one or more ethnic groups wish to expand their authority, while other groups wish to defend their identity.[88]

The single-party systems of postindependence times were often contrived to counter ethnic rivalry and to forge national unity, but to no avail, as the inequitable distribution of scarce resources perpetuated group antagonism. Moreover, political parties in democratised states have often shown a propensity for relying on and promoting the interests of favoured ethnic groups. It is correctly pointed out that: "Ethnicity and political power are closely interlinked in Africa."[89] During the past decades centralised states often created ethnic tensions through their threatening behaviour towards disempowered ethnic communities that sustained the lives of ordinary Africans. According to Wunsch: "Great ethnic conflict has usually been caused by the capture, or apparent near-capture, by one group of control over the *centralized* state."[90] The history of the civil wars in Nigeria and in Sudan illustrates this.

Within this context the politics of tribalism and ethnicity is linked to the ability of ethnic leaders, who hold positions in the state, to obtain for their regions a significant share of the collective benefits of development in infrastructure projects, such as roads, schools and dispensaries, as well the more personal rewards apportioned through discrete personal contacts.[91] To remain in power, political leaders often employ divide-and-rule tactics, where they deliberately favour one ethnic group, normally the more populous or influential group, over the other.[92] The most extreme and malignant form of ethnic mobilisation is genocide, such as the 1994 massacres in Rwanda. A major reason for these massacres was the obsession of a small group to retain power.[93] These attempts to marginalise and exclude certain regional and ethnic groups after independence had the counterproductive effect of politicising ethnicity. As Cornwall judges: using ethnic links has become a survival strategy for many Africans.[94]

Ethnocentrism is sometimes reinforced by other expressions of culture such as religion. In Nigeria the Ibos in Biafra often regarded themselves as Christians facing persecution from the Muslim north. In Sudan the ethnic divisions between the Arab-oriented north and the black-oriented south are strengthened by the religious divide between Muslims and Christians. Such ethnic divisions become more endemic and entrenched.[95]

Ethnic conflicts often also have an economic dimension. The hostilities are intensified by the economic decline linked to the deterioration of already relatively weak states. As economic resources shrink, competition between ethnic groups tends to increase, and ethnicity becomes politicised.[96] In circumstances of uncertainty, instability and intense competition for resources, people attempt to find in ethnic communities a degree of security. In circumstances of economic and political instability, where even the wealthy face daily the insecurities and uncertainties of life, kinship and ethnicity provide networks of mutual support, referred to by Simons as, "charts of trustworthiness".[97] In addition to the fierce competition for scarce resources and employment, ethnic consciousness may also be enhanced by the migration of urbanising individuals to strange environments and by education.[98]

All the abovementioned factors apply to the experiences of sub-Saharan Africans, as can be seen in the wide range of examples of ethnic competition and friction.

### 3.5.2 African ethnic competition and conflict

Ethnic diversity inevitably implies some kind of ethnic competition. Oyebade and Alao argue that, "because they are a product of artificial creation, practically no African state is immune to ethnic tension".[99] They predict: "In the years to come, ethnic problems are likely to combine with a number of other factors to cause security problems in many African countries."[100] These problems are related to the fact that to a great extent group identities depend on what the members are opposed to at any given time.[101] The significant overlap between general sub-Saharan hostilities (mentioned before) and ethnic conflicts (mentioned in this section) cannot be overlooked. Ethnic preference is a solid cause of many hostilities. In periods of fierce competition between ethnic groups, an undifferentiated mass psychology soon develops based on a strong survival instinct to destroy a collective enemy.[102]

Ethnicity was the underlying cause of secessionist tendencies in several countries, such as Congo Kinshasa, Eritrea, Nigeria, Senegal and Tanzania. It was also related to irredentism — the desire to incorporate ethnic relatives in neighbouring countries — such as in Somalia, Ghana-Togo and Nigeria-Cameroon.[103]

Ethnic differences between the north and south are most likely dominant in Nigeria. In Ghana thousands have died in clashes between the Konkomba and the Nanumba. In the 1990s, conflicts between the Hutu and Tutsi population groups in Burundi left tens of thousands dead. Ethnic hostilities occur in Kenya, Chad and Togo. Ethiopia, with fifteen major ethnic groups and up to seventy languages, is vulnerable to some form of ethnic violence.[104] The political preferences of a number of Zulu-speaking people in South Africa are sometimes cited as an example of the need for ethnocentric self-determination. Signs of this need can be detected from the traditional Zulu homeland in KwaZulu-Natal to the urban areas where many Zulus work (like the Witwatersrand) and are manifested in skirmishes that caused thousands of casualties in the 1990s.[105]

A little more will be said about Liberia and Rwanda where the societies have been torn apart by ethnic antagonism. For more than a century ethnicity provided a dividing line in Liberian politics, between the Americo-Liberians and indigenous groups. When the Liberian civil war erupted in 1990, ethnic conflict played a significant role, such as that between the Krahn and the Gio-Mano ethnic groups. This ethnocentrism bedevilled efforts to achieve representative democracy. Even the West African subregional peacekeeping force, ECOMOG, made little impact outside the district of the capital, Monrovia.[106]

Ethnicity was a major factor in Rwandan politics - even before independence in 1962 - and since then the Hutu and Tutsi ethnic groups have formed separate political movements. Within two months after the war between the Hutu majority and the Tutsi minority had erupted in 1994, one out of every sixteen Rwandans had been killed and more than two million inhabitants of the country had become refugees in the neighbouring Zaire and Uganda.[107] Although the Hutu government shared power with the Tutsis, the Tutsi Rwandan Patriotic Front (RPF) launched ongoing attacks on the country from Uganda, where there is a significant Tutsi population. Members of the same ethnic group, separated by artificial national boundaries, supported one another.

### 3.5.3 The institutionalisation of ethnicity

In the light of the competition and conflict between ethnic groups in sub-Saharan Africa, a serious policy question is whether ethnicity can be institutionalised to ensure greater security, and, if so, how.

On the one hand Ellis confirms that to a large extent nationalism, as the great mobilising ideology of the decolonisation period, has been replaced by "appeals to ethnic solidarity".[108] On the other hand and with reference to the ethnic solidarity of the same ethnic group separated by national boundaries which is a legacy of arbitrary colonial territorial divisions, Alao and Olonisakin remark prophetically: "As long as colonial boundaries in Africa continue to stay as they are, this problem will remain."[109]

Berman warns that there can be little hope of fundamental change towards modernity in African countries without limiting the patronage of the state, without displacing despotisms in the countryside and without, "effective accommodation of the reality of ethnic pluralism in formal political institutions".[110]

At the end of the twentieth century the identified sub-Saharan conflicts and the reasons underlying the propensity for conflict (such as political authoritarianism, economic underdevelopment, the weakness of states, inherited geographical boundaries and the related ethnocentrism) were creating conditions of such unbearable insecurity that members of the international community stepped in to try to secure some degree of peace. Although the aim of this chapter is not to analyse conflict resolution measures in detail, a few comments on changing approaches are essential.

*African conflict at the turn of the century*

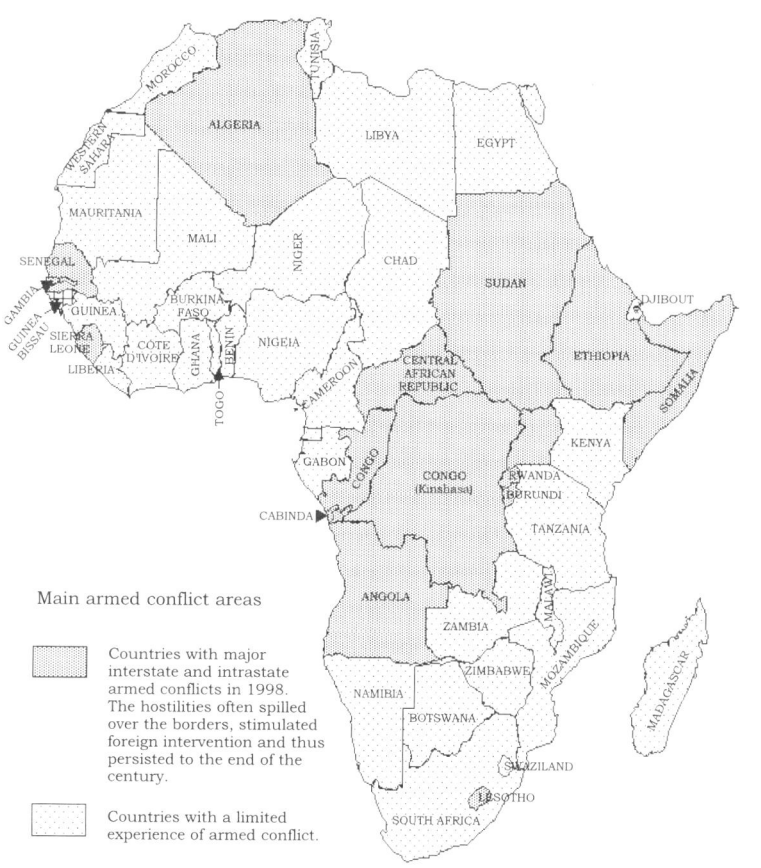

**FIGURE 4:**

**ARMED CONFLICTS IN AFRICA**

MAIN AFRICAN CONFLICT AREAS IN 1998

Main armed conflict areas

Countries with major interstate and intrastate armed conflicts in 1998. The hostilities often spilled over the borders, stimulated foreign intervention and thus persisted to the end of the century.

Countries with a limited experience of armed conflict.

Source: Hanekom, H, "The sub-Saharan African arc of conflict", *Africa Insight* 28 (3/4), 1998, p 157; International Institute for Strategic Studies, "Map: Status of armed conflict 1994-1997 - Sub-Saharan Africa", *Strategic Survey 1996/97*, Oxford University Press, London, 1997.

## 4. THE CHANGING APPROACH TO CONFLICT RESOLUTION

During the last decades of the twentieth century several factors impacted on the manner in which Western and African societies approached the resolution of the conflicts Africans were engaged in. Some of these factors will be identified.

### 4.1 Declining international commitment

One factor is the financial and strategic marginalisation of Africa by the developed world. The strategic importance the Cold War accorded Africa has, for the most part, declined.[111] At the end of the Cold War Africa's problems suddenly seemed even more remote than before. The French paper Le Monde accurately articulated the perception in the West when it argued: "Our priorities are elsewhere in Europe. At a time when our brothers on the other side of the iron curtain desperately need us, why continue favouring African regimes? Why not spend elsewhere the funds we spend there in vain?"[112] Consequently, France, Britain and the United States, among other countries, drastically reduced their aid packages to Africa in the 1990s.[113]

Moreover, negative experiences with peace missions in disorganised sub-Saharan conditions quickly convinced the Western electorates that such operations may not be in their national interests. In fact, during their intervention in the interclan conflicts in Somalia in 1992 and 1993, United States troops became so embroiled in the conflict that they eventually left Somalia with considerable casualties and a damaged reputation. Since that ill-fated intervention, even the United States has been cautious about becoming involved in African conflicts.[114] The French president articulated the rationale for the Western disengagement clearly when he suggested that "the time has come for Africans themselves to resolve their conflicts and organise their own security".[115]

In many ways the other member states of the United Nations shared this view, especially after UN peacekeeping and peace enforcement misfired, not only in Somalia and Angola, but also in traumatised Central Africa. In Rwanda, for example, a three-year UN peacekeeping operation failed to halt the ethnic genocide that resulted in between 500 000 and one million deaths.[116] The fiasco of the UN peacekeeping operation in Somalia and its inability to contain the conflict in Rwanda negatively impacted on the willingness of the international community to become involved. There was no eagerness to repeat either experience.[117]

Gradually African states became more independent from immediate and forceful international interference in conflict areas. However, contrary to some expectations, an Africa omitted from the calculations of external rivals has not become a more peaceful place. Local disputes are now receiving less global attention, are more removed from the world centres of power, and have become insignificant in terms of the global system. Consequently African states can no longer rely on outside assistance to end local wars that are not a threat to vital foreign interests. This implies that local conflicts are now given freer rein.[118]

After the Cold War more and more African voices pleaded for self-reliance in conflict management and warned that it would be "naive to continue to expect extra-African military intervention".[119] According to Oyebade: "African conflicts with international ramifications, like the crisis in Rwanda, could compel external intervention. However, such intervention would seldom be military in nature, but humanitarian."[120] Western powers have stated in no uncertain terms that they would be more interested in preventive diplomacy in early conflict situations. This would entail assisting African states to respond to early signs of conflict before conflicts escalate.[121] Rather than direct military intervention, the aim of current Western policy is to provide financial and technical aid to bolster Africa's crisis management capacity. Bekerie considers the actualisation of a united Europe at the turn of the century a lesson for Africa and a call to pursue more vigorously pan-African unity. He sees such unity as the only option for Africa to safeguard its security in the twenty-first century.[122]

## 4.2 Growing regionalisation of conflict management

Regionalisation is itself a new trend in conflict prevention, management and resolution. With the realisation that the United Nations is unable to intervene in every conflict, regional organisations have been slowly but surely improving their own capabilities, focusing on their areas of greatest perceived need. While Europe currently has the entire range of conflict resolution capacities, Africa has concentrated on establishing a conflict prevention capacity within the Organisation of African Unity (OAU) and lately on improving African peacekeeping capabilities. More generally its focus has been on the growth of civil society, democratisation and general nation building and development. African subregional bodies are showing considerable inventiveness and agility in these areas.[123]

In the first decades after the establishment of the OAU, the principal regional organisation in Africa, the members condemned the interference of non-African powers, as well as of other African states, in the internal affairs of African countries. The emphasis was on a strategy of non-interference. The initial ideal was that African countries should address their own internal problems. However, it later emerged that certain inhuman policies demanded action. The Rwandan crisis, for example, exposed the inability of both individual African states and the OAU to deal with even extreme disasters. Beyond endless calls to end the crisis, the OAU did practically nothing.[124]

However, while the OAU continued to struggle to revamp and revitalise itself in order to meet the grave challenges facing African peace and security, it gradually became aware of the need to address security interests on the African continent empathetically and systematically. The organisation became involved in a series of well-planned negotiations, such as those to restore peace to conflict-ridden states (such as Liberia, Rwanda and Somalia), and has taken part in monitoring elections in many subregions of the continent. Since 1994 the OAU has established and developed a formal Mechanism for Conflict Prevention, Management and Resolution.[125]

The 33rd OAU summit meeting, held in Harare, Zimbabwe, in June 1997, was exceptional. For the first time in its history, it mandated a regional African force to undertake peace enforcement. In response to the military *coup* in Sierra Leone in late May 1997, which overturned a recently elected government, the OAU authorised the ECOWAS Monitoring Group (ECOMOG) peacekeeping force based in Liberia to remove the illegal government of Major Johnny Koroma by force. As demonstrated by its action over Sierra Leone, the OAU appeared to be overturning its traditional reluctance to countenance intervention in the internal affairs of its member states, at least in the case of military *coups*. Zimbabwean Prime Minister Robert Mugabe declared in closing the summit meeting that future *coups* in Africa would be handled in a "hard way".[126]

Towards the end of the 1990s it became apparent that gradually developing multilateral security structures in sub-Sahara are indeed defining joint interstate peacekeeping operations as a new and decisive role. Several sub-Saharan states expanded their conventional military training programmes by presenting dedicated training for peace missions provided at military training institutions. A number of sub-Saharan states, such as Nigeria, Ghana, Ethiopia, Kenya, Zimbabwe and Tanzania, have furthermore contributed troops to peacekeeping operations.

Perhaps ECOMOG, the West African peacekeeping mission in Liberia, best demonstrates some of Africa's developing conflict resolution abilities. Member states of the Economic Community of West African States (ECOWAS) constituted this mission following their concern about the adverse regional effects of the escalating conflict in Liberia. At the initiative of Nigeria, its own troops were supplemented with those of other West African countries, such as Ghana, Gambia and Guinea.[127] Although not regarded as "terribly successful", ECOMOG contributed to securing some kind of peace for Liberia.[128] Thus sub-Sahara was taking steps to develop the capacity to manage its own conflicts.

At the turn of the century a select group of sub-Saharan states, such as Nigeria, South Africa, Kenya and Zimbabwe, proved themselves capable of providing manpower and logistics to sustain an extended foreign peace operation.[129] In addition, a few countries conducted combined operations for what they defined as "intervention missions" in support of democratically elected governments against armed rebellions or planned military *coups* (as will be discussed in following chapters). While Nigeria became involved in West Africa supported by countries such as Ghana and Gambia; Zimbabwe, Namibia and Angola played a role in the DRC; and South Africa and Botswana in Lesotho.

Joint ventures also originated from individual governments. In some subregions cross-border conflict made room for co-operation. During the first decades after independence a few states took cautious steps in the direction of joint regional security structures. Slowly but surely external military co-operation took root, firstly in the form of signing defence agreements and then, more tangibly, in the form of military assistance to protect endangered neighbours — often against the aspirations of their own military forces. Consequently, at the end of the twentieth century, the OAU as a regional organisation was responding faster to sub-Saharan conflicts through bodies such as the OAU Mechanism for Conflict Prevention, Management and Resolution. In addition, sub-regional structures, which promote defence co-operation and peace keeping, such as the Economic Community of West African States (ECOWAS) and the Southern African Inter-State Defence and Security Committee (ISDSC), were becoming more effective.

## 5. CONCLUSION

In this chapter conceptual distinctions were made between different kinds of conflict such as intrasocietal and intersocietal armed conflict; conflicts were classified according to levels of violence; and a long series of manifestations of sub-Saharan armed conflict was identified. It was pointed out that the propensity for sub-Saharan strife had serious effects on human and animal life and on living standards. In addition to the loss of life as a direct result of military action, hostilities often destroyed food supplies and livestock.

One of the main arguments was that sub-Saharan violence could not be understood without investigating the underlying demographic, political, geographical and ethnic realities. These societal characteristics, especially when viewed against the background of a modernising continent, provide some insight into the resilience of conflicts. This was not only true for the last decades of the twentieth century, but will also apply to the first decades of the twenty-first century. Without exploring societal characteristics, no amount of good intent will ever be able to effect peace in conflict areas. This is especially true of the belligerent Central African subregion, stretching from northern Angola and Congo Brazzaville through the DRC, Burundi, Rwanda and Uganda to Somalia, Ethiopia, Sudan and Eritrea.

When analysing the manifestations of African conflict, note should be taken of the negative impact of the population explosion in the conflict areas. One of the most underestimated facts is that Africa's experience of having the world's fastest population growth, exerts tremendous pressure on stability and increases the competition for scarce resources. This situation is aggravated by the parasitical authoritarianism of political leaders and the centralisation of the few assets that are available. As was pointed out by the Sipri analysts, Sollenberg and Wallensteen, a striking feature of Africa is the link between armed conflict and underdeveloped, weak states.

Manifestations of sub-Saharan conflict are increasingly influenced by the rigidity of political boundaries and the related growing power of ethnicity. As was illustrated, ethnocentrism was the underlying cause of secessionist tendencies in several countries, such as Congo Kinshasa, Eritrea, Nigeria, Senegal and Tanzania, and was also related to irridentism – the desire to incorporate ethnic relatives in neighbouring countries – such as in Somalia, Ghana-Togo and Nigeria-Cameroon. Ethnic differences between the north and south are most likely dominant in Nigeria and in Ghana, where thousands have died. The same is true of many other sub-Saharan societies such as Chad, Togo, Liberia, Kenya, Burundi and Rwanda. If African specialists, such as Berman, Alao and Olonisakin, are taken seriously, the first decades of the twenty-first century may see a growing influence of ethnic consciousness on conflict.

The third perspective in the conflict triangle model is that of conflict management. From the point of view of the resolution of conflict, it may be argued that the financial and strategic marginalisation of Africa by the developed world may, in a certain sense, be a mixed blessing. While countries such as the United States, France and Britain have reduced their aid packages to Africa and have been cautious about becoming involved in African conflicts after burning their fingers in hostilities such as in Somalia, African states on the other hand have become more self-reliant in conflict management. In fact, the OAU as the principal regional organisation, which for years followed a strategy of non-interference in conflicts, has revamped and revitalised itself in the 1990s. The organisation became involved in a series of well-planned negotiations, such as those to restore peace to conflict-ridden states (such as Liberia, Rwanda and Somalia), and has taken part in monitoring elections in many subregions of the continent. Since the mid-1990s the OAU has developed a formal Mechanism for Conflict Prevention, Management and Resolution.

Slowly but surely several states began to implement conflict resolution measures jointly in their subregions. Some signed defence agreements. Nigeria, Ghana, Ethiopia, Kenya, Zimbabwe and Tanzania started to train soldiers for peace keeping. A few countries also conducted combined operations for what they defined as, "intervention missions" in support of democratically elected governments against armed rebellions or planned military coups (as will be highlighted in the following chapters). With reference to the conflict triangle model, it can be concluded that long-term societal development inevitably influences the level of conflict propensity and thus the manifestations of conflict in sub-Saharan Africa. At the same time, the changing approach of African political leaders contributes directly, often immediately, to conflict management, sometimes through international military intervention. The future will reveal the relative strength of these forces in the various conflict areas.

## ENDNOTES

1. Chabal, P, "The (de)construction of post-colonial order in Black Africa", *AI Bulletin*, Vol 35, No 6, 1995, p 1.
2. Du Pisani, A, "Security and peace in post-apartheid Southern Africa", *International Affairs Bulletin*, Vol 13, No 3, 1992, pp 5-6.
3. Van Aardt, M, "In search of a more adequate concept of security for southern Africa", *South African Journal of International Affairs*, Vol 1, No 1, 1993, p 84, p 89.
4. Centre for Intergroup Studies (CIS) (now Centre for Conflict Resolution), *Annual Report 1993*, University of Cape Town, 1993, p 13.
5. Baynham, S, "Regional security in the Third World with specific reference to Southern Africa", *Strategic Review for Southern Africa*, Vol XVI, No 1, 1994, pp 84-111.
6. Van Aardt, M, "Security for Southern Africa", *Outline of paper presented at Conference on peace and security in Eastern and Southern Africa*, Centre for Foreign Relations, Dar es Salaam, 22 August 1994, pp 1-3.
7. Sipri (Stockholm International Peace Research Institute), *Yearbook 1998: Armaments, Disarmament and International Security*, Oxford University Press, 1998, p 24.
8. *Ibid*, p 17.
9. *Ibid*.

10. Cornwall, R, "Democratisation and security in Africa", *African Security Review*, Vol 6, No 5, 1997, p 16.
11. Heitman, H, "Security and Africa's armed forces at the end of the 1990s", *ISSUP Bulletin*, 4/95, Pretoria, p 5.
12. Thom, W G, "Sub-Saharan Africa's Changing Military Capabilities", in Arlinghaus, BE and Baker, PH, *African Armies: Evolution and Capabilities*, London, Westview Press, 1986, p 104.
13. Williams, G, "Africa in retrospect and prospect", *Africa South of the Sahara 1997*, Europa Publications, London, 1997, p 4.
14. Oyebade, A and Alao, A, "Conclusion: A short peep into a long future", in Oyebade, A, and Alao, A, (eds), *Africa After the Cold War – The Changing Perspectives on Security*, Africa World Press, Asmara, Eritrea, 1998, p 195.
15. *Ibid*, pp 195-196.
16. Sipri, *op cit*, p 23.
17. *Ibid*, pp 17, 22. For a comparison of casualties in the 1997 African conflicts, see Table 1A, pp 28-30.
18. Heitman, H, *op cit*, p 9.
19. Oyebade, A, "The end of the Cold War in Africa: Implications for conflict management and resolution", in Oyebade, A, and Alao, A, (eds), *op cit*, p 151.
20. Heitman, H, *op cit*, pp 6, 8.
21. Barrows, W L, "Changing military capabilities in Black Africa", in Foltz, WJ, and Bienen, HS (eds), *Arms and the African - Military Influences on Africa's International Relations*, Yale University Press, New Haven, 1985, p 105.
22. Oyebade, A, *op cit*, pp 153-156.
23. *Ibid*, pp 156-158.
24. *Ibid*, p 161.
25. Heitman, H, *op cit*, p 9; Oyebade, A, *op cit*, pp 161-162.
26. Oyebade, A, *op cit*, pp 162-163.
27. *UN Chronicle*, Vol 31, No 4, December 1994, p 8.
28. Oyebade, A, "The end of the Cold War in Africa", *op cit*, p 159.
29. *Ibid*, pp 160-161.
30. Heitman, H, *op cit*, p 11.
31. Du Plessis, L, "The changing historical roles of sub-Saharan armed forces", in Du Plessis, L and Hough, M (eds), *Protecting sub-*

Saharan Africa: the Military Challenge, HSRC Publishers, Pretoria, 1999, pp 79-88; and Arlinghaus, BE, "African Armies - An Analytical Approach", in Arlinghaus, BE and Baker, PH, *African Armies: Evolution and Capabilities*, London, Westview Press, 1986, p 5.

32. Barrows, WL, *op cit*, pp 118-119.
33. Thom, WG, *op cit*, pp 108-109.
34. Cornwall, R, *op cit*, p 18. Compare Clapham, C, *The African State*, presentation to the Conference of the Royal African Society on Sub-Saharan Africa: The Record and the Outlook, St John's College, Cambridge, 14-16 April 1991. For an enlightening discussion, see International Institute for Strategic Studies, *Strategic Survey 1996/97*, Oxford University Press, London, 1997, pp 212-224.
35. *Ibid*, p 17.
36. Ranger, T, "Africa", in Howard, M and Louis, R (eds) *The Oxford History of the Twentieth Century*, Oxford University Press, New York, 1998, p 269.
37. "Geography and population" in Esterhuysen, P (eds), *Africa A-Z: Continental and Country Profiles*, Africa Institute of South Africa, Pretoria, 1998, pp 13-14.
38. "Africa's growing population" in Esterhuysen, P and Botha, P (ed), *Africa at a Glance: Facts and Figures: Quality of Life and Political Change: 1997/8*, Africa Institute of South Africa, Pretoria, 1998, p 16.
39. "Geography and population", *op cit*, p 14.
40. Boahen, AA, *African Perspectives on Colonialism*, Johns Hopkins University Press, Baltimore, MD, 1987, p 95.
41. Ellis, S, "Africa after the Cold War: New patterns of government and politics", *Development and Change*, 27, 1996, p 10.
42. Fuglestad, F, "The Trevor-Roper Trap or the imperialism of history: An essay", *History in Africa*, 19, pp 309-26.
43. Clapham, C, "The Longue Durée of the African state", *African Affairs* 372, 1994, pp 433-9.
44. Oyebade, A and Alao, A, "Conclusion: A short peep...", *op cit*, pp 193-194.
45. Laakso, L and Olukoshi, AO, "The crisis of the post-colonial nation-state project in Africa", in Laakso, L and Olukoshi, AO

(eds), *Challenges to the Nation-state in Africa*, Nordiska Afrikainstitutet, Uppsala, 1997, pp 14-15.

46. Chabal, P, *op cit*, p 2.
47. Olowu, D and Wunsch, JS, "Conclusion: Self-governance and African development", in Wunsch, JS and Olowu, D (eds), *The Failure of the Centralized State: Institutions and Self-Governance in Africa*, Westview Press, Boulder, Colorado, 1990, p 298.
48. Chabal, P, *op cit*, pp 2-3.
49. Olowu, D and Wunsch, JS, "Conclusion: Self-governance...", *op cit*, p 310.
50. Berman, BJ, "Ethnicity, patronage and the African state: the politics of uncivil nationalism", *African Affairs*, Vol 97, No 388, July 1998, p 333.
51. Chabal, P, *op cit*, p 3. Great human disasters such as the German Third Reich, the Russian Stalinist purges, the Chinese Cultural Revolution and the Cambodian holocaust are often linked to the complete domination of other social institutions by the state. Where there was resistance to the terror of the state, it came from organizations that preserved some measure of autonomy, such as the church and the military in Nazi Germany. See the sound arguments by Wunsch, JS and Olowu, D, "The failure of the centralized African state", in Wunsch, JS and Olowu, D (eds), *The Failure of the Centralized State: Institutions and Self-Governance in Africa*, Westview Press, Boulder, Colorado, 1990, pp 1-22.
52. Wunsch, JS and Olowu, D, "The failure...", *op cit*, p 18.
53. *Ibid*, pp 5, 18.
54. *Ibid*, p 12.
55. Ranger, T, *op cit*, p 273.
56. Wunsch, JS and Olowu, D, "The failure...", *op cit*, p 4.
57. Cornwall, R, "The collapse of the African state", *Paper presented at the SA Defence College*, Thaba Tshwane, Feb 1999, p 3.
58. Bayart, J-F, *The State in Africa: The Politics of the Belly*, Longman, London, 1993, p 78.
59. Olowu, D and Wunsch, JS, "Conclusion: Self-governance...", *op cit*, p 298.
60. "Developing economies" in Esterhuysen, P (ed), *Africa A-Z: Continental and Country Profiles*, Africa Institute of South Africa, Pretoria, 1998, p 51.

61. *Ibid*, p 53.
62. *Ibid*, p 49.
63. Olowu, D and Wunsch, JS, "Conclusion: Self-governance...", *op cit*, p 310.
64. Wunsch, JS and Olowu, D, "The failure...", *op cit*, p 16.
65. Olowu, D and Wunsch, JS, "Conclusion: Self-governance...", *op cit*, p 293.
66. Sollenberg, M and Wallensteen, P, "Major armed conflicts", in Sipri (Stockholm International Peace Research Institute), *Yearbook 1998: Armaments, Disarmament and International Security*, Oxford University Press, 1998, p 23.
67. Cornwall, R, "The collapse of the African state", *op cit*, p 2.
68. United Nations Secretary-General, *The Causes of Conflict and the Promotion of Durable Peace and Sustainable Development in Africa*, Report of the Secretary-General, New York, 23 April 1998, p 3-4.
69. Chazan, N; Mortimer, R; Ravenhill, J; and Rotchchild, D, "The diversity of African politics: Trends and approaches", in *Politics and Society in Contemporary Africa*, Lynne Rienner Publishers, Boulder, Colorado, 1992, pp 25-26.
70. "Colonial to present times" in Esterhuysen, P (ed), *Africa A-Z: Continental and Country Profiles*, *op cit*, pp 34-36.
71. Lonsdale, J, "States and social processes in Africa: A historiographical survey", *African Studies Review*, Vol 24, No 2/3, 1981, p 139, quoted in a very informative paper by Cornwall, R, The collapse of the African state, *op cit*, p 2.
72. Hargreaves, JD, *Decolonization in Africa*, Longman, London, 1996, pp 249-250.
73. Oyebade, A and Alao, A, "Redefining African security", in Oyebade, A and Alao, A (eds), *op cit*, p 5.
74. *Ibid*, p 7.
75. Cornwall, R, "The collapse...", *op cit*, p 2.
76. *Ibid*, p 3.
77. Oyebade, A, and Alao, A, "Redefining...", *op cit*, p 8.
78. Alao, A and Olonisakin, F, "Post Cold War Africa: Ethnicity, ethnic conflict and security", in Oyebade, A and Alao, A (eds), *op cit*, p 121.

79. Ngari, I, "African military perspectives", *African Armed Forces*, December/January 1995, p 13.
80. Oyebade, A and Alao, A, "Conclusion: A short peep into a long future", *op cit*, p 194.
81. *Ibid*, p 202.
82. Alao, A and Olonisakin, F, "Post Cold War Africa", *op cit*, p 121.
83. "Peoples and origins" in Esterhuysen, P (ed), *Africa A-Z: Continental and Country Profiles*, *op cit*, p 22.
84. *Ibid*.
85. *Ibid*.
86. *Ibid*.
87. Alao, A and Olonisakin, F, "Post Cold War Africa", *op cit*, p 121.
88. Gurr, T and Harf, B, *Ethnic Conflict in World Politics*, Westview, Boulder, 1994, p 15.
89. "Peoples and origins", *op cit*, p 22.
90. Wunsch, J, "Beyond the failure of the centralized state: Toward self-governance and an alternative institutional paradigm", in Wunsch, JS and Olowu, D (eds), *op cit*, p 284.
91. Berman, BJ, *op cit*, p 335.
92. Alao, A and Olonisakin, F, "Post Cold War Africa", *op cit*, p 136.
93. Ellis, S, *op cit*, p 11.
94. Cornwall, R, "The collapse of the African state", *op cit*, p 6.
95. Alao, A and Olonisakin, F, "Post Cold War Africa", *op cit*, p 124.
96. *Ibid*, p 126.
97. Simons, A, "Democratization and ethnic conflict: the kin connection", *Nations and Nationalism*, Vol 3, No 2, 1997, p 276.
98. Cornwall, R, "The collapse of the African state", *op cit*, p 6.
99. Oyebade, A and Alao, A, "Conclusion: A short peep...", *op cit*, p 201.
100. *Ibid*, p 201.
101. Cornwall, R, "The collapse of the African state", *op cit*, p 6.
102. Rothchild, D, "Interactive models for state-ethnic relations", in Deng, FM and Zartman, W (eds), *Conflict Resolution in Africa*, Brookings Institution, Washington, 1991, p 194; and Van Horne, W (ed), Ethnicity and War, University of Wisconsin, Madison, 1984.

103. "Peoples and origins", *op cit*, p 22.
104. See the thought-provoking analysis of present sub-Saharan ethnic tensions, called "Africa's simmering conflict areas" in Alao, A and Olonisakin, F, Post Cold War Africa, *op cit*, pp 136-140.
105. Alao, A and Olonisakin, F, "Post Cold War Africa", *op cit*, p 128.
106. *Ibid*, pp 129-131.
107. *Ibid*, pp 131-132.
108. Ellis, S, *op cit*, p 11.
109. Alao, A and Olonisakin, F, "Post Cold War Africa", *op cit*, p 132.
110. Berman, B J, *op cit*, p 341.
111. Ellis, S, *op cit*, p 15.
112. *Le Monde*, quoted in Time, 7 September 1992, p 31.
113. Oyebade, A, and Alao, A, "Conclusion: A short peep...", *op cit*, p 197.
114. Alao, A and Olonisakin, F, "Post Cold War Africa", *op cit*, p 135.
115. Pres Francois Mitterand quoted in the *Washington Post*, 10 November 1994.
116. Malan, M, "Treading firmly on the layered response ladder: From peace enforcement to conflict termination operations in Africa?", *African Security Review*, Vol 6, No 5, 1997, p 47.
117. Heitman, H, *op cit*, p 12.
118. Cornwall, R, "The collapse of the African state", *op cit*, p 13.
119. Oyebade, A, "The end of the Cold War in Africa", *op cit*, p 168.
120. *Ibid*, p 168.
121. Neethling, TG, "The US response to African peace-keeping requirements: Perspectives on the African Crisis Response Initiative and beyond", *Strategic Review for Southern Africa*, Vol XX, No 1, May 1998, pp 91-113.
122. Bekerie, A, "Beyond the Cold War: Pan-Europeanism and the challenge of African unity", in Oyebade, A and Alao, A (eds), *op cit*, pp 183-190.
123. Sipri, *op cit*, p 71.
124. Alao, A and Olonisakin, F, "Post Cold War Africa", *op cit*, p 133-136.
125. Oyebade, A, "The end of the Cold War in Africa", *op cit*, pp 172-173.
126. Sipri, *op cit*, p 59.

127. Oyebade, A, "The end of the Cold War in Africa", *op cit*, p 171.
128. *Ibid*, p 176.
129. Heitman, H, *op cit*, pp 14-15.

# Chapter 4

# MILITARY INTERVENTION IN SUB-SAHARAN AFRICA: A HISTORICAL OVERVIEW

## Michael Hough

## 1. INTRODUCTION

It has been stated that the most common form of intervention in African conflicts has been by superpowers and regional hegemons. The interventions have ranged from conventional war to low-intensity conflicts, and have mainly occurred in the context of domestic conflict. In some cases, external intervention contributed to de-escalating the conflict, while in other cases, the scope and intensity of conflicts were expanded. Requests to intervene, treaties that provide for military assistance, the national interests and foreign policy objectives of the intervening power and superpower rivalry in the Cold War period, have been some of the main considerations underlying external military intervention in African conflicts. Intervention has occurred primarily in internal conflicts, although in some cases there has been an interstate component in the form of counterintervention, for example French intervention in Chad during 1983 to counter Libyan intervention.

In this chapter, an overview of the Cold War environment and its effect on direct overt military intervention (involving deployment of foreign troops either in support of governments or dissidents) in sub-Saharan Africa, in the period 1960-1990 will be given, followed by a discussion of foreign military intervention by extracontinental powers, including previous colonial powers. This is followed by an overview of military intervention by African states in internal armed conflicts in sub-Saharan Africa in the period under discussion. Finally, the policies of the Organisation of African Unity (OAU) and the Economic Community of West African States (ECOWAS) towards military intervention are discussed in the corresponding period, and some conclusions regarding the heritage and consequences of external military intervention, drawn. Interventions are not exhaustively described on a country-by-country basis, but by way of examples. Military interventions by dissident factions in one country to assist dissident groups in another country are not included, and neither are military interventions by mercenary forces, whether in support of the incumbent government or rebel factions. The emphasis is therefore on intervention by states whether acting alone or in concert with other states. Peace support operations under United Nations (UN) or OAU auspices are also excluded.

## 2. THE COLD WAR ENVIRONMENT AND MILITARY INTERVENTION IN SUB-SAHARAN AFRICA

Between 1960 and 1990, 18 fully-fledged civil wars were fought in Africa south of the Maghreb. Civil wars in Africa have seldom been a purely internal affair, and have been one of the conditions conducive to external military intervention.[1] The question that arises is why the Cold War period was particularly conducive to external military intervention in independent African states, particularly by extracontinental powers?

## 2.1 East-West rivalry

It has been noted that since 1975, external military interventions in Africa caused greater international concern than the interventions in the 1960s. This concern was especially linked to the deployment of Cuban and East German troops in Angola, following the outbreak of the civil war in 1975.[2]

In this context, competition between East and West in various spheres was seen as an important reason for external military intervention in Africa in the 1970s, and more specifically by Soviet surrogates. Political, ideological, strategic and economic considerations, or combinations of these, played a major role in these interventions.[3]

The two examples of direct extracontinental military intervention in sub-Saharan Africa in the Cold War period, excluding military intervention by former colonial powers, are Cuban intervention in Ethiopia during 1977 in reaction to the activities of the Somali Liberation Front in the Ogaden region of Ethiopia, subsequently also supported by regular Somali armed forces, and Cuban intervention in the civil war in Angola which was waged from 1975 to 1988. By the end of the 1970s, it was calculated that some 19 000 Cubans and 2 500 East Germans were operating aircraft and heavy equipment with the Angolan armed forces, while about 16 500 Cubans served with the Ethiopian armed forces.[4]

Although Soviet military personnel were also deployed in sub-Saharan Africa in the 1970s and 1980s, they assisted mainly in training and acted as military advisors. The Soviet Union also gained access to military facilities, for example in Ethiopia.[5]

It has been observed that Cuba's activities in Africa have been closely co-ordinated with those of the Soviet Union. Cuba was, however, not involved only because of its links with the Soviet Union. Its foreign policy developed from a revolutionary orientation, and the desire to diminish Western influence in Third World countries. However the Soviet Union played a major role in supplying arms and logistic support to Cuba.[6]

Although the United States (US) also provided military assistance to the UNITA rebels in Angola, the US Congress subsequently defeated an appropriation bill for military aid to UNITA and the FNLA movement in Angola. The 1976 Clark Amendment forbade military assistance to any party in the Angolan conflict. In February 1986, President Reagan, however, announced that the United States would provide arms to UNITA. This included Stinger surface-to-air missiles and anti-tank missiles. In this regard it has been observed that US military aid to UNITA assisted in establishing a military stalemate that helped convince the various parties involved in the war that military victory would not be easily attainable.[7] During the second crisis in the Shaba province in Zaire during 1978, the United States made aircraft available to fly in Belgian and French forces, but no US troops were deployed.[8]

## 2.2 Military intervention by former colonial powers

Three former colonial powers were involved in direct military intervention in sub-Saharan Africa in the period between 1960 and 1990, namely France, Britain and Belgium. Compared to French military intervention, interventions by the two other former colonial powers were limited.

### 2.2.1 France

France was the former colonial power most frequently involved in direct military intervention in Africa in the period 1960-1990. All of these, except for the French role in the second conflict in the Shaba province of the former Zaire, occurred in former French territories.[9]

More than any of the other former colonial powers, France had established close relations with many of its former colonies. Large numbers of French citizens also continued to live and work in Africa. French policies resulted in a continuing economic, political and military role, linked to the French view of its role in the global system, and the economic stake it has in many African countries. France also enjoyed a virtual monopoly over arms sales and military training in many of its former colonies.[10]

The fact that France retained a military presence in many of the former colonies, was of course also a factor that facilitated French military intervention. Intervention has for instance been unilateral to replace a regime as was the case in the Central African Republic, or on behalf of regimes requesting direct military assistance.[11]

Defence and military co-operation agreements cemented the ties between France and its former colonies in West and Equatorial Africa. This also involved the retention of military bases, and the French government saw these bases and the defence agreements as a means of maintaining its influence over the new states and their armies. By 1970, French troops in Africa were reduced from 58500 in 1962, to 6400, but the creation of a French intervention force with the primary role of supplying military assistance to former colonies and to support French troops still stationed in Africa, balanced the withdrawal to some extent. Of the 11 bilateral defence agreements signed between former colonies and France between 1960 and 1963, five still remained in force by the end of the 1970s, namely with the Central African Republic, Gabon, Ivory Coast, Togo and Senegal. A sixth agreement was signed with Djibouti in 1978, following the attainment of independence.[12]

A rise in African nationalism coincided with the reduction of French military presence in Africa, and in some instances as in Guinea, Mali, Algeria and Mauritania, there was open hostility towards France. The period between the end of the 1960s and the beginning of the 1970s was characterised by little direct intervention, in contrast to the immediate post-independence period which saw French intervention on several occasions.[13]

However, in the mid-1970s, following Soviet-Cuban intervention in Angola, the French and newly elected French president, Giscard d'Estaing, in particular, perceived new threats to their interests in Africa. Outbreaks of hostilities or resumptions of hostilities in Chad, Zaire, Western Sahara and the Horn of Africa resulted in an increase of French troops in Africa to an estimated 10000. This was, however, not regarded as a permanent military presence, but between 1977 and 1985, France intervened directly in Africa on a number of occasions.[14]

The following table depicts French troop levels stationed in sub-Saharan African countries at the end of the 1980s.

Certain constraints on external military involvement in Africa's wars, however, also existed in the period 1960-1990. The countries which were invaded, presented serious obstacles to military operations, both geographically as far as terrain is concerned, as well as in terms of long supply lines that had to be created. Counterintervention from other sources, such as in the case of Angola and Chad, limited the success of the initial intervention. Financial and political constraints also played an important role. South African and Cuban withdrawal from Angola are instances where a combination of international

## TABLE I
### FRENCH TROOP PRESENCE IN SUB-SAHARAN AFRICA: 1990

| Country | French Troops |
| --- | --- |
| Central African Republic | 1 200 |
| Chad | 1 100 |
| Côte d'Ivoire | 500 |
| Gabon | 550 |
| Senegal | 1 200 |

**Source**: IISS, London, *The Military Balance, 1990-1991*.

pressures, financial considerations and in the case of South Africa, public opinion, played a role in the decision to withdraw militarily.[15]

In France, traditional Gaullists started attacking Giscard d'Estaings' military policies in Africa *inter alia* on the grounds that France could not afford such commitments to Africa and that the pursuit of military solutions tended to exclude political solutions. These pressures played some role during 1979 when the French announced their intention to withdraw from Chad.[16]

Following the election of Francois Mitterand in 1981, it was stated that France would honour arrangements already made with African countries. France, however, remained neutral when in September 1981, the president of the Central African Republic, David Dacko, whom the French had installed as leader, was overthrown in a military *coup*.[17]

France experienced military manpower shortages due to its overseas commitments, and during the 1978 invasion of Shaba province had to call on the French Legionnaires. It also became apparent that France suffered from deficiencies in logistical equipment and capabilities. Setbacks experienced by the French military in Chad in 1978 revealed shortcomings in French military equipment as well. French military policy in Africa also complicated relations with certain African states, notably Algeria and Libya. French interests in Africa were increasingly perceived as corresponding with Western interests.[18]

Towards the end of the 1970s, France proposed a permanent non-African force to multilateralise African security problems. There was, however, little African support for the proposal. Similarly the idea of a co-ordinated Western response to destabilisation in Africa was received with scepticism by Western countries. Subsequently, Mitterand's initiatives in this regard, although contributing to the deployment of an African peacekeeping force in Chad, equally showed few practical results.[19]

Conditions facilitating interventions by extracontinental powers like France, however, also existed, such as the weakness of African armed forces, and the relatively low threat environment where interventions took place. During 1979, French foreign minister, De Guiringaud, stated that "Africa is the only continent that is still to the measure of France, within its reach. It is the only one where it can still, with 500 men, change the course of history".[20]

In the case of Belgium and Britain, military interventions had also always taken place with the approval of the affected country, while France intervened on only two occasions (in Gabon in 1964 and in the Central African Republic in 1979) against the authorities in power.[21]

It has been noted that extracontinental defence agreements could more readily be invoked against both external aggression and against internal threats, than was the case with regional agreements, contributing to the frequency of especially French military intervention in Africa.[22]

## 2.2.2 Britain

Although British military intervention in sub-Saharan Africa was on a far smaller scale than that of France, troops were deployed in Kenya, Tanzania and Uganda during 1964 to quell army mutinies. In Tanzania, President Julius Nyerere had attempted to end the mutiny through negotiations, but was eventually compelled to appeal to Britain for assistance. The operation was carried out simultaneously in all three countries, lasted only one morning, and involved 350 British troops.[23]

Analysts have stated that Britain has the military means to project power to Africa, but that it lacks the political will to become involved in direct military intervention in the continent.[24]

## 2.2.3 Belgium

Belgium has intervened militarily in Central Africa on five occasions since 1960. It has, however, been observed that domestic political constraints in Belgium prevented any type of military action in Central Africa except when emergency humanitarian reasons could be invoked. This implies that unless expatriates are threatened, Belgium will not intervene. All the Belgian interventions, namely in the Congo in 1960, 1964 and 1978; in Rwanda in 1990; and in Zaire in 1991, involved the protection and evacuation of Belgian (and other European) expatriates.[25]

The fact that Belgium had lost access to overseas military facilities; had limited defence budgets; and did not have a favourable domestic and international political environment to operate in, placed a relatively high burden on the country as far as military intervention in Africa was concerned. There were also no armed forces units specifically allocated for overseas deployment. Despite these handicaps, Belgian armed forces had developed the required military expertise and obtained appropriate equipment to carry out these interventions. Due to its military assistance programme, which was implemented in the post-colonial period, Belgium also remained acquainted with the operational environment in Central Africa. The result was that Belgian troops accomplished their objectives in the five instances of intervention with limited casualties.[26]

Military involvement (and specifically military intervention) by France, Britain and Belgium in sub-Saharan Africa followed divergent patterns. In the case of France, regulating the levels of violence and disorder in their zone of influence, formed a distinct pattern. Stability was the central theme, because this helped maintain the close links between France and her former colonies. The general support received by France from Francophone African countries and even beyond, facilitated intervention, although on occasions the reaction was hostile.[27]

In contrast, Belgian military interventions were reactive rather than preventive, and followed as a response to a specific crisis and threats to Belgian citizens in the affected countries. France had also started taking the initiative in protecting the former Belgian colonies, and three interventions (Shaba in 1978, Rwanda in 1990 and Zaire in 1991) were undertaken in conjunction with Belgium.[28]

Britain has, excepting for the three simultaneous interventions in East Africa during 1964, largely disengaged militarily from Africa, although certain military assistance programmes continue.[29]

Military intervention by former colonial powers in sub-Saharan Africa in the period 1960-1990 is depicted in the following table.

## TABLE II
## DIRECT EUROPEAN MILITARY INTERVENTION IN AFRICA: 1960-1990

| Country | Year | Intervener | Objective |
|---|---|---|---|
| Cameroon | 1960/1961 | France | Restoration of order and counter-revolution |
| CAR | 1979 | France | Support of a military *coup* |
| Chad | 1960 | France | Suppression of riots |
| Chad | 1960/1963 | France | Restoration of order |
| Chad | 1968 | France | To contain a rebellion |
| Chad | 1977-1980 | France | Support of government against rebellion |
| Chad | 1983-1984 | France | To counter Libyan-sponsored insurgents |
| Congo | 1960 | Belgium | Evacuation of Belgian nationals, restoration of order |
| Congo | 1964 | Belgium | Evacuation of Belgian nationals |
| Congo | 1978 | Belgium | Evacuation of European citizens |
| Congo-Brazzaville | 1960/1962 | France | Restoration of order |
| Djibouti | 1976/1977 | France | To counter Somali irredentism |
| Gabon | 1960 | France | Restoration of order |
| Gabon | 1962 | France | Restoration of order |
| Gabon | 1964 | France | To prevent a military *coup* |
| Gabon | 1990 | France | Protection of expatriates |
| Mauritania | 1961 | France | Restoration of order |
| Mauritania | 1977-1979 | France | Containment of the Polisario Front |
| Niger | 1963 | France | Restoration of order |
| Rwanda | 1990 | Belgium and France | Evacuation of Belgian and French citizens |
| Senegal | 1962 | France | Support against attempted *coup* |
| Uganda/Tanganyika/Kenya | 1964 | Britain | Suppression of mutinies |
| Zaire | 1977 | France | Restoring stability; support to Mobutu |
| Zaire | 1978 | France | Restoring stability; support to Mobutu |

It is sometimes difficult to distinguish between a regime stabilisation operation and military intervention. The French "humanitarian" operation in Gabon during 1990 was also highly effective in restoring order. The French intervention in Rwanda in 1990 was initially aimed at the protection of European expatriates, but due to the fact that French troops stayed on for longer than a year, the intervention became regime supportive.[30]

## 2.3 Intervention by regional actors

A number of factors conducive to intervention by extracontinental as well as by regional actors have been identified. These factors are not confined to the Cold War period under discussion, and continue to play a role in post-1990 military interventions.

The first factor is internal division within a country, which makes it difficult to resist external intrusion. Secondly, external assistance is often solicited by parties engaged in internal conflicts. This may also involve prior commitments to supplying military assistance. Thirdly, cross-border ethnic or religious affinities serve as justifications and opportunities for military intervention. Fourthly, regimes that suffer from internal instability and problems of legitimacy, tend to compensate for this by achieving success in foreign policies. Fifthly, interventions in an attempt either to pre-empt or end initiatives by other countries to take advantage of internal instability. Finally, the emergence of a number of regional powers in Africa in the 1970s resulted in a tendency towards military intervention by regional powers with superior military capabilities.[31]

In addition to the factors mentioned above, the perceived national interests of regional interveners, including their economic interests, have been important factors in decisions to intervene militarily. Specific local issues have also played a role in regional interventions. These include disputes over colonial borders, where for instance dissident movements in neighbouring countries are supported as a bargaining chip to support territorial claims. Protection of critical supply lines running through a neighbouring country is another example of a specific local issue that has been a factor in military intervention.[32]

African countries have on occasion provided support for extracontinental military intervention. Morocco, Senegal, Ivory Coast, Togo and Gabon for instance provided troops for the French-inspired African intervention force to Zaire, during the second Shaba invasion in 1978.[33]

The following table provides a selective overview of regional military intervention in sub-Saharan Africa in the period 1960-1990.

## 3. CONSEQUENCES OF MILITARY INTERVENTION

It has been noted that violence and conflict would have occurred in the African countries afflicted by war, even in the absence of external military intervention. However the international factor helped escalate the conflict in many instances. In other cases, it constrained the participants and promoted negotiation and conflict resolution. The Angolan/Namibian regional accord achieved in 1988 is seen as an example of the positive effect of international factors in conflict in Africa.[34]

Regarding the consequences of extracontinental military involvement in sub-Saharan Africa, in some countries where France has maintained a troop presence, such as Senegal, Gabon, and later also in Djibouti, there has been uninterrupted civilian government. The same applies to Cameroon, where there is no French troop presence, but where a defence

## TABLE III
### SELECTED OVERVIEW OF DIRECT MILITARY INTERVENTION IN SUB-SAHARAN AFRICA BY REGIONAL ACTORS: 1960-1990

| Country | Year | Intervener | Purpose |
| --- | --- | --- | --- |
| Angola | 1975-1988 | South Africa | Support for UNITA, anti-Cuban |
| Ethiopia | 1977-1978 | Somalia | Support for dissidents |
| Uganda | 1979 | Libya | Support for Idi Amin |
| Uganda | 1979 | Tanzania | To overthrow Idi Amin |
| Chad | 1980 | Libya | Support for dissidents |
| Mozambique | 1980 | Zimbabwe | Protection of critical supply lines |
| Gambia | 1981 | Senegal | To counter a military *coup* |

agreement with France was concluded. Togo and the Central African Republic are instances where defence agreements with France and uninterrupted civilian rule do not correlate. Compared to the colonies of Belgium and Britain, the incidence of political instability has been lower in previous French colonies. This is particularly so with regard to reducing the level of political instability in cases of civil wars, rebellions and ethnic strife. In the case of instability as a result of *coups* and attempted *coups*, the French stabilising effect is less marked. In this regard, it has been observed that where France intervened to protect or install regimes and to unseat others, it has been useful for regime security rather than national security. "They merely promote a neo-colonial situation in which the regimes in power exist mainly to fulfil the wishes of their foreign protectors instead of aspiring to minister to the needs of their people."[35]

France's political and economic role in Africa should of course also be taken into account in conjunction with its military role when assessing stability/instability in former French colonies.

It is generally maintained in Africa that during the period under discussion intervention affected African security negatively. This seems to be based on the evaluation that intervention prolongs and intensifies conflict; it could provoke counterintervention; it increases casualties and numbers of refugees as well as physical destruction; it threatens economic development; erodes national sovereignty; and it is politically destabilising. These judgements pertain to interventions by African as well as extracontinental powers. However, these criticisms do not hold true in all situations. Relatively short, intense interventions may be preferred to lower level, but prolonged conflicts.[36]

Intervention can have little economic effect in areas where there is limited economic activity, for example Libya's intervention in the northern and central parts of Chad, and if the intervening power is seen to protect economic activity in the affected country, foreign investors could be reassured.[37]

Foreign intervention need also not compromise independence over the longer term, especially if the source of the threat to the affected regime is removed. It is for instance argued that Soviet/Cuban intervention in Ethiopia to counter the threat of a Somali invasion, assisted in maintaining the sovereignty and territorial integrity of Ethiopia. Hence, depending on the situation, and seen from the point of view of the incumbent government, foreign interventions can either be politically stabilising or destabilising. However, if the underlying causes of conflict remain in the affected state or states where the intervention took place, the longer-term prospects for stability are uncertain. This is especially so where external intervention reduces the possibility of peaceful conflict resolution as the incumbent government may no longer see a need for compromise with its opponents. The legitimacy of the incumbent government may also be undermined in the perceptions of the population due to its reliance on foreign assistance.[38]

The frequency of foreign military intervention in Africa in the period 1960-1990 did, however, in certain instances, contribute to neighbouring countries increasing their defence expenditure (for example Kenya in response to the conflict in the Horn of Africa in the 1970s). The increased availability of arms also reduced one of the major constraints on conflict in Africa and increased defence spending affected expenditure on socio-economic priorities.[39]

The normative basis of interstate relations in Africa has also been affected by military interventions. Since the mid-1970s the majority of interventions (in the broader sense) have involved African states intervening in other African states. These norms, as enshrined in the OAU Charter, for example non-interference in the internal affairs of African states, will subsequently be discussed.[40]

Although intervention may be more of a manifestation than a cause of insecurity, it is clearly in the interest of Africa to minimise external intervention, whether or not it serves a specific purpose in terms of the core interests of the country or region where intervention takes place. The revival of the capacities of the OAU regarding conflict resolution and the emergence of a strong system of collective security, are viewed as preferable to military intervention.[41]

## 4. POLICIES AND VIEWS OF THE ORGANISATION OF AFRICAN UNITY AND ECOWAS REGARDING MILITARY INTERVENTION

The majority of principles contained in the Charter of the OAU are clearly opposed to intervention, including military intervention. It could of course be argued that this is specifically aimed at intervention in the internal affairs of African states, and not military intervention in an interstate war. Co-operation for defence and security is indeed listed as one of the purposes of the OAU.

Article III of the OAU Charter states:

> The Member States, in pursuit of the purposes stated in Article II, solemnly affirm and declare their adherence to the following principles:
> 1. the sovereign equality of all Member States;
> 2. non-interference in the internal affairs of States;
> 3. respect for the sovereignty and territorial integrity of each State and for its inalienable right to independent existence;
> 4. peaceful settlement of disputes by negotiation, mediation, conciliation or arbitration;
> 5. unreserved condemnation, in all its forms, of political assassination as well as of subversive activities on the part of neighbouring States or any other States;
> 6. absolute dedication to the total emancipation of the African territories which are still dependent;
> 7. affirmation of a policy of non-alignment with regard to all blocs[42].

Resolutions were passed at the OAU summit held in Libreville (Gabon) during 1977, condemning all non-African interference in the African continent. Following the 1978 summit in Khartoum, committees were established to resolve conflicts between African states that tended to invite external military intervention. One of the resolutions adopted at the Khartoum summit also declared that "the summit strongly condemns the policy of force and intervention in Africa, regardless of the source...". Simultaneously, however, the Khartoum summit "upheld the right of every independent African state to call upon friendly countries outside the continent to come to their assistance if they perceived that their security and sovereignty were under threat". It has been observed that the OAU unwittingly legitimised external intervention in the latter resolution.[43]

The OAU for instance did not condemn the extracontinental military interventions in Shaba province in Zaire to support Mobutu during 1977 and 1978 respectively, presumably because the interventions did not threaten the integrity of neighbouring states; they supported the government in power; and the OAU, due to its weak military and political power base, and constrained by its own non-intervention clause, was unable to protect member states. Reservations were, however, expressed at the Khartoum summit that each invitation for intervention is followed by an invitation for counterintervention, and that African leaders should not use the right to invite military intervention as a pretext for suppressing legitimate political opposition.[44]

During the 1960s and 1970s, various proposals for an African High Command were made in the OAU, based on the concept of a continental defence agreement. It was, however, not made clear whether this would pertain to external aggression against OAU member states only, or also internal threats.[45] The *Kampala Document* of 1991, although not an official OAU document, repeated the call, but specifically referred to external military aggression against the continent or any member state. The military operations envisaged under these structures were distinguished from peace support operations.[46]

Regarding regional organisations and military intervention in sub-Saharan Africa, the Protocol on *Mutual Assistance and Defence* adopted by the Economic Community of West African States (ECOWAS) during 1981 *inter alia* provides for military intervention on behalf of a member state to counter aggression or any armed threat. In a conflict between two member states of ECOWAS, the Allied Forces of the Community (AAFC) would at most be interposed between the troops engaged in the conflict. In situations where an internal conflict in a member state is actively maintained and sustained from outside, a request for assistance to the appropriate ECOWAS organ can be made by the head of state of the affected country, as in the case of external aggression. ECOWAS will not intervene if the conflict remains purely internal. During 1998, an ECOWAS Mechanism for Conflict Prevention, Resolution, Peacekeeping and Regional Security was decided on, but still has to be implemented.[47] ECOWAS also adopted a *Protocol on Non-Aggression* during 1978, which specifically relates to direct military intervention by member states in support of, for instance, dissident groups in another member state, or the provision of facilities to foreigners to intervene:[48]

### Article 1

Member States shall, in their relations with one another, refrain from the threat or use of force or aggression or from employing any other means inconsistent with the Charters of the United Nations and the Organisation of African Unity against the territorial integrity or political independence of other Member States.

### Article 2

Each Member State shall refrain, from committing, encouraging or condoning acts of subversion, hostility or aggression against the territorial integrity or political independence of the other Member States.

In view of the frequency of military interventions in Africa during the 1970s and the 1980s, it has been stated that "it is legitimate to question whether the conventional characterizations of inter-African relations in terms of principles such as the non-use of force, non-interference in internal affairs ... and multilateral conflict resolution are still valid ...".[49]

Especially as far as extracontinental intervention in Africa is concerned, the political fragility of some African states, their economic and military weakness, and ideological divisions within the OAU, have been said to underly the fact that opposition to external intervention in Africa has had little effect.[50] Nevertheless the OAU was relatively successful in insulating disputes, such as the Nigerian civil war, from external military intervention.[51] The OAU Conflict Resolution Mechanism of 1993 contains no reference to an African High Command, but only to peace support operations. The principle of non-interference in the internal affairs of states was specifically emphasised once again.[52]

The OAU Secretary-General however made the following comment during the OAU summit held in Senegal in July 1992:[53]

> It is arguable, therefore, that within the context of general international law as well as humanitarian law, Africa should take the lead in developing the notion that sovereignty can legally be transcended by the "intervention" of "outside forces", by their will to facilitate prevention and/or resolution, particularly on humanitarian grounds. In other words, given that every African is his brother's keeper, and that our borders are at best artificial, we in Africa need to use our own cultural and social relationships to interpret the principle of non-interference in such a way that we are enabled to apply it to our advantage in conflict prevention and resolution.

Although the above statement refers to collective intervention and appears to be linked to peace support operations and not military intervention *per se*, it does present some shift in emphasis regarding the non-interference principle. To a large extent, however, the initiative as far as military intervention and peace support operations are concerned, seems to have passed to regional organisations such as ECOWAS and even individual countries such as Nigeria.

## 5. CONTINUING MILITARY INTERVENTION AFTER 1990

In addition to the interventions in West Africa, Lesotho and the Democratic Republic of the Congo (DRC), which will be described in subsequent chapters, the post-Cold War period saw violence erupt in a number of former French colonies, for instance Zaire in 1991. A joint French and Belgian operation was limited to evacuating expatriates, although President Mobutu may also have been partly saved by the intervention.[54]

The United States deployed armed forces in a joint UN-US operation in Somalia in December 1992, preceding the deployment of UNOSOM II, but this was seen as a peace support operation and not military intervention as discussed elsewhere in this chapter. During 1994 the United States also sent marines to Burundi to evacuate American and foreign nationals.[55]

During 1996, French troops intervened in the Central African Republic to prevent the destabilisation of the government by a group of rebel soldiers. France also intervened in the Côte d'Ivoire in 1996 to protect the civilian government.[56]

During 1997, Angola entered the civil war in Congo-Brazzaville on the side of former president Denis Sassou-Nguesso, who had been defeated by Pascal Lissouba in the 1992 elections, which subsequently led to fighting between his Cobra militia and government forces. Lissouba fled from Brazzaville and Sassou-Nguesso had himself installed as president.[57]

During 1998, Senegal and Guinea intervened in Guinea-Bissau to support the government against an armed forces mutiny, and in May 2000, British troops were deployed in Sierra Leone to evacuate British and other citizens.[58]

It is therefore clear that foreign military intervention continued despite the ending of the Cold War. French intervention has increased dramatically since democratisation swept over Africa. It has also been noted that French interventions depended less on precise criteria and legal obligations than on circumstances. However in 1997 President Jacques Chirac indicated that France no longer wanted to be the gendarme of Africa. This has been interpreted as implying that France will gradually withdraw its troops from African countries, and will intervene in internal conflicts only under the auspices of the UN or the OAU.[59]

At the end of 1998, France still had 800 troops stationed in Chad; 500 in Côte d'Ivoire; 1500 in Djibouti; 600 in Gabon; and 1300 in Senegal.[60]

During 1991 three basic rules of intervention for Western powers were identified.

> Whenever possible, be [sure] that the people on whose behalf the intervention is contemplated really want it.
> Be certain that the intervener can win.
> Don't engage in an intervention unless it also serves a clear and demonstrable self-interest.[61]

Although these guidelines clearly do not cover all situations, particularly instances of humanitarian intervention, they are nevertheless valuable.

## 6. CONCLUSION

Since the 1960s, and even after the end of the Cold War, direct foreign military intervention in sub-Saharan Africa by extra-continental actors as well as continental actors has continued. The end of the Cold War has diminished the incentive for many Western powers to intervene militarily in Africa, although a continued pattern of French military intervention in the post-1990 period has been evident. This may, however, also now change. Intervention by Western powers will most likely still occur to evacuate their own nationals from conflict areas. Military intervention by African states in other African states, particularly where civil wars are being waged, either to support the government in power or the rebels, and counter-intervention, however, seems set to continue, and there seems to be a trend towards formalising this through the conclusion of mutual defence pacts.[62] These pacts, or envisaged pacts, unlike the norm, do not always seem to distinguish between military intervention in an interstate conflict and in an internal conflict especially where there has been prior external intervention by a third party.

The distinction between humanitarian intervention and UN peace enforcement on the one hand, and military intervention that does not form part of peace support operations on the other, also seems to be blurring. This occurred to some extent in South Africa and Botswana's military intervention under the auspices of the Southern African Development Community (SADC) in Lesotho during 1998. The fact that UN approval of military intervention has in some instances been sought after a specific deployment, has reinforced as well as undermined Chapter 52 of the UN Charter. In the 1990s military intervention was often disguised as "humanitarian" or "peace support operations".[63]

In the following chapters, military intervention in West Africa, the DRC and Lesotho in the latter half of the 1990s will be analysed and assessed as case studies of recent foreign military intervention in sub-Saharan Africa.

## ENDNOTES

1. Smock, D R and H Gregorian, "Introduction", in Smock, D R (ed), *Making War and Waging Peace: Foreign Intervention in Africa*, United States Institute of Peace, Washington, 1993, p 2.
2. Aluko, O, "African response to external intervention in Africa since Angola", *African Affairs*, Vol 80, No 319, April 1981, p 159.
3. *Ibid*, p 163.
4. Copson, R W, *Africa's Wars and Prospects for Peace*, M E Sharpe, New York, 1994, pp 36 and 43; IISS, *The Military Balance*, 1980-1981, p 52.
5. Sarris, L G, "Soviet military policy and arms activities in sub-Saharan Africa", in Foltz, W J and H S Bienen, *Arms and the African: Military Influences on Africa's International Relations*, Yale University Press, New Haven, 1985, pp 46-49.
6. *Ibid*, pp 34-35.
7. Papp, D S, "The Angolan civil war and Namibia: The role of external intervention", in Smock, D R (ed), *op cit*, pp 168, 172, 180 and 185.
8. Somerville, K, *Foreign Military Intervention in Africa*, Pinter, London, 1990, p 103.
9. *Ibid*, p 171.
10. *Ibid*.
11. *Ibid*, p 172.
12. Moose, G E, "French military policy in Africa", in Foltz, W J and H S Bienen, *op cit*, p 62; and Somerville, K, *op cit*, p 22.
13. Moose, G E, *op cit*, p 65.
14. *Ibid*, pp 66-68.
15. Copson, R W, *op cit*, pp 115-116.
16. Moose, G E, *op cit*, pp 85-87.
17. *Ibid*, p 88.
18. *Ibid*, pp 90-92.

19. *Ibid*, pp 94-96.
20. Rouvez, A, "French, British and Belgian military involvement", in Smock, D R (ed), *op cit*, pp 28-29.
21. *Ibid*, p 29.
22. Immobighe, T A, "Security in sub-Saharan Africa", in Singh, J and T Bernauer (eds), *Security of Third World Countries*, UNIDIR, 1993, p99.
23. Somerville, K, *op cit*, p 23; and Rouvez, A, *op cit*, p 40.
24. Rouvez, A, *op cit*, p 40.
25. *Ibid*, pp 42-45.
26. *Ibid*.
27. *Ibid*, pp 45-46.
28. *Ibid*, p 47.
29. Copson, R W, *op cit*, pp 112-113.
30. Rouvez, A, *op cit*, p 36.
31. MacFarlane, S N, "Africa's decaying security system and the rise of intervention", *International Security*, Vol 8, No 4, 1984, pp 129-135. Also see, Somerville, K, *op cit*, pp 183-188.
32. Copson, R W, *op cit*, pp 108-109.
33. Foltz, W J, and Bienen, H S, *op cit*, pp 71-72.
34. Copson, R W, *op cit*, pp 103-105.
35. Rouvez, A, *op cit*, pp 48-49; and Immobighe, T A, *op cit*, pp 100-101.
36. MacFarlane, S N, "Intervention and Security in Africa", *International Affairs*, Vol 60, No 1, Winter 1983/4, pp 56-57.
37. *Ibid*, p 58.
38. *Ibid*, pp 60-61.
39. *Ibid*, pp 62-63.
40. *Ibid*, p 63.
41. MacFarlane, S N, "Africa's decaying security system...", *op cit*, p 149.
42. Naldi, G J, *Documents of the Organisation of African Unity*, Mansell, London, 1992, pp 4-5.
43. Sesay, A (ed), *Africa and Europe: From partition to interdependence or dependence?*, Croom Helm, London, 1986, p 170.
44. *Ibid*, pp 169 and 171.

45. Hough, M, "Armed conflict and defence co-operation in sub-Saharan Africa", in Du Plessis, L and M Hough (eds), *Protecting sub-Saharan Africa: The military challenge*, HSRC Publishers, Pretoria, 1998, pp 222-223.
46. OAU, *Kampala Document for a Proposed Conference on Security, Stability, Development and Cooperation in Africa (CSSDCA)*, Kampala, Uganda, 23 May 1991.
47. ECOWAS, *Protocols annexed to the Treaty of ECOWAS*, undated, pp 130-139; and ECOWAS, *Declaration of the Ad Hoc Committee of ECOWAS Heads of State and Government, Final Communique*, Abuja, 16 September 1999, http://www.cedeao.org/sitecedeao/english/pub-7.htm.
48. *Ibid*, pp 81-86.
49. MacFarlane, S N, "Africa's decaying security system ...", *op cit*, p 147.
50. Aluko, O, *op cit*, p 175.
51. MacFarlane, S N, "Intervention and security in Africa", *op cit*, p 56.
52. OAU: *Declaration of the Assembly of Heads of State and Government on the Establishment within the OAU of a Mechanism for Conflict Prevention, Management and Resolution*, Cairo, 30 June 1993.
53. OAU: *Resolving Conflict in Africa: Proposals for Action*, 1992, p 17.
54. Rouvez, A, *op cit*, p 36.
55. Copson, R W, *op cit*, p 142; and IISS, *The Military Balance*, 1994/95, p 224.
56. IISS, *The Military Balance, 1996/97*, p 236.
57. Esterhuysen, P (ed), *Africa A-Z: Continental and Country Profiles*, Africa Institute of South Africa, 1998, pp134-135.
58. IISS, *The Military Balance*, 1998/99, p 235; and *The Star* (Johannesburg), 24 May 2000.
59. *Beeld* (Johannesburg), 29 August 1997; and *The Star* (Johannesburg), 9 October 1997.
60. IISS, *The Military Balance*, 1998/99, pp 235-268.
61. Rouvez, A, *op cit*, p 37.
62. *Business Day* (Johannesburg), 26 August 1999.
63. Sesay, A, "Between the Olive Branch and the AK-47: Paradoxes of Recent Military Intervention in West Africa", *ISSUP Bulletin*, 6/99, p 17.

## Chapter 5

# WEST AFRICAN MILITARY INTERVENTIONS IN THE 1990s: THE CASE OF ECOWAS IN LIBERIA AND SIERRA LEONE

## Amadu Sesay

## 1. INTRODUCTION

It would be wrong to give the impression that local military interventions, that is interventions by an African state (or group of African states) in the domestic affairs of one another, is a post-Cold War phenomenon. For the most celebrated case of local military intervention occurred twenty years ago, when Tanzania's Julius Nyerere sent troops to Uganda to overthrow the regime of self-styled Field Marshal Idi Amin Dada in 1979. That was ten clear years before the collapse of the Berlin Wall in October 1989. Earlier in 1971, Guinea, under President Ahmed Sekou Toure, sent troops to Freetown, Sierra Leone, to restore Siaka Stevens to power after his All Peoples' Congress (APC) government had been overthrown by his force commander, Brigadier John Bangura.[1] More instances can be cited, but the above examples will suffice to prove the point. In other words, the use of the military by an African state to bring about desired changes in another African country did not start with the end of the Cold War. Perhaps what is really different, is that such actions, especially when carried out under the rubric of "humanitarian intervention" or "peace support operations" have become in the 1990s much more blatant and frequent than ever before.

However, West Africa presented the first example of a subregional organisation that was set up to promote economic integration among its members, intervening militarily in the domestic affairs of member states at different times in the 1990s. By so doing, the ECOWAS Monitoring Group, ECOMOG, put in place by the Economic Community of West African States, ECOWAS, in August 1990 to restore peace in Liberia following the bloody civil war in that country, and later to bring down the renegade regime of Major Paul Johnny Koromah in Freetown, Sierra Leone, in May 1997, seemed to have opened up a Pandora's Box. For in December 1998, South Africa under the democratically elected government of Nelson Mandela, sent troops to neighbouring Lesotho to prop up the government of that country which was coming under increasing pressure from the army and the opposition. Then in early 1999, there was what looked like a local scramble by the neighbours of the Democratic Republic of the Congo (DRC) to meddle with its internal affairs and politics. What is responsible for this phenomenon?

## 2. FACTORS INDUCING POST-COLD WAR INTERVENTION

Several factors can be identified. First, are the separate but interconnected events that took place in eastern Europe in the late 1980s and early 1990s: the collapse of state communism, the fall of the Berlin Wall, and the collapse of the Soviet Union. These events unexpectedly brought down the iron curtain which had divided the world into two dangerously armed ideological blocs the East and the West led by the Union of Soviet Socialist Republics (USSR) and the United States (US).

The second development was the emergence of the United States as the sole military superpower and the diversion of its attention away from peripheral areas such as Africa, which led to the political marginalisation of the continent. The third factor was the outbreak of the Gulf crisis in 1990, which was spawned by the unexpected invasion of Kuwait by Sadam Hussein, and the oldfashioned manner he later incorporated it into Iraq as its 29th province. The Gulf brought into bold relief the shift in the attention of the great powers away from Africa in the 1990s. The war suggested that there were no longer political protégés in Africa; that is states which for one reason or the other were protected by the great powers. Contending forces, sometimes fuelled by primordial considerations, were therefore let loose in many parts of the continent. Individuals and groups who believed they were marginalised in the old order now openly bid for power by means other than through the ballot box. The net result was unprecedented civil strife, war and even state collapse. West Africa was one of the most affected subregions, with two wars going on simultaneously, in Liberia, 1989-1997, and Sierra Leone, 1991-1999.[2] The withdrawal of the great power political shield from the continent, then, also denied the continent the much talked about post-Cold War peace dividend, as it became the most violent and conflict-ridden region in the 1990s. Under the circumstances the onus was on Africans to find lasting solutions to their local problems.

From such a perspective the military interventions in West Africa in the 1990s were simply a much more robust manifestation of an old concept and strategy, "try Africa first". As a political strategy, "try Africa first" dates back to the early 1960s, predating the formation of the Organisation of African Unity (OAU), in 1963. In fact, the OAU was simply a manifestation, at a much higher level, of the concept itself, because a major objective of the founding fathers was first and foremost to shield the continent from the raging Cold War politics and conflicts. Whether the OAU has successfully done this or not, is a moot point. What is important for this purpose, is that West Africa put that concept into practical use at the most opportune time by mounting the ECOMOG operations in Liberia and Sierra Leone.

The third factor was the presence in Nigeria, West Africa's superpower, of a military dictator, General Ibrahim Babangida, a close friend of the embattled Liberian president, Samuel Doe. The Nigerian leader used his high standing in West Africa to skilfully manipulate ECOWAS into putting in place first a Standing Mediation Committee (SMC), and later ECOMOG which was deployed in Liberia in August 1990, ostensibly on a "humanitarian" mission, although the operation was very unpopular at home where it was perceived largely as an unnecessary drain on the country's already weak economy. According to his successor, General Sani Abacha, the Liberian operation cost some $7 billion. That notwithstanding, in May 1997 Abacha, generally regarded as one of Nigeria's most repressive rulers, almost single-handedly sent Nigerian troops to Freetown under the auspices of ECOWAS/ECOMOG, to topple the regime of Major Johnny Paul Koromah who had ousted the democratically elected government of Ahmed Tejan Kabbah on 25 May 1997. Koromah, it would appear, believed rather naively that involving the rebel Revolutionary United Front (RUF) in his new government would bring the increasingly barbarous civil war in the country to an end.

The final factor was the lively global debate on intervention which reflects two broad contending perspectives: the "realists" or the "international society" perspective on the one hand, and "the globalists" or "world society" view on the other, in the 1990s. More to the point, the realists are of the view that states are not necessarily altruistic in their actions, as they are usually designed to achieve selfish and rather parochial interests. Thus "governments have found it desirable to justify intervention in the name of the international community in order to build up the broadest possible political support".[3] For Hedley Bull, interveners "almost vicariously seek some form of collective authorisation, or at least post facto endorsement of their policies".[4] Unlike the globalists who believe in what one can call "the common humanity" argument for intervention, the "realists [are] sceptical of the notion of international community and hold that international intervention can still be best understood in terms of the power and interests of particular nation states, especially the great powers, acting individually or collectively. Such states may cloak their interests in the language of the common good and may claim to be acting in the name of the international community".[5]

From such a standpoint, great powers, be they global or merely local, often try to obtain multilateral consensus after initiating and orchestrating such interventions, in order to achieve their hidden agendas in the target states. For example, the US-led intervention in Kosovo, and Nigeria's prolonged presence in Liberia and Sierra Leone.

This is one of the main points of departure between the realists and the globalists. Unlike the realists, the globalists believe in the emergence and efficacy of a global community, and are supportive of humanitarian intervention and peace support operations aimed at alleviating human suffering. The globalist school of thought is perhaps epitomised by Damrosch, who contends that we are "currently witnessing the emergence and recognition of a legitimate 'right' to intervene in the domestic affairs of [other] states in the name of [international] community norms, values or interests". For him, "[in]stead of the view that intervention in international conflicts must be pre-emptively illegitimate, the prevailing trend today is to take seriously the claim that the international community ought to intercede to prevent bloodshed by whatever means are available".[6]

Under such circumstances, a state's claim to sovereignty can be set aside especially if the issues are bloodshed and genocide, massive refugee outflows and other forms of human suffering. In other words, if developments within a particular state give rise to humanitarian emergencies, its sovereignty is no longer sacrosanct. The Economist of London took a similar posture when it noted, rather emphatically, that we "are increasingly concerned not just to see countries well governed but also to ensure that the world is not irreparably damaged– whether by global warming, by the loss of species, by famine or by war..."[7]. The implication of the Economist's position is obvious, at least in theory: whenever and wherever such occurrences take place, "national sovereignty [should] be damned"; other countries should feel free to take any actions necessary to restore law and order in the affected state or states.

Finally, Bhikhu Parekh, has pushed the globalist argument even further by contending that in the post-Cold War international system, the citizens of any nation, irrespective of where they are located, are not moral orphans. Rather, they are governed in trust on behalf of the international community. Consequently, humanitarian intervention can be justified "when the state has virtually ceased to exist, when there is no effective civil authority, and when the subjects are in quasi state of nature. Since there is no state, the question of respecting its autonomy simply did not arise. Its subjects are rendered political orphans and need a period of time to sort out their collective affairs ... (or when) a state engages in acts of genocide or massive exploitation of minorities or perpetrates a reign of terror against its citizens".[8]

Bhikhu's position is supported by Nicholas Wheeler who says "The fundamental argument in favour of a right of humanitarian intervention is that the principles of sovereignty and non-intervention — the cornerstones of the international legal order — cannot be sacrosanct in the face of massive human suffering caused by either the collapse of a state into civil war and anarchy or a government's oppression of its people. Those who support a right of humanitarian intervention do so on the grounds that we all have moral obligations to do what we can to alleviate human suffering wherever it occurs."[9]

Implicit in the globalists' argument and plea for humanitarian intervention, thus, is an acknowledgement of the pervasive and inescapable consequences of the globalisation imperative in international relations, a phenomenon that gathered unprecedented momentum in the 1990s. Globalisation has not only given rise to extensive and complex forms of economic interdependence, but also to a "share(d) sense of view, duties, values, and obligations", and "moral interdependence" among the states and citizens of the world. The end result is an expanded "humanitarian space"[10] in the 1990s. Thus, what happens in some parts of the world is thought also to affect other parts, no matter how remote they may be geographically.

The globalists' viewpoint, it would appear, held sway within the UN system. This is evident in the creation of a Department of Humanitarian Affairs in the Secretariat in 1992, the expansion of the Security Council's definition of threats to global peace and security to include "non-military sources of instability in the economic, social, humanitarian and ecological fields"[11] and, more recently, the creation of a Permanent

International Court to try crimes against humanity. The new orientation of the UN also resulted in Security Council Resolution 688, which "linked internal repression with refugee flows to define threats to international peace and security".[12] This resolution was invoked by the UN to mount UNISOM in 1994, the most elaborate peacekeeping operation at the time, following the withdrawal of the US-led task force code named "Operation Restore Hope".[13] The UN position brought into sharp focus a fact that was accepted by students of foreign policy long before globalisation became a buzz word: that in an increasingly interdependent world, the divide between what is "domestic" and what is "external" to a state is a very thin one.

A related consequence of the globalists' "victory" is that many key concepts and principles that have guided international relations since the dawn of the Westphalian system, such as "sovereignty" and "non-interference", have either been drastically revised or even set aside completely, depending on the situations and circumstances. And with that, the way was paved for regional agencies to play a role in the maintenance of international peace and security which was not envisaged by the founding fathers of the United Nations. It was certainly this window of opportunity that was seized by President Ibrahim Babangida of Nigeria in 1990, when he convinced the regional body to mount the Liberian operation. The NATO action in Kosovo presents the clearest example, so far, of this opportunism in state behaviour in the 1990s.

In the rest of the chapter, the experiences in Liberia and Sierra Leone are used as case studies to explore critically the veracity of the various facets of the arguments advanced so far in the debate between the realist and globalist schools. An attempt is made to provide answers to several pertinent questions: To what extent were the interventions humanitarian or peace support operations? That is, were they designed to promote a common internationalist goal such as the maintenance of global peace and stability in West Africa as the globalists would suggest? To what extent were the operations a re-enactment of hard-nosed Realpolitik especially by the sub-regional giant, Nigeria? Put differently, were the two operations contrived by the interveners to promote their parochial national interests as the realists would have us believe? Did they comply with the International Committee of the Red Cross's (ICRC) definition of humanitarian intervention: "to prevent and alleviate human suffering... protect life and health and ensure respect for the human being... [and] work for the prevention of disease and for the promotion of health and social welfare"?[14] What were the consequences of the interventions? What was ECOMOG's impact on the situation in the two countries? Did intervention lead to real political, economic and social transformations and stability in the target states? Did the actions of ECOWAS and its surrogate ECOMOG, improve the situations in Liberia and Sierra Leone or did they make them much worse than they were before? If yes, in what ways? What challenges, if any, did the two operations throw up? What lessons can be learnt from ECOMOG's experiences in Liberia and Sierra Leone for the maintenance of post-Cold War peace and security in the West African subregion and elsewhere in the world, at the beginning of the new millennium? Finally, did the two operations shed any light on the understanding of the meaning and operationalisation of terms such as "sovereignty", and "international society" in the post-Cold War international system?

## 3. SETTINGS FOR INTERVENTIONS

On 24 December 1989 a civil war broke out in Liberia following a series of attacks on security posts on the

Liberia/Ivory Coast border by a band of armed men led by Charles Taylor in the name of the hitherto unknown National Patriotic Front of Liberia (NPFL). Charles Taylor, erstwhile head of the powerful General Services Agency (GSA), had been disgraced by the government of Samuel Doe for allegedly misappropriating huge sums of money, and was wanted in Liberia to stand trial on corruption charges, when he fled to the United States of America to escape arrest. Less than six months after the invasion, Taylor's rag tag forces were in control of about 95 per cent of the country, leaving President Doe and the rump of his Armed Forces of Liberia (AFL), holed in the Executive Mansion, seat of the Liberian government. In fact, by the time the summit of ECOWAS took place in May 1990 in the Gambian capital, Banjul, much of Liberia was under the control of the NPFL and Doe's government had to all intents and purposes collapsed. There followed an orgy of killings: mainly of civilians, women, children and foreign nationals, some in sacred places such as churches, mosques and embassies. There was a massive outflow of refugees into neighbouring countries, especially Côte d'Ivoire, Guinea and Sierra Leone, but also into more distant countries like Ghana and Nigeria.[15]

The background conditions that set the scene for the civil war in Liberia are already familiar. Suffice it to say, however, that they can be traced to Liberia's historical experiences, of which only a few will be highlighted here. Liberia was never colonised by a European power as had been the case with almost all other African states. Rather, it was a depressing example of what one can call "black on black" imperialism and domination, the country having been occupied by a handful of free slaves from America in 1822 under the auspices of the America Colonization Society. The original settlers and their descendants, popularly called Americo-Liberians, spent the next century or so pacifying the indigenous people, while warding off attempts by Britain and France to take over the new republic. Before 1980, it had the oldest *de facto* one-party system in the continent: the only officially recognised political party, the True Whig Party, ruthlessly and tenaciously clung to power continuously from 1877 to 1980.[16]

The domination by just five per cent of the population and the contradictions that this spawned became much more pronounced under President William Tolbert who succeeded Tubman in 1971. Under him, the True Whig Party could no longer respond fully to the political yearnings of the educated indigenous Liberians. During the economic boom of the late 1960s, it was still possible for the government to present a facade of political stability. But even then, the gains from the boom were not evenly spread among the people; two per cent of the Americo-Liberians controlled about 60 per cent of the local wealth. Thus, while they grew richer and richer, the majority of the people grew poorer and poorer, a situation captured graphically by Glower et al. in *Growth Without Development.*[17]

The oil crisis of the early 1970s had a devastating impact on Liberia as it exposed not only the fragile calm but also the extremely dependent nature of the agro-allied and mineral-based national economy. Expectedly, the external debt also rose steeply, reaching an all-time high of $168 million in 1976, while inflation stood at 11,4 per cent in a country where the average wage was $70 a month. It was against this gloomy economic background that President Tolbert offered to host the 16th summit of the OAU in 1979 at a cost of over $100 million.[18] And as if that was not enough, in April 1979, three months to the summit, the president announced an increase in the price of rice, the national staple food, from $22 a bag to $30, provoking spontaneous demonstrations in the streets of

Monrovia led by the Progressive Alliance of Liberia (PAL) of Baccus Mathews. As expected, they were brutally suppressed leaving over 200 people dead and the leadership of PAL arrested and detained. They were later to be charged with treason and sedition,[19] but were released on the eve of the OAU summit to placate the "august" visitors. The honeymoon with the government was short-lived. An abortive strike call by Mathews on 7 March 1980, led to an uncompromising speech from Tolbert during which he vowed to put a final end to what he described as leftist associations. "The time", he said, was ripe "for extreme rigidity and in the extreme interest of the people, no act of clemency will be exercised".[20]

The speech fuelled speculation in Monrovia, especially among the indigenous people, that the government was about to secretly try and execute the ring leaders of the abortive general strike. The rumours filtered through to the rank and file of the Liberian army, especially among the indigenous men. And in what looked like a well co-ordinated rescue plan, a group of 17 non-commissioned soldiers led by Master Sergeant Samuel Doe, attacked the presidential mansion in the early hours of 12 April 1980, killed Tolbert and arrested several senior government officials, 13 of whom were later publicly executed. Thus, the long America-Liberian domination of Liberia spanning over 130 years was brought to an unexpected and undignified end.[21]

Doe's presidency gave hope to the majority of Liberians that many, if not most of the ills of previous regimes would be corrected in their favour. The perception was reinforced by the appointment of progressives to his cabinet, men like Tipoteh and Boima Fanhbulleh, among others. But it was an illusion, as the revolution soon started to consume its own children. In 1981, Doe executed his second in command, Thomas Weah Seyen on spurious charges of planning to overthrow his regime. At the same time, most of the progressives left the government thus giving him a free hand. By 1984, Doe had succeeded in either physically eliminating or forcing his close associates in the 12 April 1980 *coup* into exile. And with that, Doe imposed a crude and corrupt dictatorship on the country centred on his clan, the Khrans. His civilianisation in 1985, after massively rigged elections, was perhaps the last straw. In what looked like a desperate attempt to prevent him from returning to power, Thomas Quiwonkpa, erstwhile force commander and close friend of Charles Taylor, entered Monrovia from Sierra Leone and succeeded in holding onto power for several hours before he was overpowered by pro-government troops, tortured, killed and his badly mutilated body openly displayed on the main streets of Monrovia for several hours "to teach others a lesson".[22]

The abortive *coup* was followed by persecution of the Gio and Mano ethnic groups from Nimba Country, Quiwonkpa's home. Houses and other properties were set ablaze indiscriminately. Meanwhile, Charles Taylor, wanted on corruption charges at home, slipped out of the country into Sierra Leone and later into the US where he escaped from prison custody and settled in Côte d'Ivoire. From here he established contacts at the highest political levels, especially with the aged Ivorian president, Felix Houphouet Boigny, his son-in-law, Blaisse Campaore, in Burkina Faso, and the Libyan president, Muammar Gaddafi. Taylor later received military training in Libya. All along, he was given moral and material support by Côte d'Ivoire and Burkina Faso. (See map of West African military interventions.)

Less than two years into the Liberian civil war, a related war broke out in neighbouring Sierra Leone in March 1991. A renegade ex-soldier, Corporal Foday Sankoh, launched an attack on security posts in the eastern part of the country

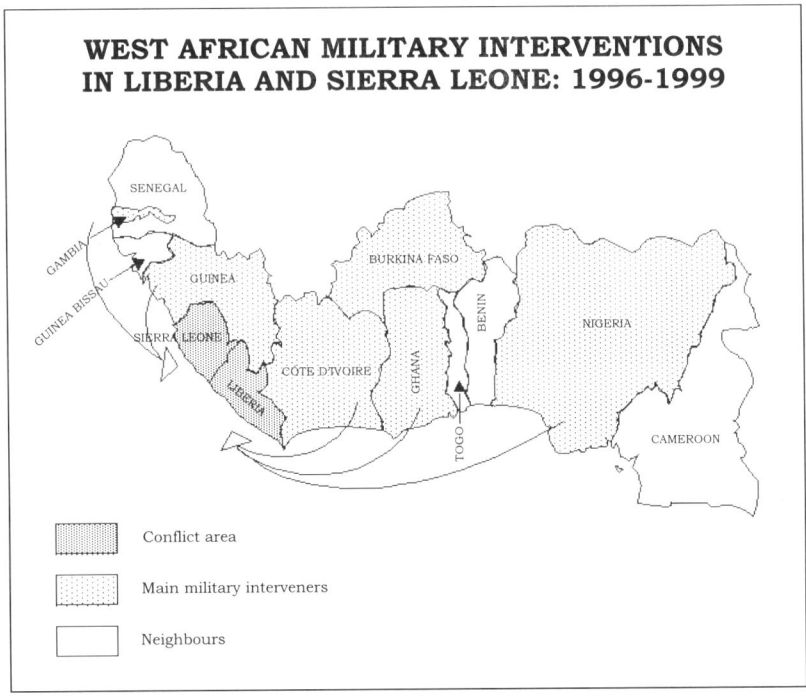

bordering Liberia, under the auspices of the Revolutionary United Front (RUF). The main targets of the rebels were the key economic areas where diamonds and gold were mined, and where coffee, cocoa, ginger, etc., all foreign exchange earners, was grown. Like its NPFL counterpart in Liberia, the RUF was noted for its lack of a coherent political agenda or blueprint.[23] Although the immediate cause of the war in Sierra Leone was the massive corruption, economic mismanagement and ethnic bias in favour of the Limba group during Siaka Stevens' APC regime, the grievances were only used as an excuse by Foday Sankoh to justify the war. The movement and its leaders were in fact far more interested in exploiting the mineral resources to enrich themselves like their mentor, Charles Taylor. In other words, the war was a massive buccaneering enterprise, pure and simple.[24]

The escalation of the war to Sierra Leone was hardly surprising. Firstly, Sierra Leone had joined Nigeria in putting together ECOMOG, which Taylor accused of denying him access to the Executive Mansion in Monrovia. Secondly, Foday Sankoh, the RUF leader, had lived in Liberia for many years, during which time he established a close personal relationship with Taylor. Both men received military training from Libya after which they settled in Côte d'Ivoire. Sankoh was also a member of Taylor's NPFL forces. More importantly, Taylor was never happy with the close links between prominent Liberian refugees in Freetown and the government of Joseph Momoh. The war in Sierra Leone could thus be seen as revenge for the tacit support Momoh gave to the formation of the United Movement for Democracy (ULIMO) in Sierra Leone under the leadership of Alhaji Kromah. The movement later opened an anti-Taylor front on the Sierra Leone-Liberia border, making it increasingly difficult for the ambitious Charles Taylor to realise his plan of seizing power in Monrovia by force.

Both wars were characterised by widespread atrocities, human rights violations and sheer human misery on a scale never before witnessed in West Africa. There was total disregard for international conventions and civilised conduct of war by the government and rebel forces. There was extensive recruitment of children as soldiers the so-called child soldiers who were noted for their cruelty to unarmed civilians, especially women and children — by the rebel factions and the governments of Liberia and Sierra Leone. The killing of patients in hospitals, for instance, moved the Italian ambassador in Monrovia to make a passionate appeal to the United States, Liberia's benefactor, to intervene and put an end to the carnage. At about the same time, five other European ambassadors issued a statement that Liberia was sliding into "anarchy and national suicide".[25] But America was more interested in the Gulf crisis. Under-secretary of State for African Affairs, Herman Cohen, told the House Sub-Committee on African Affairs pointedly that "Liberia's problem must be settled by Liberians".[26]

Meanwhile, there was an unprecedented outflow of refugees from Liberia. The United Nations High Commissioner for Refugees (UNHCR) estimated in 1992 that there were 480 000 refugees in Guinea, 175 000 in Côte d'Ivoire, 12 000 in Ghana, 6 000 in Sierra Leone, 3 000 in Nigeria and 320 and 60 respectively in the Gambia and Togo, a total of 676 380.[27] Under the auspices of the Standing Mediation Committee which the Nigerian leader, General Ibrahim Babangida, had proposed at the Banjul summit of ECOWAS in May 1990, ECOMOG was sent to Liberia on 24 August 1994. Its mandate: to secure a cease-fire, provide humanitarian assistance to the hundreds of thousands of Liberians and foreigners who had been trapped in Monrovia, and evacuate ECOWAS citizens and foreign nationals.[28] In short, ECOWAS and troop-contributing states cited the appalling humanitarian emergency/tragedy in Liberia as the main reason for their intervention in the country.

ECOMOG intervened in Sierra Leone for entirely different reasons. In fact, there was a twist of irony in the ECOWAS operation in Sierra Leone: to reinstate the democratically elected government of Ahmed Tejan Kabbah which had been overthrown by Major Johnny Paul Koromah in May 1997. Nigeria, which spearheaded the intervention, was at the time ruled by General Sani Abacha, who himself was responsible for the suppression and deaths of many people, and whose poor human rights record was epitomised by the judicial murder of Ken Saro Wiwa, playwrite, minority rights activist and environmentalist, together with eight other Ogonis in November 1995. There are thus important questions that beg for urgent answers: why did an undemocratic military regime lead a crusade on behalf of democracy, against another military regime? Why would an illegitimate military regime champion the cause of a democracy in a neighbouring state?

The first and perhaps the most important answer is that Abacha wanted to divert attention from his regime which had come under increasing pressure both at home and abroad, especially after the hanging of Ken Saro Wiwa. By leading ECOMOG into Sierra Leone, Abacha probably expected some concessions from the European Union and the United States which were not only critical of the poor human rights record of his regime, but had also headed the crusade to isolate Nigeria, leading to the imposition of limited sanctions against his government and country. Second, and at a more idiosyncratic level, for Abacha the *coup* in Freetown shifted attention once again to the destabilising role of West African armies in the politics of the subregion. According to this line of reasoning, the development also pointed directly to his own succession bid which was bitterly opposed at home. The Sierra Leone adventure was expected to provide some respite, albeit only temporarily.

## 4. JUSTIFICATIONS FOR THE INTERVENTIONS

What principles and norms were invoked in support of the interventions? How credible were these excuses? Several entities intervened in Liberia and Sierra Leone, but the focus here is mainly on state actors and their surrogates, although other actors will be identified and their roles discussed fully, as and when appropriate. By and large, however, the discussion will be centred on ECOWAS, its surrogate, ECOMOG, and the key state actors, Nigeria, Gambia, Ghana, Guinea and Sierra Leone, on the one hand, and Côte d'Ivoire and Burkina Faso on the other. The first set of states formed the core of the Liberian enterprise, and remained in that country throughout the seven-year war. Côte d'Ivoire and Burkina Faso, both members of ECOWAS, were in the forefront of the anti-Nigeria/ECOMOG coalition, and were the main backers of Charles Taylor and to a lesser extent, Foday Sankoh's RUF. Unlike ECOWAS/ECOMOG, the motives of Côte d'Ivoire and Burkina Faso were overwhelmingly idiosyncratic and political, and this point will be made clear in the relevant sections of this chapter.

The explanations put forward by ECOWAS and Nigeria are many but they can be classified under two broad headings, namely humanitarianism/globalism rationalisations, and the "legalistic" arguments. Nigeria, expectedly, turned out to be the unofficial spokesperson for ECOWAS, and also put forward a variety of explanations to justify the operations in Liberia and Sierra Leone. In the main, the justifications were cast in language that presented Nigeria as selfless and globalist. For instance, it stressed its concern for peace and security at the subregional, continental and global levels, and not at the parochial national level. Again, President Babangida was quick to say that Nigerians were only "being our brothers' keeper". The implication is that since the rest of the world had turned its back on Liberia in its darkest hour, it was left to Africans to come to their rescue.

The Nigerian predicament is understandable. First, the country provided the core of the force behind the two interventions. It contributed about 70 per cent and 90 per cent of the men and financial outlay in Liberia and Sierra Leone respectively. Second, apart from the first couple of weeks in the Liberian operation when Ghana provided the force commander, Arnold Quanoo (only to be summarily dismissed in September 1990 following the arrest and murder of Samuel Doe by Prince Yeduo Johnson of the Independent

National Patriotic Front of Liberia — INPFL), all the other commanders were Nigerian.[29] Third, opposition to the ECOMOG operation was for obvious reasons more vocal in Nigeria than in any other troop-contributing state. Thus, much of the onus was also on Nigeria to sell the operation not only to its own citizens, but to the whole of West Africa and, indeed, the rest of the world, to defuse the criticisms. Significantly, ECOWAS itself said very little directly in this period, but the few statements that were issued on its behalf focused mainly on the legal aspects of the intervention in Liberia.

## 4.1 Legal arguments

The two foundations on which the ECOWAS legal argument stood are the *1981 Protocol on Mutual Assistance on Matters of Defence* (MAD), and a letter from Doe to the ECOWAS foreign ministers requesting the intervention. ECOWAS' main point of departure was the preamble setting up the Standing Mediation Committee (SMC), the precursor to ECOMOG. The operation's legality was predicated on

> the Protocol Relating to Mutual Assistance on Matters of Defence; general concern... about... the wanton destruction of human life and property and the displacement of persons... the massive damage in various forms being caused by the armed conflict to the stability and survival of the entire Liberian nation;... concern... about the plight of foreign nations, particularly citizens of the Community who are seriously affected by the conflict; and considering that law and order in Liberia had broken down; and... to find a peaceful and lasting solution to the conflict and to put an end to the situation which is seriously disrupting the normal life of innocent citizens in Liberia.[30]

It is doubtful if the provisions of the protocol were complied with *in toto*. For sure, the document did make provision for intervention in a member state under specific conditions, but certainly not before three important organs had been put in place by the community. These were: a Defence Council; a Defence Commission; and an Allied Armed Forces Council (AAFC). Significantly, none of the organs was in place when the intervention occurred. Thus, the intervention could not be justified purely within the context of either the ECOWAS treaty or the MAD protocol.

Furthermore, even the MAD "trigger clause" was not complied with. According to the protocol: ECOWAS members "accept that any armed threat or aggression directed against any member state will constitute a threat or aggression against the entire community" (Article 2). However, Article 16 of the same document also stipulates that the attack must be external to the requesting state.

> when an external armed threat or aggression is directed against a member state of the Community, the Head of State of that country shall send a written request for assistance to the current Chairman of the Authority of ECOWAS ... the request shall mean that the Authority is duly notified and that the AAFC are placed under a state of emergency ...[31]

But as pointed out earlier, the procedures were not adhered to strictly in Liberia and Sierra Leone. The deficiency was pointed out by the Burkinabe leader, Blaisse Campaore, but he was politely ignored. Again it is doubtful if the invasion of Liberia by NPFL forces can be regarded as external simply because Taylor had the backing of some states in the subregion. This did not amount to external armed aggression in the spirit of Article 16 of the MAD protocol.

This leads to the letter from Doe, which was apparently meant to provide either a device for the embattled president or to buy him time to regroup his men. The letter was alleged to read "... it would seem expedient to introduce an ECOWAS peacekeeping force into Liberia to forestall increasing terror and tension and to ensure a peaceful transitional environment".[32] However, no official of ECOWAS, to the best of the writer's knowledge, has ever acknowledged receipt of such correspondence. But even if one assumes for argument's sake that the letter does exist, it still raises a number of fundamental issues. First, whether Doe was still the "legal" authority in the country at the time the letter was written. As noted earlier, he had been holed up at the Executive Mansion with the rump of his troops and, to all intents and purposes, his authority did not extend beyond the perimeter of the Executive Mansion fence. Second, the letter was addressed to the Council of Ministers and not to the Heads of State or the Assembly, the supreme policy-making organ of ECOWAS, as provided for under the MAD protocol. This is an important point because ECOWAS is above all an economic community, and is concerned mainly with economic matters between and among its members. Besides, Doe's letter made it categorically clear that he was requesting an orthodox peacekeeping operation to separate the warring factions, and not a peace enforcement force as ECOMOG turned out to be at critical phases in the operation.

Another controversial issue that cropped up as a result of the hurried deployment of ECOMOG was the absence of a command and control framework within the ECOWAS secretariat. According to Iweze, the force's first chief of staff, this was due to the "failure of ECOWAS members to ratify the 1981 MAD Protocol which provided for the formation of a Defence Commission and Allied Armed Forces of the Community consisting of earmarked units from the forces of member states, under a force commander, that would report to the Defence Council".[33]

The omission seriously affected the operation of the force in several important ways. First, there was near total breakdown of the central command as troops received instructions from their home countries which were sometimes in conflict with the ECOMOG mandate in Liberia. Second, for understandable reasons, the cohesion and morale of the multilateral force was also adversely affected. Because each troop-contributing state was responsible for the welfare of its men, some contingents were better provided for than others. For instance, the Ghanaian contingent in Liberia was reputed to have the best medical facilities, but was reluctant to make them available to troops from other countries. Third, the absence of a central command structure adversely affected not only the speed with which the force was deployed, but also its response to situations within Liberia and Sierra Leone. Coupled with the absence of effective communication between the force headquarters in Monrovia and the ECOWAS secretariat in Lagos, it was left to the field commander either to use his initiative or wait for orders from Lagos. But even contacts with Lagos were not always prompt. This weakness impacted on the operations of the force in diverse ways. And as Iweze pointed out, "the overall effect of this was that we could not get responses in good time. A case in point was a vital decision taken by ECOWAS which did not get to us until a month later".

If the argument that the Liberian operation, in particular, was a true humanitarian venture, is accepted, then one would also expect its sponsors to make adequate provision to meet the myriad needs of hundreds of thousands of displaced persons who had converged on Monrovia. But this was not the case. The plight of displaced persons was discussed only at the planning phase of the operation. Consequently, ECOMOG was not in a position to provide significant succour to the people of Monrovia and its environs. Finally, because the force was hastily put together, it did not gather the intelligence that would have enabled it to operate effectively, and with minimum body bags. Again, according to Iweze, "the ECOMOG operations [are] a classical case of launching troops into a theatre of operation without any form of intelligence. If the saying that 'a general who goes into battle without intelligence is like a blindfolded boxer in the ring' is true, the inception of ECOMOG proves the point".[34]

In summary, then, the justifications for intervention provided by ECOWAS are open to serious question.

## 4.2 Humanitarian arguments

In the circumstances, the gauntlet was taken up by the Nigerian president, Ibrahim Babangida, who provided the most robust and comprehensive justification for the Liberian operation. At a World Press Conference in Lagos the president based his explanation mainly on humanitarian considerations:

> ... we are in Liberia because events in that country have led to the massive destruction of property by all parties, the massacre by all parties of thousands of innocent civilians including foreign nationals, women and children some of whom had sought sanctuary in the churches, mosques, diplomatic missions, hospitals and under Red Cross protection, contrary to all recognised civilised behaviour... I ask; should Nigeria and other responsible countries in the sub-region stand by and watch the whole of Liberia turned into one mass graveyard?... we also know that there are those who are waiting to see the Liberian crisis as a concrete indicator

of Africa in disarray and despair, purposeless and without any direction or control... in Liberia, we are first and foremost reflecting the love we have for our respective countries, our sub-region, Africa, the black world, and mankind... If the 1990s... demand a redefinition of what constitutes national security, does Nigeria's position in the West African sub-region also entail certain specific roles and responsibilities? Consequently, the reasons for our presence in Liberia are not mysterious. They are simply our national obligations voluntarily contracted... or would the position of ECOWAS be more noble and much better understood if because one faction refused to cooperate... we had abandoned Liberians to fate?[35]

The Nigerian leader was to return to this theme again in another famous speech in 1992. On that occasion, he argued that "while Nigeria respects the principle of non-interference in the affairs of a member state, we believed very strongly that the crisis in Liberia, the oldest independent country in West Africa, demanded the attention of ECOWAS. This was because the killings were getting out of hand as there was no longer a credible authority to establish order in the country".[36]

The Nigerian position was supported, rather surprisingly, by the then chairperson of the OAU, Uganda's Yoweri Museveni, who apparently set aside one of the most revered concepts in inter-African relations: non-interference in the internal affairs of one another. This injunction, contained in Article 3(2) of the Charter, held sway up to the time of the Liberian civil war, and had been blamed, in part, for the organisation's poor record especially in maintaining peace and security in the continent, since it barred other states from responding unilaterally, either individually or collectively, to adverse developments in other member states. The convention was set aside in Liberia because, according to the Ugandan leader, "when we talk of non-interference in the internal affairs of one another, we mean one state which is functioning not interfering in another functioning state... we are not interfering in the internal affairs of Liberia because there was no longer any central authority in that country".[37]

Finally, General Yakubu Gowon, who ruled Nigeria from 1966 to 1975, joined the fray on the side of Nigeria and ECOWAS when he told airport correspondents in Lagos "I am sure any responsible leader in a country like Nigeria... that is faced with a problem in the region that may threaten the existence of peace or stability of a member country and possibly may spread to others should stop it because if not stopped, it could set the region ablaze with instability, revolution, etc, ..."[38]

What is clear from all the quotations is that they are quintessential globalist in rhetoric: Nigeria was in ECOMOG in response to a humanitarian emergency and disaster; to relieve human misery and stem large-scale violations of human rights by all sides in the civil war.

## 4.3 Analysis

To what extent do these justifications hold water under closer scrutiny? This is a difficult question to answer. For one, it is impossible to read the innermost motives of decision makers even in the most transparent societies. The problem is multiplied several times over in developing countries where the head of state epitomises the state itself. To paraphrase Louis XIV, African leaders are the state in their respective countries. As such, even major policy decisions could be made merely to satisfy their whims and caprices, no matter what the long-term consequences might be for the state and its citizens. The situation is exacerbated in crisis periods, and under military dictatorships, because there is relatively little or no time for broad-based consultations. In West Africa, and indeed in much of Africa, leaders have a wider margin of freedom for unilateral action than their counterparts in advanced democracies.

For another, it is incredibly difficult to identify all the subterraneous linkages between one leader and another, especially in developing countries where corruption at the highest levels is rampant. The problem is often compounded by the absence of memoirs that could shed more light on the rationale for state actions. Consequently, there is a large element of speculation in reading motives.

Nonetheless, an attempt will be made to examine critically Nigeria's justifications in the light of its relations with Liberia and Sierra Leone before and after ECOMOG was sent into the two countries in 1990 and 1997 respectively. For obvious reasons, which included its novelty and the controversy it generated in Nigeria, the rest of West Africa and the world at large, most of the justifications were in respect of the Liberian operation. Besides, unlike Sierra Leone which had close historical ties with Nigeria, Liberia was above all an American protégé per excellence. As a result, most commentators could not understand Nigeria's stake in that country. In fact, the general expectation was that the lead would be taken by the United States, Liberia's benefactor. The failure of America to do so, made the Nigerian action much more suspicious. The Nigerian justifications will be elaborated on later in the chapter. For now, the reasons advanced by the junior partners in the operation: Gambia, Ghana, Guinea, and Sierra Leone, can be examined.

### 4.3.1 Objectives of the junior partners

Gambia's participation in the venture is understandable from at least two broad perspectives. First, as the ECOWAS chair, it was expected that Banjul should set a good example by participating in the operation. Second, Nigeria and the Gambia had had close ties for many years. Abuja has provided the Chief Judge of Banjul in the last fifteen or more years. In addition, the strong military ties between Nigeria and Gambia made provision for Nigerian soldiers at the senior officer level to be seconded to the Gambian army for several years. These considerations may have persuaded the then Gambian leader, Dauda Jawara, to participate in the "humanitarian" intervention in Liberia. However, these are merely plausible conjectures for the Gambian action as the former president, Jawara, has remained largely silent since his overthrow in 1994.

Ghana's participation in ECOMOG is perhaps the most difficult to explain. Ghana is not a contiguous neighbour of Liberia, so the diverse adverse impacts of the civil war on Ghana were not as severe as those on immediate neighbours like Guinea or Sierra Leone. Again, Ghana is known to have leadership aspirations in West Africa, and is highly suspicious of Nigeria's intentions in the subregion. The rivalry between the two countries dates back to the days of Nkrumah. Thus, playing second fiddle to Nigeria in ECOMOG could only enhance Abuja's hegemony in the subregion to the detriment of Accra. It may be that Ghana's support for the operation was secured once Nigeria conceded the post of Commander of the Force to it. Finally, it is conceivable that the Ghanaian leader, Jerry Rawlings, was genuinely moved by what was happening in Liberia and thought his country should do something to alleviate the human suffering; an act that would also enhance his country's stature in the subregion and elsewhere.

Although Sierra Leone and Liberia are linked by the Mano River Union (MRU), a micro-integration and political project,[39] incessant political instability in Liberia, especially after 1980, rendered the MRU useless as a vehicle for meaningful economic and political co-operation. Relations between Sierra Leone and Liberia remained poor and reached an all-time low point after the abortive *coup* of Quiwonkpa in 1985, which was allegedly launched from Sierra Leone, and with the knowledge of Sierra Leonean authorities. Ties between Liberia and Guinea, a francophone country and member of the MRU, were more distant and tenuous. In short, then, common membership of the MRU was not a strong enough reason for the participation of Conakry and Freetown in the ECOMOG operation in Liberia.

The two countries may have decided to participate once it was clear that the bulk of the financial cost and troops would be provided by big brother, Nigeria. It is also likely that Nigeria used its economic and political leverage in the two countries to secure their participation. Abuja is known to have fledgling economic and political interests in Conakry: some small investments in its iron ore mines which were to supply raw materials for the Ajaokuta Steel Rolling Mill in Nigeria. Conakry is also a recipient of modest economic and technical assistance from Abuja. Again, Guinea was the country most affected by the refugee crisis in Liberia. This could have been a decisive factor in the country's participation in ECOMOG, especially if the operation was considered as capable of bringing the civil war to a speedy end. Pronouncements by Guinean authorities on the Liberian operation are hard to come by. However, in a statement released to the press in August 1990, a few days after ECOMOG was deployed in Monrovia, the Guinean head of state, Lansana Conte, was quoted as saying defiantly "we do not need the permission of any party involved in the conflict to implement the ECOWAS decisions in Liberia".[40]

If for nothing else, the statement is important for at least two reasons. First it is couched, although indirectly, in globalist terms: Guinea did not need approval from Liberia or any other authority to send its troops to Monrovia. Second, is the apparent determination of Guinea to honour the "consensual" decision to send troops to Liberia. Significantly, in sending troops to Monrovia in 1990, President Conte was repeating history as Guinea had sent troops to Freetown in 1971, as noted earlier, to prop up the tottering government of Siaka Stevens. On that occasion, President Sekou Toure invoked a little-known mutual defence treaty with Sierra Leone to justify the intervention.

Perhaps Sierra Leone's position is at face value the more difficult to understand. For sure, the country has had long and close historical ties with Nigeria. Many of the Creoles in Freetown can still trace their lineage to Nigeria, having been captured on the high seas by British naval ships on their way to slavery in the Americas, and taken to the then British protectorate. A whole community, Fourah Bay, is settled mainly by people whose ancestry is Yoruba, one of the three main nationalities in Nigeria. But apart from that, there is little else in the relations between the two countries. A tiny country even by African standards, in fact, the sixth smallest on the continent; with an army of less than five thousand men, and economically dependent on the West, especially the United Kingdom, the former colonial metropole, Sierra Leone cannot in reality support a foreign military adventure. Yet, it not only sent troops to Liberia, but kept them there for over seven years, even when it was fighting its own civil war. What was responsible for this paradox?

Several explanations are possible. First, fear of the contagion effect of the Liberian war. And second, like Guinea, it was perhaps also conscious of the negative impact the large

Liberian refugee population could have on its political and economic stability. However, the strongest and most plausible reason for its participation in ECOMOG can be found in the very close ties between its leader, Joseph Momoh, and Nigeria's Ibrahim Babangida. The friendship was struck at the Nigerian Defence Academy in Kaduna, where both men were students. This point is important, as Momoh used the connection to procure crude oil from Nigeria at concessionary rates, several years before the outbreak of the Liberian civil war. Sierra Leone was also a net recipient of other forms of economic and technical assistance from Nigeria in this period. Besides such considerations, it is possible also that the Sierra Leonean leader subscribed to the Nigerian president's disdain for civilians.[41] As such, he supported Babangida's view that another military man, Doe, should not be forced from office by a "bloody" civilian, Charles Taylor. A distress call from the Nigerian leader would therefore be difficult to ignore in Freetown. Of course, this does not rule out the possibility that Babangida also made financial and other inducements to the Sierra Leone leader and government, including offsetting and/or subsidising its contingent in ECOMOG.

### 4.3.2 Nigerian and ECOWAS objectives

Having examined the motives of the "junior partners" in the operation, attention can now be turned to those of ECOWAS and Nigeria. Interestingly enough, both used legalistic and internationalist rationales to explain their actions in Liberia. Were these watertight reasons?

The "internationalist" argument, or being one's brother's keeper, was perhaps the strongest of all in the Nigerian position. Since independence in 1960, but especially during the oil boom years in the 1970s, Nigeria had been playing the role of "big brother" to, and protector of the interests of all black peoples whether in Africa or in the diaspora. This commitment explains in part, Nigeria's unswerving support for the liberation struggles on the continent and, in particular, its bitter opposition to apartheid. Successive governments in Lagos invested a lot of energy, time and resources to this end, so much so that for many years Nigeria was unanimously chosen to chair the UN Committee against Apartheid, a position it held from 1972 to 1991 when apartheid collapsed. Nigeria also became an honorary frontline state in recognition of the important role it played in the liberation struggles in Southern Africa generally, and in Zimbabwe, Angola and South Africa in particular. It could therefore be argued that the "being my brother's keeper policy" was reinvigorated in the 1990s, more so in view of Africa's marginalisation by the great powers. However, many astute Nigerians doubted the sincerity of this philosophical commitment by their president. They were not sure if that foreign policy plank was strong enough to warrant the financial and human sacrifice the country was making in Liberia and Sierra Leone. This is perhaps the main reason why the new government of Obasanjo wanted to disengage from Sierra Leone as soon as possible.

Another argument advanced by ECOWAS and Nigeria was that the conflicts in Liberia and Sierra Leone posed a serious threat to state and subregional security. This was in fact the case, but only to the extent that contiguous states were experiencing a huge influx of refugees which threatened to destabilise them politically and economically. As it turned out, only Sierra Leone was in serious danger, but that was due to the close relationship between its government and some prominent Liberian refugees who subsequently formed ULIMO, a development interpreted by Charles Taylor as a coalition against his NPFL faction. This perception made it easier for Taylor to support the extension of the war into Sierra

Leone through the RUF. The fact that Guinea, which received most of the refugees from Sierra Leone and Liberia, remained relatively stable, proves the point.

As for the claim that the Liberian war was a threat to the subregion, this was so only indirectly. A far more direct threat came after the deployment of ECOMOG as a result of strong opposition to the force from two members: Côte d'Ivoire and Burkina Faso. Both countries were strong supporters of Charles Taylor and the RUF. There was a real danger that the operation would again open old wounds and rivalry between the anglophone and francophone states, especially between Nigeria and Côte d'Ivoire. The threat quickly faded the moment the Ivorian leader, Houphouet-Boigny, agreed to participate in the Liberian peace processes that led to the Yamoussoukro 1-1V peace accords as well as the Geneva Agreement. The expansion of ECOMOG to include two other francophone states, Senegal and Mali, also reduced the tension between the troop-contributing states on the one hand, and the francophone states on the other.

Did the war in Liberia pose a serious threat to world peace and security as was claimed by ECOWAS and Nigeria? Not really. Yes, there was a massive refugee outflow from Liberia and later from Sierra Leone into neighbouring countries. Many Liberians also found their way to the United States, the motherland, while a few went to Europe. There was certainly no flood of refugees into these countries that could have presented a threat to world peace and security. It surely would have been a different story if it were Nigeria that had erupted the way Liberia and Sierra Leone did. That was why the great powers were prepared to accept any arrangement that would give the semblance of peace in Africa's most populous country. Or how else does one account for the neglect of the war in Liberia and in Sierra Leone by the great powers for so many years? Surely, it was only because the two countries were of lesser strategic and economic importance to the West. Even the UN's attention was not gained by the Liberian war until late in 1993, four years after Taylor's *coup*, and even then, the response was rather disappointing. The global body remained peripheral to the search for peace in Sierra Leone despite the atrocities committed by all sides in the war. Not only that, UN monitors were the first to leave Freetown in the wake of the 6 January 1999 infiltration of the RUF. The point, really, is that the international system has a large capacity to successfully isolate a member for several years without fundamentally affecting its structure or operations, especially if the member is judged economically and politically unimportant. Unfortunately, Liberia and Sierra Leone were not vital to the rest of the international society. Viewed from this angle, the ECOWAS/Nigerian interventions on behalf of the international community become more understandable, if not more acceptable. But even then, they had to resort to various arguments to make their actions more palatable to cynical and sceptical national and international audiences.

Of all the justifications advanced by ECOWAS and Nigeria for the interventions, the humanitarian one is perhaps the most enduring. Surely, Liberia had at some point degenerated into the classical Hobbesian state of nature, especially after the murder of Doe. In Sierra Leone gruesome atrocities were committed by all sides in the conflict: crude amputations of the most bizarre forms, disembowelments, rape, murder and even cannibalism, were frequently reported. Thus according to advocates of humanitarian intervention such as Bhikhu Parekh, other states "now have a duty to intervene... but whether or not they should do so depends on a number of other factors".[42] In particular, they must take into account the comparative cost in human lives; their chances of success; the kind of precedent they are likely to set; and the future expectations they are likely to arise and the attitude of the people in question... (Besides, those intervening in the domestic affairs of other states)... must bear in mind that their knowledge of the country is bound to be limited, that they are likely to fall victim to... moral arrogance... that their actions must not prevent the natural realignments of forces, prop up those too weak to survive their departure or so internationalise the conflict that it becomes even more intractable.[43]

Intervention must therefore significantly improve the lot of the people or the strategic situation in the target state, at least in the very short term. When the interventions in Liberia and Sierra Leone are weighed against the above scale, they become difficult to justify or defend for at least two reasons. First, the operations merely prolonged the humanitarian tragedies in both countries. In Liberia, it is argued, Taylor would have seized control of the Executive Mansion and he would have imposed his will on the other factions, thereby bringing the war to an early end. In Sierra Leone, it is believed that after the Johnny Paul Koromah *coup* in May 1997, the invitation to the RUF to join his government would have also brought the war in that country to an end. It is not easy to substantiate these contentions. What is incontrovertible is that in Sierra Leone, the atrocities against the civilian population became more frequent and more bizarre after ECOMOG's intervention. Perhaps it is because the force was never perceived as impartial by faction leaders. That was certainly the conclusion of Charles Taylor in Liberia. Unfortunately, some of the actions of the force did not instil confidence in the rebels. For example, ECOMOG was accused of committing atrocities in Liberia by the London-based Africa Economic Intelligence Unit, just like the rebels. The accusation tarnished its image, and severely weakened its mission mandate and ability to broker peace in the country.[44] Again, the force was accused of openly taking sides with various factions in Liberia, depending on the strategic situation it was confronted with, that is ULIMO, the INPLF and the Liberia Peace Council (LPC), etc. ECOMOG was also alleged to have been involved in providing arms and ammunition to favoured factions to enhance their fighting capacity against Taylor's NPFL. As Iweze, ECOMOG's first chief of staff, rightly noted: "At a stage rather than act as a tool for conflict resolution, ECOMOG itself became a party to the conflict, especially when enforcement orders were given ... to persuade Charles Taylor to go to the negotiation table."[45]

Other commentators are less charitable:

> ... the inability of the force to maintain neutrality in its endeavours created a situation in which the factions lost faith in the peace-keepers. Rather than serving as an organisation maintaining peace for the good of Liberia, ECOMOG appeared to be a mere cover for foreign exploitation. ECOMOG deteriorated into an 'inadequate peace-keeping force'... which prolonged the war and weakened regional security ... its intervention only delayed the inevitable; Taylor's ascension to the presidency.[46]

Whether deliberately or inadvertently, ECOMOG aligned itself politically in Liberia and in Sierra Leone. By putting in place an interim government in Monrovia whose survival it was committed to, the force unwittingly appeared to confirm Charles Taylor's worst fears that it was not an impartial arbiter but a major party to the conflict. This perception was echoed by the Minister of Information in Amos Sawyer's Interim Government of National Unity (IGNU) in late 1993, in reaction to a statement credited to Nigeria's interim president, Ernest Shonekan:

> If Nigeria leaves, it is finished for us. We cannot understand why Nigeria which has done so much and very well for Liberia, had to reach such a decision especially at a time when the peace process is at its crucial stage. Maybe Shonekan wants (the NPFL leader) Charles Taylor to kill us. I hope our Nigerian brothers will reconsider their decision. They must not leave us in the middle of the road ...[47]

Taylor's intransigence and calculated violations of several peace accords brokered by ECOWAS, was in part due to his perception of the force as partial in the conflict.

In Sierra Leone, ECOMOG took sides with pro-government militias commonly known as Kamajos and Kapras. Perhaps that was inevitable given the circumstances that led to its deployment in that country in the first place. Of much more significance, though, was the impression that it could win the bush war against the RUF. In doing so, it gave Ahmed Tejan Kabbah a false sense of security and made it difficult for him to opt for an early peaceful resolution of the war. Meanwhile, the commitment of the military to the defence of his regime was questionable, as it was frequently alleged that senior officers were engaged in illicit diamond and gold mining. The surprise attack on ECOMOG's main barracks at Hastings, a few kilometres from Freetown and the subsequent invasion of the capital on 6 January 1999, proved this point beyond doubt. The mayhem that followed left over 6000 dead, and many houses and other valuable properties were also destroyed by the rebels.[48]

Secondly, the intervention prolonged the conflicts by internationalising them, thereby making the search for peaceful solutions more arduous because of the diverse interests involved. Côte d'Ivoire and Burkina Faso apparently had an axe to grind with Doe. For President Houphouet-Boigny, the intervention was sweet revenge for the brutal murders of President William Tolbert, his father-in-law, and AB Tolbert, his son-in-law, in the April 1980 *coup*. For the Burkino Faso leader, Blaisse Compaore, it was solidarity with his father-in-law, Houphouet-Boigny. Thus, he was a willing recruit to the anti-Doe camp in the conflict. Compaore later used his close ties with the Libyan leader, Maommar Gaddafi, to facilitate the training of Taylor and some of his commanders, including Foday Sankoh, in Libya. Burkina Faso also became a conduit for arms and ammunition to Charles Taylor's NPFL. The hostile attitude of these countries made ECOMOG's mission in Liberia not only very difficult, but also undermined the search for an early peaceful settlement of the war.

In Sierra Leone, British influence, albeit restrained, complicated the peace process. The British not only supplied arms and advisers to Tejan Kabbah's forces, but also gave the erroneous impression that the war could be won on the battlefield with superior fire power. But of course history is replete with examples that do not support such optimism. The defeat of the Americans in Vietnam, and the exit of the Soviet Union from Afghanistan in 1989, are eloquent testimonies to the limitations of superior firepower in a bush war like that in Sierra Leone. It is significant to note that the turning point in the peace process came after the January 1999 invasion of Freetown, and the election of a civilian president in Nigeria in February that year, who was committed to withdrawing Nigerian troops from ECOMOG at the earliest opportunity. The two developments considerably weakened Tejan Kabbah's position, and made him much more receptive to a peaceful end to the war with the RUF. The result was the Lome

Agreement of June 1999, which apparently established a mutually acceptable framework for power sharing between the SLPP government of Tejan Kabbah and Foday Sankoh's RUF.

It is clear from the above analysis that the interventions were flawed in many ways, and cannot therefore be presented as wholly altruistic. Apart from the reasons suggested above, several other factors, mainly domestic to Nigeria, account for this assessment. In the first place, General Ibrahim Babangida was known to be a close friend of Samuel Doe and his government. Many informed Nigerians believed that their president was not transparent enough, and that he had a hidden agenda in Liberia. According to this line of thinking, ECOMOG was more than just a clever device to save a friend's neck. For the African Economic Intelligence Unit, the intervention in Liberia was the result of Babangida's obsession with making himself a political power broker in the subregion. Besides, the president was said to be understudying Doe who had successfully transmuted from a military to a civilian president in 1985. Babangida had a similar ambition and agenda in Nigeria. Accordingly, the fall of Doe would deprive him of a mentor and a source of inspiration. Babangida, as already pointed out, was also noted for his contempt of civilians. A military leader, no matter how obnoxious his regime, should not be hounded out of office by a rag-tag army under civilian command. It was hardly surprising, therefore, that Babangida threw the entire weight of the Nigerian state behind ECOMOG in Liberia.

Nigerians also wondered why their government was willing to sacrifice innocent Nigerian lives – especially those of civilians trapped in Liberia – if their president had nothing to hide, when other countries had already evacuated their own citizens from that country. These issues were dealt with in an editorial in the country's most reputable daily, the *Guardian of Lagos*:

> Our government's failure to make arrangements to evacuate stranded Nigerians from Liberia is counted as evidence of Nigeria's support for Doe's regime. According to this view (which was widespread at a time), Nigeria has refused to evacuate her citizens to create a facade of stability in Liberia. Government did not want to give the impression that Doe had lost control of the situation which could have a negative psychological effect on the war effort.[49]

The critics of ECOMOG also pointed to Doe's visit to Nigeria in May 1990, and media reports that he had been given a planeload of arms to bolster his war effort against Taylor. The Liberian leader denied any connection between the war and said the trip which was essentially to "show our solidarity with the Nigerian leader in the wake of the abortive coup against him, and to reassure President Babangida of our support, and to encourage him to continue to do the good work for our people and lay a solid foundation for democracy in Africa".[50]

In his defence, Babangida said "there was nothing wrong in lending an ear to a brother in distress, that did not signify acquiescence". As to the allegation that he deliberately refused to evacuate Nigerians trapped in Monrovia, the president's response was: "Liberians are our brothers and Nigerians over there (Liberia) live together with them and see themselves as part of the society. I don't think it is right for any government to create a distinction between fellow Africans over the evacuation exercise."[51]

However, the hollowness of the logic was too glaring. Any serious government should regard the safety of its citizens abroad as a primary responsibility. Thus American and

British governments are usually among the first to evacuate their citizens in crisis-ridden states or regions. The Nigerian leader's argument was even more illogical given the fact that Nigerians were targeted by Charles Taylor in retaliation to the deployment of ECOMOG, which stood between him and the Executive Mansion in Monrovia.

Apart from these considerations, Babangida worked to reinstate Samuel Doe as a respectable member of the African leadership and Nigeria was responsible for the fence-mending between Liberia and both Sierra Leone and Guinea, especially after the abortive *coup* by Quiwonkpa in 1985.[52]

The more the government tried to wriggle out of the crisis of confidence regarding the way it had handled the evacuation of Nigerians from Liberia, the more details were made available by the media about the close ties between Nigeria and Liberia under Samuel Doe. For instance, it was disclosed that Babangida bought Liberia's $30 million loan with the African Development Bank (AfDB) for reasons that have never been made known to the Nigerian public. And when Doe wanted to pursue postgraduate studies in Political Science in Liberia, he convinced the Nigerian president to finance the establishment of a Graduate School of International Affairs to the tune of $8 million. Nigerian professors were seconded to the school which had been renamed the "Babangida School of International Diplomacy", and were paid in US dollars by the Nigerian government. Finally, Nigeria contributed the bulk of the troops in ECOMOG as well as 70 per cent of the total financial cost of the operation, some $7 billion, according to General Abacha, although many Nigerians believe the figure is grossly understated.

ECOMOG is then the result of a complex mix of circumstances which are both domestic and external to the subregion, such as leadership idiosyncrasies, especially on the part of Nigeria's leaders; the domestic politics of member states; the end of the Cold War; and the withdrawal of great power interest in Africa. It is also significant that at the time it was created, many of the troop-contributing states did not have democratically elected governments. This lack of accountability made it possible for the leaders to commit their citizens in ways that would not have been possible under transparent and accountable regimes.

## 5  SOME CONSEQUENCES OF THE INTERVENTIONS

ECOMOG has been the subject of scholarly studies and criticisms, both informed and uninformed. But it is generally acknowledged that ECOMOG succeeded in stabilising the appalling humanitarian situation in Liberia, especially around Monrovia, the haven for hundreds of thousands of displaced persons. ECOMOG put a check on the most brutal and barbaric phase in the civil war by separating the warring factions in Monrovia. To be sure, its control over the rest of the country was not total, but it nevertheless facilitated the delivery of humanitarian assistance by international aid agencies in Monrovia, its immediate environs and, indeed, in other parts of the country when that was possible. This limited achievement has been acknowledged by many individuals and studies. According to the permanent representative of the United States to the United Nations:

> In a country where anarchy reigned, ECOMOG provided order and bastion of security in Monrovia and hundreds of thousands of Liberians flocked to the relative safety of the city ... ECOMOG remains virtually the only force in Liberia unblemished by serious human rights abuses and is the one military force not motivated by personal aggrandisement.[53]

And according to Mackinlay and Alao:

> In the African context ECOMOG's intervention has been, on balance, successful. ECOMOG demonstrated a rough and ready capability to take on the factions and restore a relative degree of order. In this way it has been a vital element of the peace process. But even in the most optimistic circumstances, ECOMOG did not have sufficient forces in Liberia to maintain a reasonable level of security...[54]

This was vital in a country that had entirely collapsed. However, it is not clear if ECOMOG achieved the same feat in Sierra Leone.

The force represented in an unprecedented fashion, African states' resolve to participate fully in the new international order in spite of their apparent strategic devaluation and marginalisation. In fact the Liberian operation, in particular represented a brave attempt by West African countries at collective problem solving.[55] Thus some of ECOMOG's limitations are better appreciated from such a perspective. Nonetheless, the force was largely accepted by the international community as a major stabilising factor in the subregion, a model to be emulated by other regions in Africa, if not the rest of the developing world. ECOWAS/ECOMOG facilitated the initiation of peace processes in Liberia and Sierra Leone. Many accords were signed by the parties between 1990 and 1997 in the case of Liberia, and up to the Lomé Accords of July 1999, in respect of Sierra Leone. In Liberia, ECOWAS/ECOMOG also moderated the general elections that led to the installation of a democratic government headed by former rebel faction leader, Charles Taylor.

ECOWAS/ECOMOG undoubtedly set a very important precedent; namely that a peacekeeping force can, in the post-

Cold War era, be mounted by a subregional body without the prior approval of the United Nations. The two operations were not directly sanctioned by the world body, but they both not only received retroactive approval from New York, the UN even played second fiddle to both ECOWAS and ECOMOG in the two countries. By so doing, it is posited here that the UN not only reinforced Chapter 52 of the Charter, but also indirectly undermined its own control over similar operations in future, whether in Africa or elsewhere. In particular, the endorsement of the ECOWAS initiative in Liberia can be seen as a tacit devolution of responsibility for the maintenance of global peace and security by the UN, one of its primary missions. Perhaps that was inevitable, given the selective support of peacekeeping and peace support operations by the great powers especially in regions/states they considered peripheral to their national interests.

At a more general level, the two ECOMOG operations established a new triangular co-operation between ECOWAS, the OAU and the UN. Such a tripartite working relationship had not been anticipated by the founding fathers of the UN, a point that did not escape the then Secretary General, Boutros Boutros-Ghali:

> The peace process in Liberia poses a special opportunity to the UN in that UNOMIL would be the first peace-keeping operation undertaken by the UN in co-operation with a peace-keeping mission already set up by another organisation, in this case a sub-regional organisation ... This relationship potentially present some challenges but I am confident that with goodwill ... this relationship will be successful and may even set a precedent for future peace-keeping missions ...[56]

Other important outcomes of the interventions already pointed out are that they internationalised the wars in the two countries and by so doing, prolonged them and the hardships of their citizens. In the case of Sierra Leone, the presence of ECOMOG seemed to exacerbate the atrocities committed by the RUF fighters – for the maiming and amputations, kidnapping, rape, etc. became more frequent and gruesome after February 1998 when Johnny Paul Koromah's government was flushed out of Freetown. Again, the mayhem unleashed on the population of Freetown in January 1999 reinforces the point.

There is no doubt that the interventions have militarised civil society in Liberia and Sierra Leone. Because thousands of young men were drafted into the wars as child soldiers, there has been a proliferation of small arms and ammunition not just in the principal countries, but also in contiguous neighbours. All troop-contributing states and those bordering on Liberia and Sierra Leone have experienced a wave of crime-related urban violence due to the relative ease with which guns are now available in the subregion in general, and in the participating states especially. For instance, armed robbery cases have increased significantly in Côte d'Ivoire and Guinea, while in Nigeria, which has had a long history of urban violence, armed robberies committed with ECOMOG weapons are a common occurrence.[57] In Liberia, ex-combatants roam the streets freely terrorising innocent citizens and visitors (as the writer discovered to his chagrin in November/December 1998 during a research field visit to Monrovia). In early August 1999, about 120 ex-combatants invaded the house of the Executive Director of the Centre for Democratic Empowerment, Conmany Wesseh, wielding knives, sticks and other dangerous weapons, in protest against a statement credited to him during a radio programme. Although he was not in the house at the time, members of his family, including his wife, were manhandled while valuable items including computers and other electronic gadgets were carted away by the hoodlums. Perhaps he would have been killed had they found him at home. Sadly, West Africa and the international community have not learnt any lesson, as the demobilisation process in Sierra Leone has been incomprehensive and half-hearted, with all the adverse consequences for effective post-war reconstruction and national reconciliation.[58]

In the absence of central funding, the financial burden of non-troop contributing ECOWAS members was minimal, while the operation imposed severe financial strains on the troop-contributing states, a main reason why it was not easy to expand the number of troop-contributing states in Liberia and Sierra Leone. In fact, fewer countries were involved in the Sierra Leone operation. The economies of troop-contributing states were hard hit, although Nigeria bore the brunt of the two operations in financial as well as human terms. It is not a coincidence, then, that calls for the withdrawal of ECOMOG were also loudest in that country.

The Liberian operation had a particularly devastating impact on Sierra Leone. Apart from the heavy financial burden arising from the Liberian venture, galloping inflation and appalling living standards for the majority of its citizens, the intervention was the immediate cause of the civil war that broke out in March 1991, and the *coup d'état* that overthrew Joseph Momoh in April 1992. The woes of the citizens were compounded by the Koromah *coup* of 25 May 1997 and the events that followed. The atrocities against the civilian population have left many people traumatised for life. Again, the *coup* that brought Yayah Jameh to power in the Gambia in April 1994 is also traceable to the presence of that country's troops in Liberia.

> Of all the 5 key sub-regional leaders who spearheaded the establishment of ECOMOG in 1990, only two: President Jerry Rawlings of Ghana and Lansana Conte of Guinea, are still in their seats ... the others have all been ousted in circumstances directly and indirectly linked to the intervention. The escalation of political instability and economic hardship in Sierra Leone, the Gambia and in the border areas of Guinea are all danger signals which the sub-regional initiative appears, inadvertently, to have exacerbated rather than alleviated.[59]

As for ECOWAS, the progenitor of ECOMOG, the implications can be itemised broadly as political and psychological. Politically, the Liberian intervention initially threatened to split the organisation along the old francophone/anglophone linguistic divide. Opposition to the Liberian peacekeeping operation especially from Côte d'Ivoire and Burkina Faso, aggravated the political destabilisation of the subregion. The danger was however short-lived as all the member states were conscious of their common vulnerability. Boigny, for instance, realised in the end that ongoing support for Taylor and defiance of ECOWAS could tempt other members to destabilise his own country. This consideration partly explains his *volte-face* and rather belated commitment to the peace process in Liberia. And with that, the francophone states and the rest of the subregion unwittingly also conceded to Nigeria's hegemony in the subregion.

The psychological impacts are short term and long term. In the short term, ECOWAS arguably set in motion what is now referred to as the African renaissance. It certainly lifted morale in the subregion, if not the whole of Africa, and reinforced the belief that Africans are their "brothers' keepers". The interventions renewed hope in Africa's future and the ability of its leaders to arrest the continent's slide into chaos in the post-Cold War international order. The long-term psychological impact is more difficult to pin down. So far, Charles Taylor had held Liberia together, albeit tenuously. The ceremonial destruction of weapons in that country in July 1999, in front of the leaders of Nigeria and Sierra Leone, demonstrated that he was ready to take his country out of isolation. ECOMOG can be credited with restoring some semblance of law and order in that country specifically, and West Africa in general. The election of Charles Taylor as executive president of Liberia rekindled hope that the subregion would not be left out of the move to democracy that swept the world following the collapse of communism in Eastern Europe. Surely, a Charles Taylor victory through the barrel of the gun would have been a serious setback for peace and a serious blow "to democratic aspirations throughout Africa and would have led to the conclusion that might is right. Dissidents throughout the region many of whom maintain connections with Taylor, would [have been] encouraged to take their battle into the streets rather than working through the political process".[60]

Finally, had ECOMOG scrambled out of Liberia, its deployment in Freetown would have been impossible. ECOMOG has set a precedent that other subregional hegemons will probably want to emulate in future. South Africa's incursion into Lesotho is already proof that regional hegemons are ready to take risks, and will move into neighbouring states if their interests are "threatened".

## 6. LESSONS FROM THE INTERVENTIONS

Several lessons are discernible. The first is that a subregional organisation can be used successfully to contain a deadly civil war and reverse a successful *coup* if some member states are prepared to make the necessary human and financial contributions and sacrifices. The willingness of Presidents Ibrahim Babangida and Sani Abacha of Nigeria to do so made ECOMOG a reality. And with that, a signal was sent around the world that Africa should perhaps not be written off yet, despite its present turmoil and apparent marginalisation in the post-Cold War order. Another lesson is that African leaders, like their colleagues elsewhere in the world, are in tune with the monumental changes that have taken place since the collapse of the Berlin Wall. These include a redefinition of some key concepts such as non-interference, sovereignty and intervention that have been central to international politics since the dawn of the Westphalian system in 1648. For almost fifty years, Cold War considerations made it hard to tinker with sovereignty. That the interventions were justified using norms that are invoked by the great powers suggests that a major political revolution is taking place in Africa. The interpretation given to concepts such as non-interference and sovereignty by no less a person than the chairperson of the OAU, suggests that they are losing their sanctity even in a continent where they have held sway since the early 1960s.

The development is in line with the trend in the wider international systems, a point reinforced by Boutros-Ghali in his *1992 Agenda for Peace*:

> The foundation stone of international society is and must remain the State, and respect for its fundamental sovereignty and integrity... the time of absolute sovereignty has passed; its theory was never matched by reality... leaders of states today must understand this and find... a balance between the needs of good internal governance and the requirements of an ever more interdependent world.[61]

Paradoxically, Africa could lose out as a result of the redefinition. As the weakest continent in the present international dispensation, the dangers are obvious since even humanitarian intervention is subject to abuse. Nicholas Wheeler has rightly warned that even if international "consensus could be established upon what principles should justify humanitarian intervention at the UN, there is always the fear that these principles might be abused".[62] The experiences of Iraq, and more recently of the former Yugoslavia, and the DRC, seem to prove him right. Thus, Thomas Ohlson's observation that "militarist interventionist advocacy and behaviour is very much on the agenda, albeit with multilateral rationales ..."[63] is correct. Such behaviour is what Nye has appropriately described as "the alternative way of exercising power, namely, to set the agenda and make others feel they accept this agenda..."[64] That was exactly what the United States did in the Gulf, Bosnia, Somalia, and Kosovo. Nigeria and its allies did the same thing in Liberia and Sierra Leone. A common factor in all these actions is that the dominant actor sought to "monopolise the right to interpret the laws and norms... to attain a situation in which it can invoke the entire international authority behind its interpretation of the rules in support of its own interests ..."[65]

It will be totally wrong, therefore, to conclude that the ECOMOG interventions or those that have taken place in other parts of the world, for that matter, portend the emergence of a "global community" as the globalists are wont to argue. The total neglect and later the slow response of the rest of the international community to the humanitarian emergencies in Liberia and Sierra Leone left much to be desired. Significantly, the United Nations is not beyond reproach in this regard. Its Observer Mission to Liberia, UNOMIL, arrived too late in the day. Besides, numbering only

303, it was in no position to effectively monitor the entire country. In Sierra Leone, the members of the Observer Mission were among the first people to scramble out of the country following the RUF invasion of Freetown in January 1999. The late arrival of the UN teams in both countries did not do much to ease ECOMOG's multiple burdens. The inability of other ECOWAS members to contribute troops to both operations created a crisis of legitimacy for the force and seriously compromised its claim to be an impartial agent. Thus, it was variously seen as a Nigerian creature and a willing tool of Abuja's hegemonic agenda in West Africa. An early response by the international community to the numerous pleas of ECOWAS and Nigeria for UN involvement in the operations would have enabled the subregional organisation to diversify both the composition and membership of the force. That way, its integrity and neutrality would have remained largely intact. In other words, as an informed observer put it: "If it had been involved earlier, the UN might have provided the neutrality and legitimacy ... to the operation that is needed from the beginning ... The early interest of the international community could [have helped] to avoid the "capture" of [the] operation by a hegemon like Nigeria".[66]

The less than enthusiastic reaction of the United Nations to the humanitarian emergencies in Liberia and Sierra Leone also confirmed the fears of skeptics that not much had changed in the behaviour of international society. It certainly did not enhance the view that globalisation was weaving a "common humanity" around the globe. ECOMOG's interventions in Liberia and Sierra Leone therefore partly supported the realists' argument that states are often driven by narrow national interests in their responses to situations in the international system. That was the lesson learnt in Rwanda and from French policies in the Great Lakes. How else does one explain the callous attitude of the major European powers toward the Liberian people? For while buccaneering warlords ruthlessly and shamelessly shared out Liberia among themselves, the leading European powers were doing brisk business with them. "France was the leading importer of the estimated 343000 cubic metres of timber that came out of Taylor's territory in 1991-1992. Germany, Britain, Italy, the Netherlands, Spain, Greece, Portugal and Turkey, being the other importers".[67]

By so doing, these states directly and indirectly empowered the rebel factions to continue the wars, and even enhanced their capacity to inflict more violence and suffering on the innocent people of Liberia. This attitude is surely incompatible with the ideals of a fledgling global community, and certainly was contrary to the spirit of humanitarian intervention and peace support operations. The conclusion can therefore be made that while the great powers may be eager to redefine the norms and principles of state behaviour in the post-Cold War era when it suits them, they are still hooked on to old and narrow national role perceptions in their actual behaviour. In this instance, Liberia and Sierra Leone were simply "ignored" because great power vital interests were not directly under threat. In short, the humanitarian tragedies in Liberia and Sierra Leone and elsewhere in Africa would have been minimised, if not entirely avoided, had the great powers reacted promptly and in unison to those crises.

This brings one to the role and behaviour of aid agencies and officials. They certainly sometimes become part of the problem and not the solution. The alleged involvement of the Red Cross in the infiltration of Freetown by rebel RUF/AFRC child soldiers on 6 January 1999 is a case in point. The agency was accused of dispensing hard drugs to child soldiers disguised as "headache" and "stomach pain" tablets.[68] There is also growing unease that aid agencies, and/or their officials, have become too sleek and professional. That is, as they move about in their air-conditioned four-wheel drive vehicles, they may inadvertently be abusing the sensibilities of their hosts. Some of these traits were observed first hand in Monrovia in November-December 1998. There is also a growing perception that aid workers/officials, like any other group of professionals, may in the end just be interested in enhancing their own personal or corporate interests. The Red Cross's alleged role in Sierra Leone, and before that in Biafra in the late 1960s, seems to support this contention. In summary, aid agencies and workers are increasingly portrayed as cultural salesmen and women of their home countries.[69]

A final lesson is that it would be much cheaper for the subregion, and indeed the international community, to prevent similar Liberian and Sierra Leonean disasters if the background conditions that usually lead to the emergence and survival of dictators and tyrants like Doe could be nipped in the bud in the first place. But that is for the future. What should be addressed immediately is the enormous post-war reconstruction and reconciliation tasks that must be carried out in Liberia and Sierra Leone if the swords are to remain sheathed. ECOMOG has done what it could in Liberia and Sierra Leone. The operations were far from perfect, but peace has been restored once again to the two countries. The ball is now squarely in the court of the rest of the world. However, the signs are ominous as the international community has no blueprint for effective post-war reconstruction and reconciliation in the countries. For instance, although ex-combatants were eager to come out of the bush and lay down their arms in accordance with the July 1999 *Lomé Agreement* between the RUF and the government of Sierra Leone, there are no funds available for the disarmament to start, and for the resettlement of these people in civil society.

Effective post-war reconstruction and reconciliation hinge on the successful rehabilitation and reintegration of ex-combatants, including the thousands of child soldiers, into civil society. The Liberian experience is instructive in that since the war formally came to an end in 1997, not much has been done in terms of effective post-war reconstruction and reconciliation. Monrovia has remained without electricity and water supply since 1992, the sewage system has broken down, and most of the houses damaged during the war have not been restored. There is also massive unemployment, especially among the youth. In other words, post-war Liberia can be described as another disaster waiting to happen. Unfortunately, the government of Charles Taylor does not have the capacity or resources to halt the disaster, in spite of the flamboyant presidential rhetoric to the contrary. In fact, Taylor conducts himself more like the president of the NPFL, rather than the father of the Liberian nation. The human rights situation in the country is still appalling. The government acts with impunity, which does not engender confidence in foreign donors who are critical of the country's post-war reconstruction programme. This is perhaps what led to the public destruction of arms and ammunition by Taylor in the presence of leaders from Nigeria and Sierra Leone. It remains to be seen if this stunt will restore confidence in his regime and attract the much-needed foreign assistance to the country. As for Sierra Leone, it is to be hoped that its post-war experiences will be more pleasant than Liberia's.

In the long run, however, the peace and security of each nation and the subregion can be guaranteed only by the establishment of democracy and good governance. Democratic governments are in a better position to cater for the basic human needs of the people and to ensure their full participation in the political process. That way, perceptions that some groups and individuals are more favoured than others, or that they have greater access to political and economic resources than others in their respective states – a major source of post-Cold War conflicts in West Africa and elsewhere in the continent – would be mitigated. Popular participation and accountability on the part of the people and office holders would minimise perceptions of marginalisation, and the desire to overthrow governments by means other than through the ballot box. This is important because the Sierra Leone precedent, that is ECOMOG 11, may not be a lasting one after all. Given the small size of the country's army, the low morale of the army and the people, coupled with the mood of the international community at the time, Nigeria, acting alone, could have achieved the same political objectives in Freetown. Put differently, multilateral intervention in a West African state in future to reinstate a democratically elected government after a successful *coup d'état à la* Sierra Leone, may not be a viable response to the peace and security dilemmas facing the subregion. For there are what one can describe as "untouchables" in West Africa. For instance, a situation where a renegade military government in Ghana or Nigeria, for that matter, would be flushed out by an ECOMOG operation similar to that carried out in Sierra Leone in February 1998, cannot readily be envisaged.

ECOWAS and its member states should therefore devote greater attention to satisfying the basic needs of all their citizens as a more reliable way of guaranteeing peace and security in the subregion and its constituent units. Perhaps the organisation should follow the road of the OAU and take a stern position on regimes that come to power through military *coups*. It should say that such governments will not be allowed to participate in its activities and programmes. Such regimes should actually be suspended from the organisation. This would be a much better deterrent than the Sierra Leone precedent.

Finally, a clear lesson from the ECOMOG experiment is the desirability of a single, subregion-wide conflict management mechanism that commands the support of all members across the anglophone-francophone linguistic divide. Happily, a step in the right direction has already been taken with the adoption of a single conflict prevention and management mechanism by ECOWAS in the first half of 1999. It follows that the existing and competitive structures: the francophone *Non-Aggression and Defence Assistance Agreement* (ANAD), and the ECOWAS MAD, will have to go. Fortunately, both organs have agreed to disband, at least, in principle. But ECOWAS should go beyond the creation of just a single conflict management mechanism in the subregion. The organ should be equipped with a practical sanctions regime to checkmate ambitious (military politicians) who might be tempted to overthrow democratically elected governments in the subregion. Civilian governments whose human rights records are a threat to security and peace should also be the subject of economic and political sanctions. They should be ostracised politically and economically. In addition, the community should not hesitate to mount a campaign of isolation from the rest of the world against such a state or group of states. All things being equal, that should not be difficult to do given the current mood and preference for democratic governments everywhere in the world. Great power backing for such sanctions could act as a credible deterrent not only to military adventurism, but also to budding civilian dictators. The overall effect would be to terminate timeously a situation such as that in Liberia before the civil war. Surely, there were clear signs of the impending disaster in that country. Only no one, including ECOWAS, cared enough to pay attention to it, or to avoid it, until it was much too late. The hope, therefore, is that after two bloody, and perhaps preventable civil wars, the lesson has sunk in properly.

## ENDNOTES

1. For more on this aspect, see Sesay, A, "Conflict and Collaboration: Sierra Leone and her West African Neighbours", in *Afrika Spectrum*, Vol 80, No 2, Hamburg, 1980, pp 31-63.

2. For more about the background conditions and the wars, see, Sesay, A, "Historical background to the Liberian Crisis", in Vogt, M A (ed), *The Liberian Crisis and ECOMOG*, Gabumo Publishing House, Lagos, 1992; and Human Rights Watch, *Easy Prey: Child Soldiers in Liberia*, Human Rights Watch, New York, 1994.

3. Lyons, G M and M Mastanduno, "Introduction", in *Beyond Westphalia*, The Johns Hopkins University Press, London, 1995, p 12.

4. *Ibid*, p 13.

5. *Ibid*.

6. *Ibid*, p 3.

7. *Ibid*.

8. Parekh, B, "Beyond Humanitarian Intervention", *Paper presented at a Workshop on Humanitarian Intervention After the Cold War*, London School of Economics, Department of International Relations, June 1995, p 23. Emphasis added.

9. Wheeler, N J, "Order, Justice, Statecraft and Humanitarian Intervention", *Paper presented at a Workshop on Humanitarian Intervention and International Society*, London School of Economics, 11 June 1994, p 49.

10. Weiss, T and J Chopra, "Sovereignty Under Siege: From Intervention to Humanitarian Space", in Lyons, G M and M Mastanduno, *op cit*, p 111.

11. *Ibid*; p 88.

12. Ducrh, W J and B M Blechman, *Keeping the Peace: The UN in the Emerging World Order*, The Henry L. Stimson Centre, Washington, 1992; and Sesay, A, "Bridges Between Peace-keeping and Conflict Resolution: Confidence Building as Strategies for Managing African Conflicts", in Vogt, MA and LS Aminu (eds), *Peace-*

*keeping as a Security Strategy in Africa: Chad and Liberia as Case Studies*, Fourth Dimension Press, Enugu, 1996.

13. For an assessment of the Operation, see Gosende, R, "Operation Restore Hope: A PostScript", in *Guardian*, Lagos, 14 May 1993.

14. Quoted by Jones, B, in "Intervention Without Borders',: Humanitarian Intervention in Rwanda, 1990-94", in *Millennium*, Vol 24, No 2, Summer 1995, p 38.

15. For more details on this, see Weller, M (ed), *Regional Peacekeeping and International Enforcement: The Liberian Crisis*, University Press, Cambridge, 1994.

16. See for instance, Liebenow, G, *Liberia: The Evolution of Privilege*, Northwestern University Press, Evanston, 1966; and Saigbe Boley, GE, *Liberia: The Rise and Fall of the First Republic*, Macmillan, London, 1983.

17. Clower, R W *et al*, *Growth Without Development*, Northwestern University Press, Evanston, 1966.

18. See Sesay, A, "The Liberian Revolution: Forward March; Stop: About Face Turn", *Conflict Quarterly*, Vol 111, No 4, Summer, 1983, pp 48-71.

19. See Sesay, A, "Societal Inequalities, Ethnic Heterogeneity and Political Instability", *Plural Societies*, Vol 11, No 3, 1980, pp 15-30.

20. *West Africa*, 17 March 1980, pp 468 and 500.

21. See Sesay, A, "The Liberian Revolution: Forward March; Stop; About Face-Turn", *op cit*, pp 48-71.

22. See Sesay, A, "The Liberian Revolution", *op cit*, for details on this.

23. See Sesay, A and A Alao, "Sierra Leone's Forgotten Civil War", *Jane's Intelligence Review*, Vol 7, No 5, May 1995, pp 234-235.

24. For details on this and other aspects of collapsed states in Africa, see Zartman, I W, *Collapsed States*, Lynne Rienner, Boulder, 1995.

25. Quoted in Nwolise, O B C, "The Internationalisation of the Liberian Crisis and its Effects on West Africa", in Vogt, MA (ed), *ECOMOG and the Liberian Crisis*, p 60.

26. Quoted in Weller, M (ed), *Regional Peace-keeping and International Enforcement: The Liberian Crisis, op cit*, p 25.

27. UNHRC, Country Report: Liberia, 18 August 1993, in Weller, M (ed), *Regional Peace-keeping...*, *op cit*, p 365.

28. For various aspects of this conflict, see Vogt, MA (ed.), *ECOMOG and the Liberian Crisis, op cit.*

29. However, to camouflage the Nigerian dominance, his replacements were tagged, "Field Commanders", for details see Adisa, J, "ECOMOG Field Commanders", in Vogt, M A (ed), *ECOMOG and the Liberian Crisis, op cit.*

30. ECOWAS Decision A/Dec. 1/8/90. Emphasis added.

31. *Protocol Relating to Mutual Assistance on Defence*, ECOWAS Secretariat, Lagos.

32. Quoted in Weller, M (ed), *Regional Peacekeeping and International Enforcement, op cit*, pxi.

33. Iweze, C Y, "Nigeria in Liberia: The Military Operations of ECOMOG", in Vogt, MA and AE Ekoko (eds), *Nigeria in International Peacekeeping, 1960-1992*, Malthouse, Lagos, 1993, p 240.

34. *Ibid*, p 245.

35. Press briefing by the President at Dodan Barracks, Lagos, October 31, 1990, titled "The Imperative Features of Nigerian Foreign Policy and the Crisis in Liberia", pp 12-14. Emphasis added.

36. Quoted in *African Concord* (Lagos), 10 August 1992, p 22.

37. Quoted in *ECOWAS Mediation in the Liberian Crisis*, ECOWAS Secretariat, Lagos, p 8.

38. Quoted in *African Concord* (Lagos), 10 August 1992, p 22.

39. For more details on the Union, see Sesay, A, "The Mano River Union: Politics of Dependence or Interdependence?", in Onwuka, R I and A Sesay (eds), *The Future of Regionalism in Africa*, Macmillan Press, London, 1984.

40. Quoted in *African Concord* ( Lagos), 27 August 1990, p 22.

41. The Nigerian leader's contempt for civilians is reflected in his reference to them as "bloody civilians".

42. Parekh, B, "Beyond Humanitarian Intervention", *op cit*, p 23.

43. *Ibid*; p 24.

44. Shaw, C and J Ihonvbere, "Hegemonic Participation in Peacekeeping Operations: The Case of Nigeria in ECOMOG", *International Journal of World Peace*, Vol Xlll, No 2, June 1996, p 45.

45. Iweze, C Y, "Nigeria in Liberia: The Military Operations of ECOMOG", *op cit*, p 245.

46. Yoroms, G and E K Aning, "From Economic to Political Integration: Towards an Analysis of ECOWAS Transition", *Africa Peace Review*, Vol 1, No 2, October 1997, p 47.
47. Quoted in Weller, M (ed) *Regional Peacekeeping and International Enforcement, op cit*, p 374.
48. See BBC and Cable Network News (CNN) Broadcasts in the first two weeks after the invasion, and *The Guardian* (Lagos), various dates after 6 January 1999, for more details.
49. *The Guardian* (Lagos) 25 June 1990.
50. *The Guardian* (Lagos), 15 June 1990.
51. *African Concord*, 27 August, 1990, p 31.
52. Vogt, M A and A.E. Ekoko (eds), *Nigeria in International Peacekeeping, op cit*, p 192.
53. US Permanent Representative to the UN's contribution to Security Council debate on Liberia, quoted in Weller, M (ed), *Regional peace-keeping and International Enforcement, op cit*, p266.
54. Mackinlay, J and A Alao, Liberia 1994: *ECOMOG and UNOMIL Response to a Special Emergency*, The UN University, Occasional Paper, No 1, 1995.
55. This perception is reflected in the title of the first local book on the crisis edited by Vogt, MA, *The Liberian Crisis and ECOMOG: A Bold Attempt at Regional Peacekeeping*.
56. UN Secretary General report to the Security Council on the Liberian situation, quoted in Weller, M (ed), *Regional Peacekeeping and International Enforcement, op cit*, pp 380-388.
57. A Roman Catholic priest was killed in the country in April 1995 in a gun attack. Incidents of armed robberies have generally increased in the country since 1989 when the Liberian war started.
58. For more on ex-combatants and child soldiers in Liberia, see Sesay, A, *et al,* "The Role of Social Support in the rehabilitation of Child Soldiers in Liberia", *Final Report submitted to the United States Institute of Peace*, Washington, D C, September 1999.
59. *West Africa*, 22-28 August 1994, p 1459.
60. US Permanent Representative to the UN, quoted in Weller, M (ed), *Regional Peace Keeping and International Enforcement, op cit*, p 267.
61. Quoted in Gow, J, in "Serbian Nationalism and the Hissssng Sssssnake in International Order: Whose Sovereignty? Which

62. Wheeler, N J, "Order, Justice, Statecraft and Humanitarian Intervention", *op cit*, p 53.
63. Ohlson, T, "The end of the Cold War and Conflict Resolution in Southern Africa", in Siddiqui, R (ed), *Sub-Saharan Africa: A Continent in Transition*, Avesbury, Aldershot, 1993, p 238.
64. Nye, J, quoted in Ohlson, T, "The End of the Cold War and Conflict Resolution in Southern Africa", *op cit*, p 239.
65. *Ibid*, p 239.
66. Article reviewed for *Journal of Conflict Studies*, "ECOMOG and Regional Peace-keeping in Liberia", 1999, p 4.
67. Lowenkopf, M, "Liberia: Putting Back the State Together", in Zartman, W I, *Collapsed States*, *op cit*, p 98.
68. Discussion with Sierra Leonean colleague in Ile-Ife, Nigeria, who was trapped in Freetown during the 6 January 1999 invasion of the city by RUF/AFRC rebels.
69. The Red Cross was also accused of supplying arms to Ojukwu's Biafra during the Nigerian civil war, 1967-1970. For an insightful study of the role of Western aid agencies in a recent conflict, see Urvin, P, *Aiding Violence: The Development Enterprise in Rwanda*, Kumarian Press, Connecticut, 1999.

(continued from previous note)
Nation?", *The Slavonic and East European Review*, 72, 3 July, p 475. Emphasis added.

## Chapter 6

# CENTRAL AFRICAN MILITARY INTERVENTIONS IN THE 1990s: THE CASE OF THE DRC

Heinrich Matthee

## 1. INTRODUCTION

Thousands of fighters from at least eight African states and several insurgent groups are involved in a war in the Democratic Republic of the Congo (DRC). This chapter investigates some of the dynamics of military intervention by foreign African governments in the Congo.

The role of regional dynamics and the successful military intervention in the Congo during 1996-1997 are discussed. The links between military intervention since 1998 and the limited authority of the state in the DRC, the weak economic base and the volatile security situation under President Laurent Kabila are investigated too.

The chapter explores the cascading conflict of foreign intervention, domestic rebellion and peasant war. The consequences and implications of foreign intervention for the DRC are discussed, as well as the resumption of winner-takes-all politics.

## 2. HISTORICAL BACKGROUND

### 2.1 Regional dynamics

The Democratic Republic of the Congo, also known as Congo Kinshasa, is situated in Central Africa. The country shares its land borders of ten thousand kilometres with eight other countries, namely Rwanda, Uganda, Burundi, Sudan, Central African Republic, Congo-Brazzaville, Zambia and Angola.

Differentiated communities like the Tutsi live on both sides of the borders, drawn by the European colonial powers during the 19$^{th}$ century. The long borders, limited policing of borders and the fluidity of populations strengthen the effect of economic and political events in one country on other countries in the region.

Tutsi-Hutu animosities in the region had such a spillover effect before.[1] Tutsis and Hutus live in the eastern DRC, western Tanzania, southern Uganda, Rwanda and Burundi. In 1994 hundreds of thousands of Tutsi and Hutu moderates were massacred by Hutu soldiers and youth militia in Rwanda. Only a Tutsi military under Paul Kagame stopped the genocide, but fear of revenge by the Tutsi caused over a million Hutus to pour into the eastern part of the neighbouring Congo.

Thousands of Rwandan Hutu ex-soldiers and militiamen settled among the unarmed Hutus in border camps, and these armed groups used the cover of the refugee camps to launch attacks against Tutsi settlements in the region. President Mobutu Sese Seko, the ruler of Congo Kinshasa, angered the rulers of Rwanda by not doing anything to separate the refugees from the insurgents or to stop the attacks from his territory.

Similarly, the Ugandan government of Yoweri Museveni had to contend with insurgent groups supported by Sudan and operating from Congo Kinshasa.[2] The Rwandese Vice-President, Paul Kagame, had been Museveni's chief of intelligence during the latter's insurgency campaign in Uganda and there was regular communication between the two leaders.

Ethnic Tutsis had resided for generations in the east of Congo Kinshasa, known as Zaïre during the rule of President Mobutu. The government of President Mobutu attempted to deprive them of citizenship and to dislodge them from the land they occupied. Local groups like the Hunde and Nande also used the opportunity to violently pursue land claims against these Tutsis. When an estimated two thousand Congolese Tutsis were massacred in 1996, the eastern Congolese Tutsis, Rwanda and Uganda became allies to end Mobutu's 30 years of rule in Congo Kinshasa.

## 2.2 Rebellion and military intervention 1996-1997

The campaign of the Alliance of Democratic Forces for the Liberation of Congo-Zaïre (AFDL) started on 10 October 1996. The AFDL consisted of several groups, including a group led by Laurent Kabila, a veteran Maoist guerrilla opponent of Mobutu. Kabila was known to Museveni and Kagame and used as a Zairian spokesman for the rebellion.[3] Nevertheless, the foreign military intervention by the Ugandan and Rwandan rulers overshadowed the domestic rebellion.

The vanguard of the AFDL forces consisted of Rwandan and Congolese Tutsis. Mobutu's undisciplined and socially fragmented army was quickly routed. Under pressure from the victorious AFDL forces, Mobutu's generals intervened domestically to end the war. Mobutu fled and the AFDL installed Kabila as the new ruler of Congo Kinshasa in May 1997.

## 2.3 The significance of the war of 1996-1997

The successful campaign of the AFDL in 1996-1997 influenced the context of the 1998 conflict. While the rebellion did not change the political system of patronage, the Tutsi group became the group favoured by the state, replacing Mobutu's Ngwandi group.

The quick and successful campaigns of the rebel forces revealed the lack of government authority outside Kinshasa. The Ugandan and Rwandan leaders also demonstrated their military ability to influence who would rule the third largest country in Africa. The rebellion did not change the historical fact that the government in Kinshasa needed foreign support and mercenaries to survive local challenges to its authority.

The rebellion of 1996-1997 left a legacy of disruption and militarisation in Congolese society. The number of refugees in the region increased. As the AFDL forces advanced through the country, they recruited and militarised the many teenagers who had marginal roles only in traditional communities and the system of patronage.

In addition, the rebellion meant that the new ruler was indebted financially to the rulers of Uganda, Rwanda, Angola and Zimbabwe. The Kabila government had to honour new contracts, entered into with mining companies in exchange for financial support during the rebellion. The cost of the war effort further depleted the limited funds of state structures and left Kabila with even fewer means to ensure allegiance by client networks.

In addition to limited funds for patronage, Kabila could not rely on a strong personal network in Kinshasa itself. Most of his officials came from the east or from exile. Many soldiers of Mobutu's army also survived, forming a nucleus of potential resistance to the new ruler. The conflict provided the opportunity to establish a distinctive Tutsi zone of influence that could accommodate the potentially disruptive Tutsi interests outside the established state. Eventually, however, the rebellion reinforced the statist framework.

## FACTORS FAVOURING MILITARY INTERVENTION

### 3.1 The limited reach of state structures in the DRC

The Democratic Republic of the Congo (DRC) is a huge territory of 2,35 million square kilometres, limited technological ability and a large diverse population of forty five million people. The vast river basins and dense rainforests of the DRC have limited roads, railways or communication links. The roads go no further than one hundred kilometres outside the capital, steamships and barges provide transport on the Congo River and less than 10 per cent of the country has electricity.[4]

Governance in this extensive postcolonial country includes colonial state structures. After coming to power, Kabila promised a list of democratic reforms before certain dates in his inaugural address. However, no deadlines were met and the security of Kabila and his regime remained predominant. Political activity was suspended and Kabila was given absolute power over policy and appointments for a two-year period before elections. Kabila appointed Sakombi Inongo, the orchestrator of the Mobutu personality cult, as his communications adviser and Maoist education was introduced for the state administration.[5]

Political opposition to strong Tutsi influence prompted Kabila to weaken the Tutsi and Kasai leadership element in the government. At the beginning of January 1998 Kabila carried out a major cabinet reshuffle in terms of which he gave fellow

Katangan decisive influence in the cabinet. Like Mobutu, Kabila started to build up a personal security unit, this time composed of his fellow Katangans. The presidential office and the military also remained the main beneficiaries of the state budget.

Kabila effectively neutralised the parliamentary opposition and controlled the capital of Kinshasa through the military and a small network of mainly Katangan associates.[6] Legitimation occurred through costly patronage to some clients while the eastern provinces were excluded from the same benefits. The presidential network had information about what was going on in the rest of the country but there was limited ability to implement policies outside the capital.

The state structures were neopatrimonial: In spite of the colonial heritage of bureaucratic state structures, there was no clear distinction between public and private spheres and a strong personalisation of power relationships around Kabila.[7] The narrow symbiosis between state structures and a limited number of social networks meant that the state was too weak to spend the limited state funds equitably and independently from these networks.[8]

## 3.2 The legacy of economic weakness

After the end of the 1980s the country experienced a rapid decline in its formal economic sphere, with a significant drop in measurable mining and agriculture output and a reduced tax base.[9] Informal markets in the country provided a means to escape taxation by a predatory state. In addition, Mobutu also sought opportunities and resources for supporters in informal markets. The state endured because of the networks and alliances that had been built, but the state's resource base remained weak.[10]

The presidential network used its links to the formal and informal economy for enrichment. The wealth was used for private purposes, to build patron-clients relations and to buy off some opposition. Money was often not used for development but rather to establish symbolic authority over competing networks by conspicuous consumption. As a result, the infrastructure outside Kinshasa was often allowed to decay, which meant that the eastern Kivu provinces became virtually cut off from central state services.

The weakness of state structures led to a loss of political control over the population and over economic space in the Kivu provinces. Commodities and the currencies of neighbours such as Rwanda and Uganda were used in a huge informal trade zone.[11] Neighbouring rulers and their clients had interests in the formal and informal markets.

Under Kabila's rule, hyperinflation of 567 per cent was cut to 14 per cent. Little money was available to help finance the state apparatus. Kabila started to cancel mineral concessions and contracts unilaterally, insisting on either nationalisation of assets or new contracts at additional payments.[12] The unilateral cancellation of mining concessions by Kabila led to legal action against his government by mining companies, but also to support from some business groups for Kabila's adversaries.

Kabila inherited an economically weakened state that remained vulnerable to the economic advances of neighbours in the border regions. Because of limited income from tax, foreign aid and mining concessions, the state structures continued to be impoverished and were unable to implement plans for economic renewal.

## 3.3 Local ambitions for wealth and power

Apart from central state structures, some local power structures from the precolonial and colonial era persisted in the postcolonial state. Regional and ethnic consciousness among the more than two hundred language groups was not only a political force in itself, but actually a channel through which competition for wealth, power and status was expressed.[13]

Some local power structures in Katanga/Shaba, Kasai and the eastern Kivu provinces crystallised around resources, trade routes and clan networks. These structures became semi-autonomous over time. Competition and conflict over resources, including three percent of the arable land and rich reserves of diamonds, cobalt and copper, remained a strong driving force in politics in local and state structures in the country.

Thanks to the military intervention by Rwanda and Uganda, Kabila came to power and changed the name of the state from Zaïre to the Democratic Republic of the Congo. However, he did not fundamentally change the political order of Mobutu's thirty two years of rule during the short period of major peace in the DRC.

The DRC was the strongest structure in a patchwork of power zones. Kabila's power in and around Kinshasa rested on military force, foreign support, patronage, a personal network and the exclusion of some groups from state service and patronage.[14] The concentration of control over many resources in state structures and the exclusion of different groups from the benefits of state patronage made it attractive to the excluded groups to try to take over Kinshasa.

## 3.4 The fragmented military

Kabila wanted to strengthen his hold on power by creating a new military structure. He had to achieve cohesion between diverse groups, including exiles from Angola, Katangese youths, Congolese Tutsis and ex-Mobutu soldiers. The challenge was even greater because military cohesion had to be improved while local conflicts still raged in the semi-autonomous Katanga and the eastern provinces.

Fighters from the Bembe, Hunde, Nande and other groups, known as Simba rebels in the 1960s and mai-mai militia in the 1990s, initially formed part of the Tutsi-driven AFDL because they wanted more autonomy to protect their resources. A number of Rwandan and Congolese Tutsis acted like occupiers after Kabila's victory in 1997, harassing and humiliating local populations, seizing movable property, demoting local chiefs and obtaining the best state administration posts.[15]

Frustrated by what they perceived as Tutsi domination, local militias increasingly helped Ugandan, Rwandan and Burundi rebel groups. In September 1997 these militias attacked Congolese Tutsis in the east and thousands subsequently fled to Rwanda. Despite signed security agreements between the Kabila government and Uganda, Rwanda and Burundi, rebel movements from these three countries continued to use Congolese territory as bases. Sometimes the rebels were even escorted by elements of the Congolese army.

During the ongoing local conflicts, Kabila's army fragmented into factions reflecting different social interests.[16] Different pay scales between Tutsi, Katangese and ex-Mobutu soldiers, and favouritism towards soldiers from Kabila's home region, provoked rivalries and clashes. Like the Mobutu regime, the Kabila government had no military hierarchy with the ability to control the situation.[17] Nonpayment of salaries also became an issue. The economic weakness of state structures made it difficult to improve the situation.

## 3.5 The allies fall out

Initially the support of the Ugandan and Rwandan governments acted as a security net for the Kabila government with its small power base in Kinshasa. According to Kabila's intelligence chief during the rebellion, Pascal Mukeba, Kabila signed a pact with the Rwandese Tutsi government on 23 October 1996, in return for military support during the rebellion. In terms of the pact Kabila would give the Congo's eastern region to the Tutsi minority on both sides of the border when he came to power.[18]

If this were true and politically feasible, it would have meant that the Congolese Tutsis would acquire their own safe haven. The Rwandan Tutsi forces would also have been able to encircle the Hutu militia that regularly attacked Tutsi settlements.

However, Kabila did not carry out his undertaking. The continued visible presence in the DRC of mainly Rwandan foreign officers and Kagame's claim that Rwanda had played a decisive role in the 1996-1997 war, started to embarrass Kabila politically, since it made him look like a Rwandan frontman.

Local discontent and conflicts with Tutsi soldiers in the new Congolese army grew steadily. Kabila started to weaken the Tutsi element in his government while strengthening the position of people from his own region, Katanga. He also planned the incorporation of Hutu fighters in his military as a counter to the Tutsi presence.[19]

Opposition to Kabila emerged inside the AFDL leadership and within the military. The political dissidents were sidelined by Kabila and closely watched. According to Ernest Wamba dia Wamba, the political dissidence was unable to assume an organisational form and never went beyond relations based on friendship and ethnic or regional belonging. The military dissidence started to focus on a coup against Kabila.[20]

The limited authority of the state in the vast DRC, the legacy of economic weakness, local ambitions for power and wealth, and the fragmented military created a power vacuum in the eastern DRC. This situation was favourable for military intervention.

## 4. THE COURSE OF MILITARY INTERVENTION

### 4.1 The threat to Kabila

By July 1998 there were rumours in Kinshasa of an invasion by the armies of Rwanda and Uganda.[21] On 11 July the Rwandan, James Kabarere, was replaced as chief of staff. Reports of a *coup d'état* against Kabila emerged and on 26 July Kabila ordered the remaining Rwandese soldiers to leave Congo Kinshasa.

Cross-border movements by Ugandan and Rwandan troops increased. On 2 August, Congolese Tutsi and Rwandan soldiers tried to take over two military bases in Kinshasa. Tutsi-led army units in the east rebelled and attacks on government installations and Hutu militia started almost simultaneously in the eastern areas of Goma, Bukavu and Uvira.[22]

Simultaneously, anti-Tutsi sentiments erupted in Kinshasa and were fanned by the Kabila government to mobilise opposition against the rebels. Hundreds of Tutsi were arrested and some lynched. On 5 August the *Rassemblement Congolais pour la Democratie* (RCD), or Congolese Rally for Democracy, emerged as the main rebel group under Ernest Wamba dia Wamba.

The roots of the conflict after August 1998 were similar to those of the conflict of 1996-1997. The Congolese Tutsis were still not recognised as Congolese citizens and were harassed while the Kinshasa government remained inactive. Insurgent groups were again allowed to attack Rwandan and Ugandan citizens from the Congo.

The course of the conflict also showed similarities with the conflict of 1996-1997. The military campaign started in the east and was conducted by an alliance of different Congolese groups. As before, the rebel alliance was fashioned by Rwanda and Uganda with Congolese and Rwanda Tutsi fighters forming the vanguard.

The rebel alliance included three political groups. Two groups focused on the overthrow of Kabila, namely ex-Mobutists who wanted to regain power and AFDL revisionists who had been sidelined by Kabila. A third group headed by Wamba emphasised the building of political institutions to create an alternative political order too.

The Rwandan military tried to maintain its hold on the RCD through the Congolese rebel forces and some leaders of the RCD. The pressing security concerns of Rwandan Tutsis and military action were prioritised, not the domestic political concerns of the Congolese participants. The RCD forces launched a quick military campaign and soon captured the capital cities of the eastern provinces, just as the AFDL forces had done before.[23] While there were pockets of resistance left in the east, the RCD forces dominated the eastern third of the country.

Early in August James Kabarere, Kabila's Tutsi chief of staff who had earlier been dismissed, hijacked three aeroplanes and dispatched four hundred Rwandese troops to the Kitona airbase, two thousand kilometres away, to open another front in the west. The twenty thousand troops from Kabila's army at Kitona, most of them ex-Mobutu soldiers not yet integrated into Kabila's new army, joined the rebellion. By mid-August the RCD forces were engaging Kabila's military reserves, only fifty km away from Kinshasa.[24]

## 4.2 New alliances and the survival of Kabila

Kabila appealed to African governments to intervene on his behalf. The Congo owed a war debt of several million dollars to Zimbabwe and the Zimbabweans were concerned about repayment in the event of Kabila's overthrow. The business interests of some of President Mugabe's associates and senior officers were at risk too.[25] Mugabe, whose prominence as a regional leader between 1980 and 1994 had been eclipsed by South Africa's President Mandela, saw the Congolese events as an opportunity to regain domestic and regional stature.[26]

No direct Zimbabwean security interests were threatened inside the Congo. Nevertheless, when approached by Kabila for help, the Zimbabwean ruler, Robert Mugabe, did not consult his parliament and ignored the Zimbabwean constitution which stated the military could be used only in defence of the country. He unilaterally commited his troops to the conflict.

The Angolan government, which had supported Mobutu's overthrow, was concerned about the involvement of Mobutist generals, soldiers and politicians in the rebellion. The Angolan government also recognised that a stable Congo Kinshasa would secure Angola's border against a growing UNITA insurgent threat from Congolese bases. The Angolan government wanted to increase its chances of restoring the Benguela railway line, and oil and diamond business.

The involvement of the Angolan government in August 1998 was contrary to an earlier arrangement with the Rwandan government not to intervene. The Angolan president, who did not want a full-scale war with UNITA in Angola, may have tried to deny hardline military figures the opportunity to move soldiers elsewhere. At the same time, depressed oil prices and tight credit lines restricted the development of offshore oilfields, which meant that Angola had limited funds for a war.[27] As the conflict continued, Kabila negotiated mining concessions with Angola to ensure continuing Angolan support.[28]

On 19 August the Organ on Politics, Defence and Security of the Southern Africa Development Community (SADC), of which the DRC had become a member, responded positively to a request for assistance by Kabila. Since there was no mutual defence pact or separate protocol, the basis for the assistance was not completely covered by the SADC framework.[29]

Nevertheless, the governments of Angola, Zimbabwe, Namibia, Sudan and Chad became Kabila's main supporters, with political support from a number of francophone West African countries.[30] The governments of Rwanda, Burundi and Uganda, however, continued to support the opposition. Kabila's successful request for foreign support led to the most spectacular example in the 20th century of direct military intervention by African governments in another African country. (See map.)

## 4.3 The experiences of the Angolan and Zimbabwean forces

The Angolan and Zimbabwean forces saved Kabila and stopped the RCD advance on the western front, where Angola suffered substantial losses. The Angolan forces were deployed

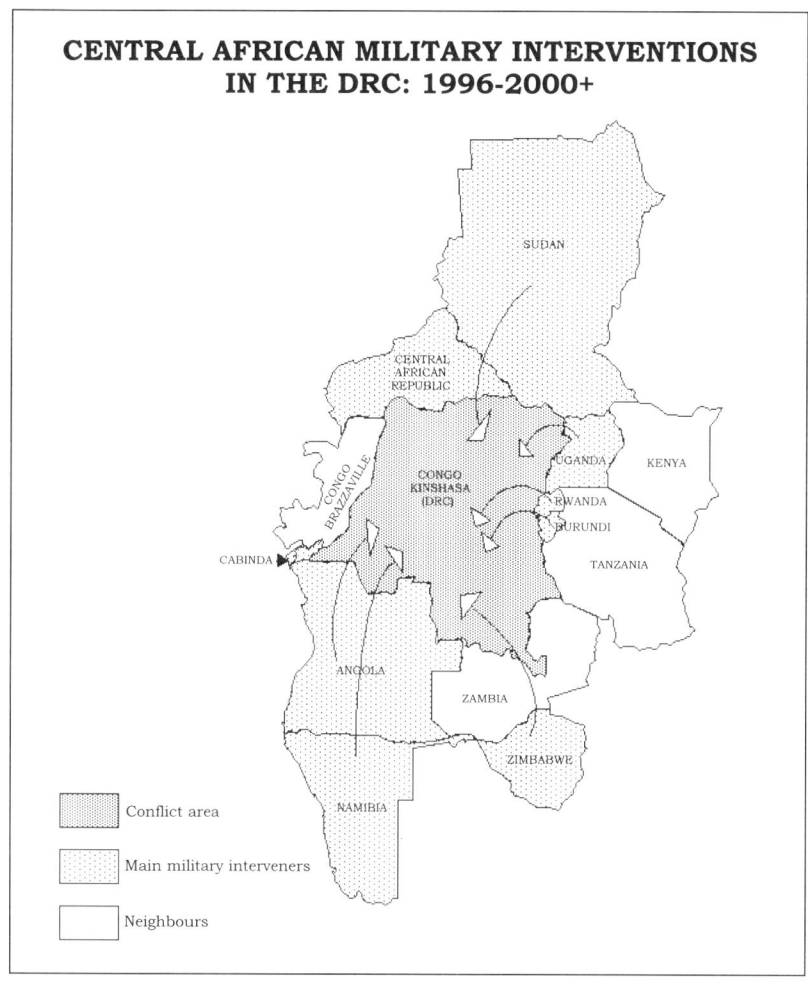

in defence of Angolan security interests in the western Congo Kinshasa, while the Zimbabwean forces were deployed in the east. By September 1998 the Angolan government indicated an interest in a ceasefire.

Differences arose between the allies on the political situation in the Congo. For example, the Angolan government, in opposition to Kabila, said that peace talks should include the issue of the citizenship of Congolese Tutsis. Kabila's allies came to his aid unilaterally, not as part of a regional structure. Military co-ordination was therefore difficult, especially because of the poor condition of the Congolese forces.

Kabila's forces had weak military intelligence following the destruction of Mobutu's intelligence service in 1996-1997. Allegations of widespread bribery by rebels, desertion and alienation of the civilian population as a result of looting were made against Kabila's troops.[31] The Angolan and Zimbabwean forces sometimes found their Congolese allies as obstructive as their rebel adversaries.

Angola allegedly had more troops and much larger military budgets than Rwanda and Uganda combined. Angola, Zimbabwe and Sudan also had some military capability in the air, whereas Uganda and Rwanda had virtually none.[32] Nevertheless, the advantages of Kabila's allies did not necessarily have a large impact.

Some of the allied troops, acquainted with the more arid bush environments of southern Africa, struggled in the Congo's tropical conditions. The tropical climate's unpredictability, heavy rains, landmines and bad roads undermined planning and impeded the large-scale movement of mechanised troops in September 1998.[33] Tropical infections and snakebites also affected the troops negatively.

The RCD often launched surprise offensives under the cover of bad weather to neutralise the air advantage of Kabila's allies. One such offensive led to the fall of the important town of Kindu to the rebels in October 1998.

The unexpected surge in UNITA activity in late 1998 influenced Angola's force deployment in the DRC. Despite UN sanctions, UNITA controlled sixty to seventy percent of diamond production in Angola, raising an estimated US $3.7 billion from diamond sales since 1992. UNITA had an edge on the government in that it did not have to run a state administration but could use all its resources for its war machine. UNITA had used the time after the Lusaka peace accord to rearm and was ready to demonstrate that it could not be destroyed by government offensives.[34]

Eventually there was a substantial withdrawal of Angolan troops from the DRC to enable the government to counter UNITA insurgents inside Angola. The December 1998 offensive against UNITA headquarters in the Angolan central highlands failed disastrously. Almost all the territory handed over to the MPLA after the Lusaka accords returned to UNITA's control. UNITA advanced on different fronts and the Angolan government requested more assistance from Cuban soldiers.[35]

In February 1999 Angola withdrew most of its troops, air support and logistical support from the Congo to resist the UNITA advance inside Angola. Unlike the Angolan forces, the Zimbabwean forces were deployed in the east of the DRC, acquiring economic benefits from hard currency allowances, black marketeering and mining ventures.[36] The number of Zimbabwean troops was eventually increased substantially to almost ten thousand. However, the departure of Angolan troops left the Kabila alliance vulnerable and many Zimbabwean soldiers were withdrawn to defend the area between the river port Matadi and the capital Kinshasa.

In financially stricken Zimbabwe, the high cost and limited success of Zimbabwean offensives against the RCD in the east strengthened Mugabe's political opposition among the population, trade unions and the military.[37] A serious Zimbabwean defeat at Manono in June 1999 increased the precariousness of the expensive and unsuccessful military venture.

## 4.4 Security and economic enterprise

On the rebel side, the military rulers of Rwanda and Uganda were the major foreign actors. Similar to the rebellion of 1996-1997, the Rwandan Tutsi rulers saw threats by Hutu fighters in 1998 as the signal to send troops to the east of the Congo. The security of Tutsi communities in the region was the prime motivation for Rwandan participation in the conflict.

Much of the fighting of the RCD forces was done by Rwandan and Ugandan soldiers. Uganda and Rwanda could count, to some extent, on indirect financial and military support from the United Stated of America (USA). The two countries also had strong logistical capabilities.[38] The early deployment of substantial Ugandan forces deep inside the Congo distinguished the 1998 conflict from the 1996-1997 conflict, when Uganda's involvement was less visible.

Similar to 1996-1997, Museveni wanted to weaken the Congo-based Ugandan rebel groups on the Congolese side of the border. The intervention of Sudan on Kabila's side constituted another direct threat to Uganda's security interests.[39] Ugandan troops also fought soldiers from Chad at Bulia, Equateur, some 1 400 kilometres from the border that had to be secured.[40] This incongruity indicated military necessity or personal animosity towards Kabila, who had turned against his erstwhile mentor Museveni.

Uganda, looking for stability in the Congo to expand its trade interests, exported more Congolese gold in 1998 than any other state in the region.[41] There were allegations that several companies operating in eastern Congo had Ugandan and Rwandan military shareholders. Rwanda, although it did not produce diamonds, exported them. The conflict enabled some actors to accumulate wealth.[42] In some areas and periods, the intervention did not aim to defeat Kabila's forces but rather to run risky economic enterprises.

## 5. DOMESTIC DYNAMICS DURING THE CONFLICT

### 5.1 Kabila as ethnic entrepreneur

To recruit people to his banner, the erstwhile Marxist Kabila became an entrepreneur of ethnic emotions. To this end, he used a dualistic discourse that divided all forces between a Bantu front and a Hima or Nilotic front. Museveni and Kagame were accused of wanting to establish a Hima/Nilotic empire in the region.[43]

Kabila's communication media promoted anti-Tutsi feelings, which led to lynchings of Tutsis in different towns in the DRC. The Hutu-Tutsi construct of antagonistic identity was eventually replaced by a regional Bantu-Nilotic construct of antagonistic identity.

The Hutus were considered part of Kabila's Bantu front. During and after the 1996-1997 conflict Rwandan Hutus suffered substantial losses at the hands of Kabila's alliance. Nevertheless, the former Hutu fighters of Rwanda, many of them involved in the anti-Tutsi genocide of 1994, were brought in from neighbouring countries. They were rearmed, retrained and deployed in the northeast and southeast of the Congo.[44]

Not only ethnic identity constructs re-emerged during the conflict. Religious identity constructs, based on understandings of Christianity or Islam, also played a role in the mobilisation of fighters. Interpretations of African traditional religion affected the conduct of members of the RCD rebel movement as well as the mai-mai militia.[45]

## 5.2 The hidden peasant war

The mai-mai militia became part of the anti-Tutsi campaign. Similar to the 1996-1997 rebellion, local Bembe, Hunde and Nande militias temporarily joined Hutu militias in attacking Congolese and Rwandan Tutsi forces in the east. In December 1998 the rebels lost the town of Fizi to anti-Tutsi local militia. In reaction, the rebel alliance negotiated with some local groups to reduce resistance to the RCD administration. Some local militia leaders became part of the RCD structures.

The local militia was perceived as consisting of three main groups. However, their leaders and numbers were difficult to identify and their fighting was often unpredictable and sporadic. The war by local militias for territory and resources, sometimes against Kabila's forces and sometimes against the rebels, had the features of a peasant war subsumed in the Tutsi-driven rebellion and the conflict between foreign interventionist forces.

The Tutsi presence was just as unpopular as Kabila's rule.[46] Nevertheless, because of business interests, ethnic links and the proximity of supportive Rwandan Tutsis, the rebel alliance was better placed to maintain some control in the east than the Kinshasa government ever was.

## 5.3 The rebel split

The rebel advance slowed towards the end of 1998. Internal factions competed for control and differed on the ways to gain the support of the populations of conquered territories. Wamba, an aged but respected African historian, did not have the charisma or shrewdness needed to keep the rebel politicians together.

Wamba's analysis of the position of the rebels was succinct: "We think that we cannot permit president Kabila to win the military victory because that is going to aggravate our problem. The dictatorship will be entrenched... This does not mean, however, that we are interested in military victory either. We are interested in political victory. So that's why we have to do all we can to pressurise and get the other side to negotiate with us."[47]

The Ugandans were not impressed by the academic approach of the Wamba leadership.[48] In October 1998 the Congolese Liberation Movement (MLC) of populist businessman-politician Jean-Pierre Bemba was established in Equateur province on the northern front. Bemba, who came from the region, was the only leader to have organised local elections in the Congo since May 1997. The MLC enjoyed ex-Mobutist and Ugandan support as well too.

On the southern front, the different factions in the RCD started to split up. Wamba denounced the looting and plundering of resources by military-business networks. Lunda Bululu, a strong leadership figure, was criticised for taking too many unilateral decisions, including the allocation of mineral concessions.

Wamba wanted the war to be conducted as a people's war: training people while also making them stakeholders in building political institutions. His goal was not merely the overthrow of Kabila, but the establishment of a new political order. The pressing short-term security concerns of the Rwandan military, the dominant actor on the southern front, contrasted with this approach.

A Rwandan-directed campaign to marginalise Wamba in the RCD started and eventually succeeded. In May the RCD officially split. Dr. Emile Ilunga, a veteran of the Katangan attacks against Mobutu in the 1970s and 1980s and a member of the AFDL, became the leader of the so-called RCD-Goma. The RCD did not represent all Congolese Tutsis. Dissident Congolese Tutsi factions led by Joseph Mutembo and Muller Ruhimbaka attempted to distance themselves from the worst anti-Hutu abuses of the Rwandan Tutsi military.[49]

Wamba established a RCD-Kisangani headquarters under Ugandan protection. His focus on a long-term development of cadres, political institutions and resistance to Kabila suited the Ugandan actors too. Uganda had less pressing security concerns than the Rwandan Tutsi military, for whom survival was literally at stake. Uganda wanted a stable Congo to strengthen Uganda's trade interests in the east.

There were rumours in Rwanda about the pre-occupation of senior Ugandan military officers with their business relationships with Bemba's rebels. Serious power clashes occurred between Rwandan and Ugandan soldiers at the end of 1998.[50]

## 5.4 Military intervention and non-combatants in the DRC

In spite of the wide-ranging military intervention in the DRC, the fighting was sporadic and the casualties relatively light. The conflict was experienced differently in different areas of the DRC.

Journalists in Kinshasa reported that citizens had to stop when the presidential cavalcade drove past and people were careful not to say anything. Outside the eastern Congo and Kinshasa some people were told that there was no war, merely an operation against traitors. In the combat areas there were periods of intense fighting and long lulls in the fighting. In contrast to the enthusiastic welcome of anti-Mobutu soldiers in 1997, the people seemed to be tired of suffering and war.[51]

The existing refugee problem in the region was exacerbated by the conflict. The extensive intervention meant that more areas were affected by the conflict than would have been the case in a local rebellion. Forces from both sides perpetrated civilian massacres and thousands of Congolese military and civilian refugees fled into neighbouring states including Zambia and Congo-Brazzaville.[52]

In the Congo, the breakdown of the health infrastructure and the depletion of medical supplies in certain areas aggravated the effect of epidemics. The conflict prevented anything being done about the pollution that was emanating from some of Kinshasa's industries. The military intervention and broader conflict therefore had many negative consequences for non-combatants.

## 6. FRAGILE PEACE IN THE DRC

### 6.1 The ceasefire process

Exhaustion of resources and the military stalemate prompted the different parties to the conflict to engage in a ceasefire process, which culminated in the signing of a ceasefire agreement in July 1999 by all governments involved. The upshot was a situation, with the rebels dominating the east and parts of the north, but far from Kinshasa, and with Kabila largely on the defensive.

Article III of the agreement, headed "Principles of the Agreement", addressed the main concerns of parties to the conflict. For Kabila, Paragraph 15 confirmed that no division of the DRC would occur along the lines of the military stalemate. Paragraph 12 stated that the final withdrawal of all foreign troops from the DRC would occur in accordance with a fixed calendar.

For Rwanda and Uganda, Paragraph 17 stated that all parties would take all the necessary steps to control the infiltration of armed groups and arms trafficking along the Congolese border. Paragraph 22, read with Chapter 8 of Annexure A, stated that militias, including those suspected of genocide, would be screened, disarmed and genocide suspects handed over to the International War Crimes Tribunal for Rwanda.[53]

For the rebel groups, Paragraph 16 re-affirmed the equal rights and protection of the Congolese Tutsis. Paragraph 19, read with Chapter 5 of Annexure A, confirmed that the Kabila government, the rebel groups, the unarmed opposition and civil society representatives would enter into an equal and open national dialogue. The Congolese actors were to agree upon the rules and timetable of the negotiations, the formation of a new amalgamated military, the new state institutions, an election process and the draft of the new constitution.[54]

## 6.2 The struggle continues

After the ceasefire agreement in July 1999, isolated incidents of violence between Kabila's forces and the rebel forces were still reported.[55] Competition over the rebel leadership and access to resources led to clashes between Ugandan and Rwandan forces in Kisangani in August 1999. Foreign African delegations visited Kisangani to gauge the level of popular support for Wamba and fighting occurred over Ugandan control of the airport and city centre. Kabila tried to deepen divisions between Uganda and Rwanda by making a separate peace offer to Uganda, but failed. At the end of 1999, the Ugandan and Rwandan governments cemented renewed political and military co-operation between the anti-Kabila forces during a series of meetings.[56]

Military mobilisation, troop movements and violent clashes occurred throughout 1999 and well into 2000. All parties breached the ceasefire agreement, and Kabila used the breathing space to rearm by bartering mineral concessions for a variety of military hardware. The arming of unemployed youths and the mai-mai militia, reinforcement of the Zimbabwean forces and the bombings of rebel positions occurred.

During late September 1999, fighters from Rwanda and RCD-Goma attacked Hutu militia and moved to the central Kasai region to counter possible new offensives by Kabila's forces. In October Kabila attacked RCD-Goma and MLC positions, and in November 1999 mai-mai militia, supplied from the air by Kabila, attacked the RCD-Kisangani. In November 1999 the RCD-Kisangani and the MLC renounced the ceasefire.

Hutu fighters from Burundi and Rwanda present in the DRC, supposed to be disarmed in terms of the peace accord, were encouraged by Kabila to relocate elsewhere. The Hutu fighters have contributed to an upsurge in fighting against the Tutsi-dominated and anti-Kabila government in Burundi.[57]

The Joint Military Council established in terms of the ceasefire was unable to resolve the siege of Zimbabwean and Namibian forces by Rwandan-backed forces at Ikela. Violations of the ceasefire have already occurred and will probably continue. Several actors perceive an advantage in continued conflict. Kabila, who distrusts the effect of a negotiated settlement on his position at this stage, has used the ceasefire merely to prepare for new offensives. Many Hutu militia, implicated in the 1994 Rwandan genocide, have much to lose from the implementation of the ceasefire. Some mai-mai militia perceive an opportunity to advance their peasant interests. Hutu and mai-mai militia have consequently become important components of Kabila's forces.

Many of the leaders of the anti-Kabila forces link the pursuit of their interests to the removal of Kabila from the political scene. They do not believe that Kabila will voluntarily relinquish power after negotiations, so military force seems the only solution.[58] In addition, on all sides there are militarised economic enterprises that profit from continued conflict and little control by the government in Kinshasa.

Civilian suffering and continued armed conflicts over wealth and power have overshadowed the ceasefire. Even an implemented ceasefire at this stage will do little more than freeze the military stalemate between the opposing forces, with the rebel alliance still occupying towns and areas in the east and northwest.

### 6.3 Limited international leverage

The Kabila government restricted the movements of the UN observer mission that was authorised by the Security Council in August 1999. The forty military liaison officers could seldom confirm the military build-up of Kabila's forces in the first months after the ceasefire agreement or local press reports of human rights abuses by various parties.[59]

In February 2000 the Security Council in terms of Resolution 1291 expanded the observer mission by authorising more than 5500 UN troops to monitor the ceasefire. If the combatants in the DRC are willing to see them deployed and if the troops are indeed contributed, the full deployment of the force may still take several months. The force will be unable to protect many civilians in the vast territory.[60]

Section 11 of Resolution 1291 requests the UN Secretary General to continue to plan for additional deployments. An expensive force of tens of thousands of troops with the ability to communicate and to move supplies and people in a large country with little infrastructure would be needed for effective peacekeeping. The most powerful UN member states are reluctant to commit their own military personnel to a peace-keeping exercise in the DRC.

A cautious and piecemeal international approach to the situation in the DRC is evident, perhaps as a result of the difficulties experienced by UN forces in Somalia, Bosnia and Angola. International leverage on the domestic and regional situation has proved very limited and will remain so for a long time.

## 6.4 Winner-takes-all struggle in the DRC

The DRC still has a neopatrimonial political order based on state patronage of select groups and networks. The concentration of control over resources in state structures makes it attractive to excluded groups not to settle for anything less than a take-over of the state. Elite political pacts and compromise settlements are difficult in neopatrimonial orders, because of few institutional channels to negotiate rules and powersharing.[61]

Kabila did not have the time, resources or inclination to change the political system in Kinshasa during his fight for survival. His allies also had other interests at heart than political reform in the DRC. On the rebel side, the Rwandan focus on immediate security concerns and the Ugandan militarised business ventures were paramount.

The new administration established after the Ugandan military intervention at Bunia, changed local patterns of power and access to resources. Local Hemu and Lendu leaders revived memories of Hemu-Lendu clashes in 1975 and identity constructs to mobilise support in the conflict over land and other commodities. In June 1999 fighting erupted between these groups. Hundreds of civilians from both groups were killed with machetes and arrows and thousands fled from their razed villages.[62]

Hostilities have not ceased since the ceasefire. If the ceasefire process eventually gets under way, the creation of consensus and statebuilding envisaged in the ceasefire agreement will have to take place with very limited resources. The ceasefire process has a state-centric focus. As a result, the peasant struggles of the mai-mai are not really addressed.

There are also issues of wealth and power accumulation, often linked to identity constructs and outside the full reach of the government in Kinshasa. Extending state authority will affect all concerned. Perceptions of central state authority as alien colonialism may become a potent force in the struggles over authority. Like the Ugandan military in Bunia, peacekeeping forces may cause power realignments and inadvertently trigger violent contests.

The vast territory of the DRC, wealth and power accumulation outside the state structures and the imbedded neo-patrimonial practices in weak state structures are likely to present problems for some time to come. The end of the military intervention will not end the winner-takes-all struggle in the domestic politics of the DRC.

## 7. CONCLUSION

Kabila's provocative behaviour, Congolese-based insurgents and the example of successful military intervention in 1996-1997 prompted the Ugandan and Rwandan rulers to intervene in the DRC in 1998. The limited authority of the state in the Congo, local struggles for wealth and power and the fragmented DRC military, created favourable conditions for such intervention.

Kabila was initially threatened by the intervention and then saved by the military intervention of Angola, Zimbabwe and others. The different interventions reinforced negative perceptions of African stability and achieved ambiguous success. For example, the costs of Zimbabwean and Angolan intervention will not necessarily be offset by the benefits.

The Rwandan and Ugandan intervention weakened the already impoverished Congolese state structures. These state structures will have to ensure in future that insurgents do not attack neighbours from Congolese bases. The Rwandan intervention on behalf of Tutsi interests included anti-Hutu abuses and may have made reconciliation between Tutsi and non-Tutsi interests in the DRC more difficult than before.

The military intervention and rebellion placed the future nature of the DRC's political order on the regional agenda. However, the intervention also highlighted the fact that no single Congolese actor can exert authority over the vast territory and diverse population. In addition, neighbouring African rulers now know their ability to establish spheres of political and business influence in the DRC by military means.

The military intervention did not create any strong political institutions in the DRC. The rulers of Rwanda and Angola focused on a quick military campaign to safeguard their security. The Ugandan and Zimbabwean interventions were aimed at acquiring business interests. The chance that strong legitimate institutions will emerge during the ceasefire process, seems remote. When there are no more foreign uniforms in the Congolese forests, intense and sometimes violent political struggles will continue to pervade the patchwork of power zones.

# ENDNOTES

1. Clarke, W, "Waiting for 'The Big One': Confronting Complex Humanitarian Emergencies and State Collapse in Central Africa", *Small Wars and Insurgencies*, Vol 19, Spring 1998, p 702. See also Nzongola-Ntalaja, G, in "Conflict in Eastern Zaïre", *Africa Insight*, Vol 26, No 4, 1991, pp 392-394.

2. *Africa Confidential*, 9 May 1997, pp 1, 5-6.

3. Rosenblum, P, "Kabila's Congo", *Current History*, Vol 97, May 1998, pp 193-199.

4. Solomon, H, "From Zaïre to the Democratic Republic of the Congo: Towards post-Mobutuism", *Africa Insight*, Vol 27, No 2, 1997, pp 91-97.

5. *BBC Focus on Africa*, July-September 1997, p 13. See also *New African*, March 1998, p 26.

6. Weiss, H, "Zaire: Collapsed Society, Surviving State, Future Polity", in Zartman, I (ed), *Collapsed States – The Disintegration and Restoration of Legitimate Authority*, Rienner, Boulder, 1995, pp 157-170. See also Chabal, P, *Power in Africa: An Essay in Political Interpretation*, Macmillan, London, 1992, p 216.

7. Williame, J-C, "Congo Kinshasa: General Mobutu and Two Political Generations", in Welch, C (ed), *Soldier and State in Africa: a comparative analysis of military intervention and political change*, Northwestern University Press, Evanston, 1970, pp 124-151. See also Callaghy, T, "The State as Lame Leviathan: The Patrimonial Administrative State in Africa", in Ergas, Z (ed), *The African State in Transition*, Macmillan, London, 1987, pp 87-115.

8. Under Mobutu the state was especially weak because the presidential network exceeded the norms of reciprocity, inherent in patron-client ties, and made excessive use of state structures for private profit. Kabila did not indulge in many excesses before the conflict. See Chazan, *et al*, *Politics and Society in Contemporary Africa*, Rienner, Boulder, 1992, p 181. See also Chabal, P, *op cit*, p 216 and *New African*, July/August 1997, pp 12-14.

9. *Africa Confidential*, 25 April 1997, pp 1-3.

10. Reno, W, *Corruption and State Politics in Sierra Leone*, Cambridge University Press, Cambridge, 1995, p 19. See also Chabal, P, *op cit*, p 227; and Bayart, J-F, *The State in Africa: The Politics of the Belly*, Longman, London, 1993, pp 237-241.

11. Turner, J, *Continent Ablaze: The Insurgency Wars in Africa 1960 to the Present*, Ball, Johannesburg, 1998, pp 221-223.

12. *Africa Confidential*, 3 April 1998, p 3. See also *Business Report* (Johannesburg), 3 September 1998.

13. Bayart, J-F, *op cit*, pp 252-259.

14. Joseph, R, "Democratization in Africa after 1989: Comparative and Theoretical Perspectives", *Comparative Politics*, April 1997, pp 363-375. See also Baker, B, "The Class of 1990: how have the autocratic leaders of sub-saharan Africa fared under democratisation", *Third World Quarterly*, Vol 19, No 1, 1998, pp 115-127.

15. Reyntjens, P, "Briefing: The Second Congo War: More than a remake", *African Affairs*, Vol 98, No 391, April 1999, pp 243-244.

16. *New African*, April 1998, p 22. See also *Africa Confidential*, 20 February 1998, p 5.

17. *Africa Research Bulletin*, 30 November 1997, p 12901. See also *Africa Confidential*, 26 September 1997, p 5.

18. Knemeyer, T, "Putsch gegen den Putschisten", *Die Welt*, 7 August 1998, p 3.

19. Misser, F and Rake, A, "Congo in crisis", *New African*, October 1998, pp 10-11. See also *New African*, June 1997, p 21, *Africa Confidential*, 10 July 1998, p 5; and *Africa Confidential*, 11 September 1998, p 4.

20. Wamba dia Wamba, E, "Crisis in the Congolese Rally for Democracy (RCD): Struggle of antagonist political lines" on the RCD website http://www.congorcd.org/statements/struggle.htm.

21. *Africa Confidential*, 10 July 1998, p 3. See also *Africa Confidential*, 28 August 1998, p 4.

22. Reyntjens, P, *op cit*, p 246.

23. *New African*, October 1998, pp 10-15.

24. Misser, F and Rake, A, *op cit*, pp 12 and 13.

25. For an analysis of patron-client networks in the Zimbabwean military, see Young, E, "Chiefs and Worried Soldiers: Authority and Power in the Zimbabwe National Army", *Armed Forces and Society*, Vol 24, No 1, Fall 1997, pp 139-149 on pp 137-140.

26. *Africa Confidential*, 20 November 1998, pp 1-2. See also *Africa Confidential*, 23 October 1998, p 8.

27. Cornwall, R, "Angola", *AM Live,* Sound Archives, South African Broadcasting Corporation, 17 September 1998. See also Cornwall, R, "Central Africa on the boil", *African Security Review*, Vol 8, No 1, 1999, p 51.
28. *New African*, October 1998, pp 14-15. See also *BBC Focus on Africa*, October-December 1998, pp 5-7.
29. Hough, M, "Armed conflict and defence co-operation in sub-Saharan Africa" in Du Plessis, L and Hough, M, Protecting Sub-Saharan Africa: *The Military Challenge*, Human Sciences Research Council, Pretoria, 1999, pp 238-240, 244-246.
30. Historically, conflict in the Congo's Shaba/Katanga region spilled over into Zambia too, but this time it mainly took the form of fleeing Congolese troops and civilians.
31. *Business Day* (Johannesburg), 20 November 1998. See also *Cape Argus* (Cape Town), 24 November 1998.
32. Hough, M, "The challenge of effective air power in sub-Saharan Africa", in Du Plessis, L and Hough, M, *op cit*, pp 120-123.
33. *Africa Confidential*, 11 September 1998, p 3.
34. Cornwall, R, "Angola", *AM Live*, Sound Archives, South African Broadcasting Corporation, 22 September 1998. See also Echevarria, V, "Unita beats the diamond ban", *New African*, March 1999, p. 33.
35. Misser, F, "Cuban troops return to Africa", *New African*, March 1999, p 24.
36. *Mail and Guardian* (Johannesburg), 21-27 January 2000.
37. *Sunday Times* (Johannesburg), 8 November 1998, p 15. See also *Africa Confidential*, 4 December 1998, pp 1-2.
38. Cornwall, R and Potgieter, J, "A large peace of Africa?", *African Security Review*, Vol 7, No 6, 1998, pp 74-86.
39. Makara, S, "Notes on Uganda's Relations with its Neighbouring States: with Specific Reference to the Conflict in the Democratic Republic of the Congo", *Southern African Political and Economic Monitor*, Vol II, No 12, October/November 1998, pp 15-17.
40. *BBC Focus on Africa*, January-March 1999, p 21. See also *New African*, October 1998, p 11 and *Africa Confidential*, 9 October 1998, p 5.
41. Michaels, M, "The Bleeding Heart of Africa", *Time*, 22 March 1999, p 39.
42. Reyntjens, P, *op cit*, p 249.

43. Vlasblom, D, "Kabila bespeelt etnische haat", *NRC Handelsblad*, 12 August 1998, p 4. See also Reyntjens, P, *op cit*, p 249.
44. UN Security Council, *Final Report of the International Commission of Inquiry (Rwanda)*, 18 November 1998, S/1998/1096, paragraphs 86-87.
45. *Africa Confidential*, 11 September 1998, p 3. See also *Cape Times* (Cape Town), 21September 1999, the interview with Professor Ernest Wamba dia Wamba on 29 November 1999 and *Peacekeeping Monitor of the Congo*, No IX, 14 January 14 February 2000 at http://www.congorcd.org.
46. *De Volkskrant*, 14 August 1998, p 4. See also *Newsweek*, 7 September 1998, p 25.
47. Ernest Wamba dia Wamba during an interview with the SABC, *AM Live*, Sound Archives, South African Broadcasting Corporation, 2 November 1998.
48. Cornwell, R, "The Democratic Republic of Congo", *African Security Review*, Vol 8, No 1, 1999, pp. 53-54.
49. Lemarchand, R, "The Fire in the Great Lakes", *Current History*, May 1999, p 200.
50. *Sunday Times* (Johannesburg), 17 January 1999. See also *Business Day* (Johannesburg), 20 November 1998; and *Cape Times* (Cape Town), 28 December 1998.
51. Mailes, S, "Congo", *AM Live*, Sound Archives, South African Broadcasting Corporation, 14 September 1998, and Mundea, M and Michaels, J, "Congo", *AM Live*, Sound Archives, South African Broadcasting Corporation, 10 December 1998.
52. *Cape Times* (Cape Town), 16 March 1999.
53. *Draft Agreement for a Ceasefire in the Democratic Republic of Congo*.
54. *Ibid*.
55. *Argus* (Cape Town), 28 July 1999. See also *Cape Times* (Cape Town), 27 August 1999.
56. *Peacekeeping Monitor of the Congo*, No VIII, January 2000 at http://www.congorcd.org.
57. *Cape Times* (Cape Town), 11 October 1999, p 4.
58. Interview with Ernest Wamba dia Wamba on 29 November 1999 at http://www.congorcd.org.

59. *Mail and Guardian* (Johannesburg), 17 November 1999 at http://www.mg.co.za.
60. *United Nations Security Council Resolution* 1291 of 24 February 2000 at http://www.un.org.
61. Marley, A, "Problems of Terminating Wars in Africa", *Small Wars and Insurgencies*, Vol 8, No 3, Winter 1997, pp 109-115. See also Bratton, M and Van de Walle, N, "Neopatrimonial regimes and political transitions in Africa", *World Politics*, Vol 46, No 2, July 1994, pp 474-477.
62. *Mail and Guardian* (Johannesburg), 18-24 February 2000.

## Chapter 7

# SOUTHERN AFRICAN MILITARY INTERVENTIONS IN THE 1990s: THE CASE OF SADC IN LESOTHO

## Theo Neethling

## 1. INTRODUCTION

On 22 September 1998 the early morning silence of Lesotho was shattered by the sounds of *Operation Boleas* when 600 South African soldiers moved into Lesotho. Thus began the Southern African Development Community's (SADC) almost seven-month long operation in an effort to deal with the deteriorating security situation in the mountain kingdom of Lesotho. Although it was said to be a combined task force, consisting of the South African National Defence Force (SANDF) and the Botswana Defence Force (BDF), it was not before nightfall on 22 September that approximately 200 Botswanan troops arrived in Maseru.

The operation resulted primarily from the dissatisfaction of the opposition parties who demanded that King Letsie III use his powers to dissolve the parliament, since they believed that its members had been fraudulently elected.[1] Mutinous members of the Lesotho Defence Force (LDF) then seized arms and ammunition and expelled or imprisoned their commanding officers. Government vehicles were hijacked, the broadcasting station was closed, the prime minister and other ministers were virtually held hostage and the Lesotho police had lost control of the situation.[2] The demonstrators congregated at various locations, denying workers entry and threatening to occupy government offices. As far as the SANDF was concerned, the situation preceding the intervention could really be considered nothing less than a *coup d'état*.[3]

The South African government insisted that the military intervention did not constitute an invasion[4] while the SANDF maintained that there was not only a proper SADC mandate, but also a moral obligation on South Africa and Botswana to intervene in Lesotho.[5] The decision was based on and justified by the fact that SADC had been directly approached by the Prime Minister of Lesotho, Mr Pakalitha Mosisili, who requested intervention;[6] that the intervention was based on agreements reached in SADC; that all attempts at peacefully resolving the dispute had failed; and that South Africa had intervened to protect certain South African interests such as the Katse Dam water scheme. It was furthermore argued that the Lesotho government had been democratically elected (despite certain irregularities during the election process) and that it was increasingly required of South Africa to play a role in regional peacekeeping efforts.[7] In addition, it was stated that the decision had notified ambitious elements in the military forces in the region that in no member state would the political aspirations of any military faction be tolerated, and that South Africa's commitment to this policy was also a commitment to development in the region.[8]

From a South African viewpoint it was not just a simple and insignificant operation in a small neighbouring state. It was a dramatic event and a milestone for the new South Africa - the first time that the democratic government had deployed troops on foreign soil in a conflict situation. By doing so, it had changed its relationship with Lesotho and the region. Another important point is that the operation was conducted in the full glare of the media. It was described in journalistic terms as "a loss of innocence" as it "announced the arrival of a very different South Africa; Big Brother is bashful no longer".[9]

A heated debate took place eliciting a variety of viewpoints from reporters, analysts and government spokespersons on the appropriateness of SADC's intervention in Lesotho. *Operation Boleas* was lauded by some and vilified by others. This chapter is an attempt to shed some light on a number of issues and questions that featured in the public debate in South Africa on *Operation Boleas*. An attempt will be made to provide perspectives from a military viewpoint, with special reference to the South African forces that participated in the operation. The operational activities during 1998 up to the point when *Operation Boleas* began displaying many of the classic hallmarks of a peace mission (i.e. November 1998) will be given special attention. Finally, the political context in which the operation took place will be discussed.

## 2. MISSION AND OPERATIONAL DESIGN

The *mission* of the Combined Task Force was "to intervene militarily in Lesotho to prevent any further anarchy and to create a stable environment for the restoration of law and order".[10] The *battle concept* was described as "[t]he deployment of forces in order to locate and identify destabilisers and destabiliser resources, to disarm and contain them and to strike where applicable with the necessary force to eliminate the threat."[11] The *desired result* was to[12]

- create a stable environment in Lesotho;

- restore law and order to enable negotiations to take place between the political parties in Lesotho.

The operational design provided for a four-stage process:[13]

Stage 1: The preparation and movement to the Forward Assembly Area at Ladybrand in the Free State.

Stage 2: The planned military intervention in Lesotho, which was divided into the following four phases:
- To move in and secure the South African/Lesotho border post.
- To move in and secure the Royal Palace, government buildings, the Ratjemose military base, the Makoanyane military base and the Birds Nest Airport.
- To stabilise the target areas and disarm dissident LDF elements.
- To establish links between the SANDF and the BDF.

Stage 3: The continuation of stabilisation operations.[14]

Stage 4: The final stage when the Combined Task Force was relieved of its duties in Lesotho and demobilised.

The following tasking priorities were defined for *Operation Boleas*:[15]

Priority 1: Securing the Maseru border post, the LDF bases, the Lesotho Broadcasting Station and various embassies.

Priority 2: Securing the Royal Palace, the airport and government buildings, as well as power and water supply facilities.

Priority 3: Securing the Maseru central business district and stabilising the rest of Lesotho.

## 3. MEDIA REACTION AND GOVERNMENT RESPONSE

According to media reports the intervention operation in Lesotho became South Africa's school of hard knocks, especially in the light of the higher rate of casualties than had been expected. Newspaper headlines referred to *Operation Boleas* as "[t]he incursion that went wrong";[16] "[f]earful milestone for South Africa"[17] and "SANDF blunder".[18] Moreover, as arson and looting in central Maseru resulted in several deaths, the effect of the operation was described as "[a] city ruined by bungled intervention" and "Lesotho tarnishes SA's peacemakers image".[19] The following reports reflected and typified the general attitude of a large part of the media:

> Burning and smouldering buildings. Indiscriminate and unchecked arson and looting. At least 66 people killed. A once-thriving city practically destroyed. These were the costs of this week's SA-led "peacekeeping" mission to Lesotho following almost two months of protests by opposition parties against the results of the mountain kingdom's May elections. During those weeks, the opposition loudly proclaims only five people were killed and 'not a single window was broken'. Anyone present in Lesotho this week would have found it difficult to argue with that point of view. The situation was rich in irony, however well-intentioned and legally correct Tuesday's dawn incursion by 600 SA National Defence Force (SANDF) troops may have been. Its legal correctness is under dispute, as is the motive behind what is variously described as an "invasion", "incursion" or "intervention", depending upon to whom one speaks;[20]

and

> Apartheid South Africa had a history of being cruel and arrogant towards this mountain kingdom that very few

> people outside South Africa ever heard of. They (our neighbours) maintain that the new South Africa is every bit as arrogant towards them as the old South Africa was... The real damage has been done at home. Mistakes that cost money can be explained away. Mistakes that send boys in body bags demand straight answers. We need some assurance that they will not happen again.[21]

The SANDF was likewise heavily criticised for (what was perceived as) severely underestimating its task against the mutinous LDF. One reporter portrayed the general outlook as follows:

> The SA forces were also dangerously understrength, more than likely because of poor intelligence about the level of resistance anticipated, and entered the country prepared for a best-case rather than a worst-case scenario. So instead of securing the capital and preserving peace and stability, as was the mission's intention, SANDF troops became tied up in a protracted battle with mutineers, giving opposition supporters the opportunity to plunder, loot and burn the city centre[22];

and

> Before entering, SA should have rattled more sabres and, if then decided that intervention was unavoidable, it should have gone in with enough force to keep casualties to a minimum and prevent the widespread rioting that has destroyed the Maseru city centre. Militarily, the operation was bungled due to poor intelligence about the likely level of resistance, inexperience and a lack of co-ordination with the Botswana forces which arrived a day late.[23]

It soon became clear that the South African media played a crucial role in interpreting news and events in respect of

*Operation Boleas.* Predictably, government spokespersons quickly responded to the abovementioned reporting. In fact, the media establishment was challenged for its (perceived) inaccurate or biased reporting on the operation. Fink Haysom, legal advisor in the Office of the President, blamed the media for its blindness "to the values and sacrifices behind the Lesotho intervention" as a result of an "unprofessional rush to fashionable and superficial judgement".[24] In addition, presidential spokesperson, Parks Mankahlana, publicly claimed the following:[25]

> The candidness of our Government does not deserve to be rewarded with verbal abuse and disingenuous disregard for facts as we saw... Neither should it legitimise sloppy comment and lackadaisical appraisal of what we believe most South Africans regard to be serious national and international developments. Perceived executive errors do not give license to the prostitution of the truth or the manipulation of fears of an impending apocalypse or even conventional stereotypes about government on the African continent as understood by cynics and detractors of both our Government and everything that is African...
>
> We all depend on them (the media) to know what is happening in the country and the world. There is therefore an obligation on the part of the media not only to report accurately, but to offer informed comment as well. True, the media has an entertainment role. But entertainment of the opponents of the Government cannot happen at the expense of decent comment.

Mankahlana rightly concluded that many and varied voices had been heard on the appropriateness of SADC's intervention in Lesotho. To this end, he stated that it was difficult to establish whether the mission could be regarded as successful or not.[26] This statement begs the following questions:

- How did the Combined Task Force and the SANDF in particular perform in the framework of challenges and perils normally associated with operations of this kind?

- Which factors were of special significance in the conducting and the outcome of the operation?

- Were the main political and military objectives of *Operation Boleas* accomplished?

Some thoughts in this regard are sketched below.

## 4. GENERAL CHALLENGES TO PEACE INTERVENTION OPERATIONS

Bir[27] describes "intervention" by today's definition as "to intervene in internal crises of a country in military, political, social fields for humanitarian purposes". Such action is often imperative when conditions require the international community or a part thereof to preserve peace. Accordingly, the characteristics and the principles of peace intervention operations are different from ordinary military operations. The nature of intervention operations is multidimensional (political/diplomatic, military/security, humanitarian/economic/social) and dictate planned co-ordination with a view to ensuring a coherent multinational effort.

To assess *Operation Boleas* as a military operation, one needs to take into account certain essential elements or requirements in any peace intervention operation or enforcement action.[28] From a theoretical and practical viewpoint, the successful conducting of such operations requires a high degree of co-ordination between various contributing nations and bodies, and also requires clear objectives and demands.

According to Bir[29] some important principles in this regard are the following:

- Political objectives: Like all military operations, intervention operations need clearly defined and attainable political objectives.

- Unity of effort: This relates to a climate of co-operation and harmonious action that is essential for ensuring that all the intervening powers work in a collective, and not a conflicting manner.

- Legitimacy: An intervention operation is likely to be accepted if it is perceived as legitimate. If not, the action may not be widely supported and may even be resisted.

- Perseverance: This implies the patient, resolute and persistent pursuit of goals and objectives. A long-term political objective should be pursued.

- Restraint: Intervention operations require the careful balancing of requirements for security, for conducting operations and for political objectives. The proper use of force is therefore essential.

Riza[30] points out that multinational action needs to be prompt, effective and sustained in order to be successful. Consequently, the following elements may be of great significance for successfully conducting such operations:

- Clarity and consensus: The primary effect of enforcement powers should be a deterring one. Such an effect is possible only if a mandate with clear goals exists, together with appropriate and transparent criteria formulated in such a manner that the precise nature of the response to be decided upon can be determined on a case-by-case basis.

- Resources: A credible deterrent and enforcement capacity depends on the reliable availability of adequately equipped and trained forces. Such a capability should be provided by all participating parties and member states.

- Political resolve: The lack of staying power in the face of adversity severely weakens the credibility of international enforcement. For collective security to be effective, a credible force should be mustered, with adequate financing from states that have sufficient political resolve to stay the course.

- Command and control: Unity of command and control should be ensured to meet the overriding concerns of mission integrity and the maximum safety of personnel.

In addition to the above, Gamba and Potgieter[31] mention the following issues as challenges at the operative level during multinational operations:

- information gathering;
- role and influence of the media;
- training of troops to meet operational challenges; and
- status of civil-military relations during an operation.

Given this background or broad framework, the following section examines *Operation Boleas* with special focus on the military and operational aspects of the intervention.

## 5. ASSESSING OPERATION BOLEAS

It needs to be noted that success in any multinational operation depends upon a broad political process. Such missions never comprise only military exercises. In fact, military operations play a distinctly supportive role, and may even produce few obvious results as regards the outcome.

Of significant importance is the broad political apparatus or institutional framework created to manage co-operative security and to co-ordinate the peace effort. Such political apparatus and institutional framework entails a complex amalgam of political, diplomatic, military and economic measures at the domestic and broader levels.[32]

## 5.1 Clarity and consensus on the mandate

It is an indisputable fact that Africa is the continent most plagued by conflict. In Africa the nature of recent and current threats relates less to conflict between nations than to conflict within states. Civil wars, fuelled by deep-seated hatred and involving armed factions and the availability of weapons and ammunition (as often experienced in Africa) present peace forces of all kinds with serious challenges and a resistant operational environment. In such volatile situations mandates must provide for sporadic change in the nature of operations and in the military action to be taken.

Accordingly, clear mandates and rules of engagement are relevant. As multinational operations in the name of peace and security reside in the interface between political and military affairs, the need for a clear mandate is paramount. Against this background, the experience of military forces in many theatres highlights a critical issue concerning the contemporary challenge of operations in internal conflicts, namely the problem of formulating mandates whose humanitarian and political objectives are effectively understood and reinforced by the forces on the ground.[33]

As far as *Operation Boleas* is concerned, the SANDF claimed that the forces were mandated to conduct a military intervention operation to establish control over the South African-Lesotho border, to protect South African assets and to stabilise Maseru in order to create a safe environment in which Lesotho's problems could be negotiated.[34] The task of the SANDF was therefore to prevent any further anarchy, negate the threat of a military *coup*, and to create a stable environment within which a political settlement could evolve.[35] From a political perspective it was also stated that the operation did not intend to "prop up" either the Lesotho government or the opposition. Intervention was intended to quash a military *coup* which would have prevented the people of Lesotho from democratically resolving any conflict dividing the majority and its opposition.[36]

In a post mortem on its foray into Lesotho, the SANDF did, however, claim that the government lacked a clear national security policy and that it had not been made clear to the SANDF that *Operation Boleas* was an intervention operation as opposed to a peace support operation.[37] Still, in the light of the above, it would be fair to conclude that the military forces were not hampered by political uncertainty or confusion about the political and strategic objectives of *Operation Boleas*. Unlike many other multinational operations - especially peace enforcement operations - previously conducted on African soil, there was no volatile operational situation that had to provide for sporadic change in the nature of the operation and the action to be taken by the military forces. In fact, the operation was conducted in a tiny country with a 909 km border where the forces clearly had to deal with a deteriorating security situation, securing South African interests in respect of the gigantic Highlands water project and preventing a military *coup* by mutinous members of the LDF.

The SANDF publicly stated that the *Rules of Engagement*, the *Status of Forces Agreement* and the mandate had been made clear before the operation began and that legal briefings had been given to all concerned prior to the deployment of forces. The only problem was that a wider mandate should have been provided to cover incidents such as the looting which took place in Maseru. Specifically, the maintenance of law and order was inhibited because the SADC forces had no powers of arrest.[38]

## 5.2 Resources, financial constraints and force levels

The participation of African forces in multinational operations to prevent, manage and resolve conflicts present a range of different problems, of which an important one is finding the necessary funds to finance such involvement. Roleplayers in sub-Saharan Africa need financial assistance to conduct regional operations in order to maintain peace and security.[39] As a result of financial constraints, many sub-Saharan African defence forces experience logistical and organisational problems. Furthermore, armed forces are generally plagued by obsolete military equipment, while training difficulties are also experienced.[40] Many sub-Saharan African countries are inhibited from participating in multinational operations, as most countries experience difficulties in respect of the ground, air or sea transportation required for timely long-distance deployment.[41]

Effective logistical support, as an essential element of any operation, cannot be overemphasised. A lack of such support leaves soldiers feeling abandoned and incapable of operating optimally. Inadequate logistical support has possibly been the most crucial handicap experienced by sub-Saharan African soldiers in the past.

In the case of *Operation Boleas*, the South African Army deployed a mechanised battalion, with an airborne company in reserve, on 22 September 1998. The South African Air Force deployed six Oryx transport helicopters, two Alouette III gunships, two Alouette III helicopters (in a command role) and a Cesna Caravan. In addition, a Botswanan mechanised infantry company joined after a 12-hour delay.[42] According to the Chief of the SANDF, General Siphiwe Nyanda, the operation cost the SANDF more than R24 million from September 22 to November 2. These costs included more than R6,2 million for personnel allowances, R1,3 million for civilian transportation and R2,7 million for air support services.[43] In February 1999, it was revealed that the total expenses of the operation amounted to R36 million and that the Lesotho government would have to bear the costs.[44] Yet, on 9 March 2000 the South African Minister of Defence, Mosiuoa Lekota, announced that South Africa would carry the cost of R57 million incurred by the SANDF.[45]

Although the SANDF claimed that operational expenses had depleted its already strained budget[46] and that the SANDF's war reserves were at low levels,[47] there is no conclusive indication that the execution of the operation was hampered by financial constraints in terms of day-to-day operational activities. In fact, the strength and capability of the South African forces in the African context is indisputable, while Botswana has become an "upper middle-income" country in terms of the World Bank definition, with one of the world's highest economic growth rates.[48] It can therefore be argued that a lack of resources and inadequate logistical support cannot be seriously considered as impeding factors in conducting the intervention operation in Lesotho. Neither were the forces troubled by difficulties as regards long-distance deployment. Certain problems, such as ineffective telecommunication during the operation, were more the result of inexperience and a lack of functionally trained and skilled personnel. Still, the SANDF's public acknowledgement that only limited reserves of ration packs, batteries, vehicle tyres, vehicle spares for Ratels, Mambas and Caspirs were available should not be taken lightly as it indicates that budget cuts had a deleterious effect on the SANDF's main and other equipment.[49]

Some analysts argue that the deployment of a force too weak to carry out its mission quickly in the face of stiff opposition influenced the outcome of *Operation Boleas*. It would also seem that the situation was aggravated by the late arrival of the BDF contingent, leaving the intervention force under-strength during the crucial early hours with no troops to handle the unexpected rioting and looting in Maseru.[50] Media reports strongly suggested that, had the SANDF entered Lesotho with a much stronger troop contingent, the city could have been flooded with patrols, obviating the need to lift a finger against civilians who ran riot, thus possibly saving Maseru from partial destruction.[51] The SANDF, however, maintained that the forces had been correctly composed in the light of intelligence reports and in view of the operational appreciation of the level of resistance expected, and pointed to the fact that the forces had been committed to the doctrine of minimum force.[52] Yet, the SANDF eventually took the step of increasing its troop numbers in Lesotho to 3 500 in the course of events during October 1998 and later admitted that there had been a perception on the part of the SADC forces that the dissident elements in Lesotho would be disorientated and that they would be easily overcome.[53]

In the final analysis, information on the run-up, planning and execution of *Operation Boleas* reveals that the preliminary decision made at the operational level was based on *Operation Kitso*, a contingency plan designed only for the evacuation of South Africa's High Commission personnel and South African citizens in Lesotho, and not for military intervention in the event of a possible *coup d'état*. Clearly, a more comprehensive operational plan should have been formulated.[54]

## 5.3 Command and control arrangements

It should be pointed out that states participating in multinational operations to prevent, manage and resolve conflicts retain their autonomy and sovereignty. Contending national priorities have the potential to translate themselves into problems as regards command and control, rules of engagement, disciplinary measures and personnel procedures. Differences of opinion in a volatile situation can result in political differences and disagreements between the participating states.[55]

Challenges concerning a lack of co-ordination between and within missions severely impinge on the processes that are often required within the mandates of missions.[56] Such lack of co-ordination can pose numerous military problems, particularly given different training standards, operating procedures and suspicions about intelligence sharing.[57]

As regards *Operation Boleas*, the SADC forces appear to have consisted almost exclusively of SANDF personnel rather than a mix of SANDF and BDF soldiers. South Africa, owing to its proximity to Lesotho and its size, contributed far greater force numbers to the operation than did Botswana. In addition, the South African forces were also "first on the scene" and, as such, they had to deal with what was perhaps the most difficult and challenging part of the operation. As already pointed out, the BDF troops arrived in Lesotho only after the SANDF had been engaged in a day-long solo effort, in combat operations against LDF elements – particularly in and around Maseru. The BDF had also been committed to southern Lesotho, where its vehicles were more suited to the terrain than the heavier South African vehicles.[58] It should also be noted that a combined joint headquarters had been established by the Combined Task Force to conduct simultaneous planning and execution and to conduct replanning during execution.[59] It would therefore seem that challenges associated with a lack of co-ordination and command and control arrangements between and within peace missions cannot be cited as factors that impinged on *Operation Boleas* in any significant way.

## 5.4 Standard of participating forces

Since the undertaking of multinational operations for the maintenance of peace and security is always a daunting challenge, proper standards of training, quality and the professionalism of soldiers can hardly be overemphasised. It is imperative that professional armed forces, commanded by professional officers, properly trained and well-disciplined for their primary mission, should be the only forces deployed for such operations.[60] Regarding the quality and standard of African armed forces, there can be little doubt that vast differences exist between the level of skills, training and education of the South African forces and those of the rest of Africa.[61]

However, in a frank *post mortem* on its foray into Lesotho, the SANDF stated that the situation in Lesotho developed quickly and that time was too short for proper planning and for deployment drills and rehearsals by the soldiers involved[62] – despite the fact that the President's Office instructed the SANDF to conduct contingency planning on 16 September 1998.[63] Participating units were not fully combat-ready, and stock-level planning for operational reserves was not done, resulting in a strain on supplies. Similarly, it was not possible to brief all roleplayers ahead of the operation, and co-ordination between the relevant functionaries of the Department of Foreign Affairs and the Department of Defence was not properly synchronised.[64] Accordingly, the subsequent media reports that the SANDF went in "too quickly and ill-prepared" cannot be slated as totally unjustified and unfounded.

To some analysts, the decision to send troops to Lesotho marked a radical change in approach by the government which, until the intervention took place, had unsuccessfully pursued the path of peaceful negotiations. Then, after failing to persuade the quarrelling political parties in Lesotho to sit down and hold talks, "it wielded the big stick"[65] — but without a contingency plan on the part of the SANDF.[66]

Another problem of *Operation Boleas* related to reports of ill discipline among SANDF soldiers. Several allegations of misconduct (especially absence without leave) were reported. However, the SANDF took a firm stand in this regard[67] and it is doubtful whether this really inhibited the ability of the SANDF to perform its task. In fact the SANDF claimed that its troops distinguished themselves by demonstrating good battle discipline.[68]

The appointment of key personnel with appropriate managerial skills and experience is vital in the context of resource requirements. In previous multinational operations in sub-Saharan Africa, for example, the failure of military planners to select officers with adequate training and expertise for vital aspects of operations, influenced the ability of forces to deal with the conflict successfully.[69] By the same token, collective operations in the name of peace and security are seldom "tidy", and "the fog of war" demands strong and competent leadership.[70]

A lack of sound leadership apparently did not jeopardise the execution of *Operation Boleas* at any stage. For example, Colonel Robbie Hartslief, Officer Commanding during the first part of *Operation Boleas*, was highly commended by the South

African media for his leadership in the operation. Hartslief, an officer who had undergone training in peace operations in Canada, Germany and Bosnia, became the Officer Commanding 43 Mechanised Brigade, a SANDF rapid deployment unit. As such, he was undoubtedly an experienced officer and was earmarked for a top command role in a SADC peacekeeping exercise that would have taken place in 1998.[71] The rest of the South African command structure in *Operation Boleas* also seem to have shown good managerial and leadership skills during the operation,[72] despite a few tactical errors in the early stages of the operation.[73]

## 5.5 Importance of meaningful intelligence

Contemporary peace initiatives have shown that politically fluid and militarily complex situations may require more advanced resources and procedures for collecting, assessing and distributing intelligence. Intelligence on the military power and disposition of forces, the location of minefields, the level of violence and other features in a deployment area are essential for planning and conducting military operations.[74] In order to exercise his or her mandate effectively, a military commander needs to be able to detect the movements of the belligerent forces, determine the location of arms caches, and anticipate the plans and tactics of those who intend to violate agreements and jeopardise the execution of the mission mandate.[75]

In almost all sub-Saharan African peace efforts, troops have been dispatched to mission areas with inadequate intelligence on the local inhabitants, their cultures, beliefs and customs. Even basic geographic information has been a problem, as few sub-Saharan African countries have up-to-date maps, especially maps providing geographic information that is essential for meaningful military planning.[76]

The provision of intelligence was one of the most controversial aspects of *Operation Boleas*. Media reports generally described the intelligence used to guide the South African troops into battle as "poor and inaccurate", and associated this with the much higher rate of casualties than had been expected.[77] Even specialised military journals reported, for example, that the underlying cause of problems encountered during the operation seems to have been the failure of South Africa's Department of Foreign Affairs and the intelligence services to provide an accurate picture of the situation. Consequently, the SANDF had made an over-optimistic assessment of the situation, resulting in the deployment of a force too weak to handle the situation.[78] One analyst expressed the opinion that "either the intelligence gathered was used poorly or the military has a different understanding of what constitutes good intelligence". Another analyst was less assertive in his approach and warned against "making intelligence-gathering the scapegoat of the Lesotho debacle".[79]

In response to media reports and speculation, SANDF spokesperson, Colonel John Rolt, stated that if there had been a problem internally with gathering intelligence, as was being speculated, then it was best that the problem was sorted out internally.[80] At the same time, Colonel Hartslief maintained that the South African forces were in a position to make use of accurate intelligence reports. He disclosed that the South African special forces were dispatched to the mission area prior to the operation with a view to providing the SADC forces with relevant information and that the SANDF did not enter Lesotho blindly. According to Hartslief, it was, rather, the "fog of war" that played a role in the operational difficulties encountered during the deployment phase.[81]

However, the SANDF eventually admitted that the degree of armed resistance encountered was greater than had been expected[82] and that the initial commitment of 600 SANDF troops was based on intelligence reports anticipating limited resistance.[83] It was also admitted that as a result of the withdrawal from Lesotho of the South African military attaché in April 1998, the SANDF had suffered a significant loss of intelligence collection capabilities in that country. By the same token, observation teams could not confirm certain critical tactical information on time and adequate aerial photographs were unavailable. It was publicly stated that the SANDF intelligence contingent was not sufficiently manned and skilled, while outdated equipment had to be used. In addition, specialised counter-intelligence was not immediately available. Intelligence liaison with the BDF was also limited.[84] In the final analysis, one can only readily agree with the observation that improvements in the SANDF's intelligence-gathering capabilities in the process of its analysis and in the transmission of intelligence to all relevant roleplayers are imperative in operations of this kind.[85]

## 5.6 Role of media coverage

Military forces engaged in peace initiatives should be seen to be efficient and effective. Accordingly, media representatives should be in a position to have a clear understanding of the operation and of the operational issues within the mission territory. Media coverage can enhance perceptions - positive or negative - among the members of the task force themselves and the people in whose area they are deployed, as well as among the public at large. The ability to deal with the media may be crucial in determining how peace initiatives are perceived.[86] The role of the media should therefore be understood and never be underestimated.

Friction between the military components of peace missions and the media has often occurred in the past. Military commanders often choose to ignore the media, which is a dangerous strategy, as the role of the media is to inform and to educate.[87] When dealt with properly, the media can be a powerful instrument for commanders in a distressful and desperate situation.

It has already been stated that *Operation Boleas* was conducted in the full glare of the media and that reporters played a crucial role in interpreting the news and events surrounding the operation. It was also pointed out that the South African government criticised the media for their assessment of the Lesotho intervention and alleged that the media were guilty of manipulating the truth. A number of opinions had also been voiced on the appropriateness of SADC's intervention in Lesotho, which made it difficult to judge whether the mission could be regarded as successful or not. Judgement was further clouded since the impression was created by the media that the intervention was unrelated to any rationale and a clear political mandate.[88] In this regard, the SANDF publicly stated that the psychological and media war had been lost "at all levels".[89] As regards media liaison the SANDF also admitted that[90]

- there was a lack of clear strategic guidelines;
- there was no cohesive corporate communication strategy;
- external communication tended to be reactive rather than proactive.

But at the same time the external communication during the operation was enhanced by[91]

- the direct involvement of commanders in this role;
- high levels of truth and transparency;
- visits to the area of operations arranged for journalists.

Much was done in his personal capacity by Colonel Hartslief to ensure that the media could cover the operation in Lesotho. In fact, Hartslief was commended for his openness towards journalists. In his dealings with the media, he also admitted that the South African government (or military) struggled to relate the intervention to a particular rationale. He argued that better communication could have tempered some of the criticism and negative reflections on the part of reporters.[92]

Thus it would seem that the South African government found it difficult to propagate a wider understanding of *Operation Boleas* in media circles. It should be noted that peace missions of all kinds reside in the interface between political and military affairs. Media reports accordingly claimed that the South African government and SADC lacked a clear policy framework in their dealings with Lesotho. Another point of criticism in respect of the political handling of the issue related to questions about payment for the operation. The official South African response that "Lesotho will have to pay"[93] was always treated with a measure of scepticism.

There was also a negative response to the fact that the Minister of Safety and Security, Mr Sydney Mufamadi, instead of the Minister of Foreign Affairs, Mr Alfred Nzo, was given the task of dealing with the turmoil in Lesotho. Similarly, the fact that Acting President Mangosuthu Buthelezi (in the absence of President Nelson Mandela and Deputy President Thabo Mbeki) took the decision that the SANDF should intervene in Lesotho was likewise questioned and widely criticised.[94] This was aggravated by a number of prominent government representatives informally alleging that they had either not been informed or only scantily informed of the plans for the Lesotho intervention. Some parliamentarians and the chairs of key parliamentary committees were angered by their exclusion from the decision-making process regarding the operation.[95] Certain reporters also maintained that a military solution was opted for, while efforts by the South African government to find a negotiated political settlement in Lesotho had not been fully exhausted.[96] Such claims were supported by the opposition parties in Lesotho, who fomented suspicion about the motives for the intervention.[97]

These critical claims pertaining to the political handling of the operation seem to have had a negative influence on the media's general attitude towards the operational aspects of the operation. Yet, it would also appear that the initial negative reports in the media on *Operation Boleas* changed somewhat over time, as could be detected in later media reports after Lesotho had returned to normal.

## 5.7 Need for sound civil-military relations

The deployment of peace forces of all kinds demands a delicate and critical relationship with the host government and other parties to the conflict, such as the local population. Any type of third-party intervention requires a sensitive approach in situations of internal conflict, as it is suggestive of the deployment of a ruling force from the outside.[98] Because peace force members are often or frequently in contact with the local population, there is a need for caution and prudence on their part to avoid misunderstandings and tension. They will be called upon to use diplomatic skills, seek compromises through negotiation and to be tolerant of others. Such attributes require an additional dimension to a soldier's professional life.[99]

In this context, the task force of *Operation Boleas* was clearly committed to the doctrine of minimum force. The SANDF maintained that a non-violent approach had been followed for as long as this was possible, even at the expense of military effectiveness.[100] For instance, blank ammunition was initially used by the Ratel 90s and, on all occasions, the South African troops were fired on first.[101] Also, it was pointed out that refugees were looked after.[102] It can therefore be concluded that the SANDF was indeed aware that the deployment of troops in Lesotho involved a delicate and critical relationship with the respective roleplayers, including the local population.

It should also be noted to the credit of the officers commanding *Operation Boleas* that a Civil-Military Operation Centre was established in Maseru early in the mission's existence. According to Colonel Hartslief, this helped to shape a more positive image of the operation from the viewpoint of civil-military relations.[103] The centre was established to co-ordinate civil and military affairs between the SADC forces and roleplayers in Lesotho. Specifically, the function of the Civil-Military Operation Centre was to oversee security-related issues in Lesotho and to liaise with government departments, the business community, non-governmental organisations and other roleplayers in security matters and humanitarian relief.[104]

## 5.8 Linguistic problems and diverse military cultures

The effective command and control of any military operation depends heavily on its communication capacity. Authorities at all levels should be provided with timely information on the direction and co-ordination of all activities at ground level.[105]

In sub-Saharan Africa, the military of the various states have inherited the languages of the former colonial powers, as well as their various military cultures. Previous command and control problems experienced during multinational operations to prevent, manage and resolve conflicts in sub-Saharan Africa were often related to linguistic diversity.[106]

Since the South African and Botswanan forces used English as a medium of command communication, any problems pertaining to command and control cannot be related to linguistic diversity. In addition, as had already been pointed out, the South African forces arrived "first on the scene" and had to deal with what was perhaps the most difficult and challenging part of the operation single-handedly. Furthermore, the BDF was deployed in southern Lesotho, where its vehicles were more suited to the terrain than the heavier South African vehicles.

It could also be argued that the Combined Task Force had a decided advantage over any other potential task force regarding its cultural background, language and knowledge of Lesotho. The culture, customs and traditions of the people of Lesotho were not unknown to the members of the Combined Task Force. They therefore had a fairly easy task as far as compatibility with the operational requirements and the local environment was concerned.

## 6. OVERARCHING INSTITUTIONAL FRAMEWORK AND POLITICAL AUTHORITY

Military operations in the realms of peace and security depend critically on the extent to which international authority underpins such operations and on the political will of participating member states. This kind of authority is needed to reduce political pressure on the countries involved; it prevents the international isolation of the participating countries if an operation aborts, and it prevents overextending the capabilities of a country's armed forces.[107] Such a political apparatus and institutional framework is also important for the legitimacy of an operation. Legitimacy is frequently a decisive element for intervention operations, and such operations are likely to be supported by other external roleplayers if they are perceived as legitimate.[108]

## 6.1 Modalities for SADC military intervention

One of the greatest difficulties pertaining to *Operation Boleas* was its political justification from a regional perspective. Much confusion surrounded the modalities for security co-operation under the auspices of SADC. In August 1998, SADC became the focus of international attention when Angola, Zimbabwe and Namibia decided to intervene in the Democratic Republic of Congo (DRC). The intervention was based on requests from President Laurent Kabila for military assistance (the DRC became a member of SADC in 1997) against advancing rebel forces.[109] Still, the undertaking was *ad hoc* and was not organised under SADC auspices, although it did receive retroactive endorsement from SADC.[110]

South Africa specifically emphasised the need for a peaceful solution and declined to send troops. It was also reported that South Africa would consider sending troops only if a peacekeeping force (presumably in accordance with a UN mandate) were deployed in the DRC. This resulted in criticism from the Zimbabwean President, Robert Mugabe, the leading figure in the mission to prop up Kabila's regime, who came to power through military force.[111]

The South African decision eventually proved to be a wise one, as Rwanda and Uganda later entered the conflict in support of the rebel movement, while Chad and Sudan were drawn in to fight on the side of Kabila.[112] Importantly, Zimbabwe and Angola were criticised: reporters claimed that Zimbabwe's main motive was to promote Zimbabwean business interests in the Congo. Similarly, it was reported that Angola's main interest was to prevent the Angolan rebel force, Unita, from using the DRC as a springboard for attacks.[113]

On 31 August, the UN Security Council called for a ceasefire in the DRC, the withdrawal of all foreign forces and the opening of political dialogue aimed at national reconciliation. There was also a renewed call for an international conference on peace, security and development in the region to be held under the auspices of the United Nations and the Organisation for African Unity (OAU).[114] However, at the 18th SADC summit held in Mauritius on 13 and 14 September 1998 the SADC heads of state and government "welcomed initiatives by SADC and its Member States intended to assist in the restoration of peace, security and stability in the DRC."[115]

In September 1998, shortly after Kabila's request for assistance, South Africa and Botswana intervened in Lesotho to help the Lesotho government restore law and order following election-related unrest. The undertaking was labelled a "SADC force" after a series of phone calls between the concerned heads of state.[116] The intervention was immediately questioned as some observers argued that its only validity in international law was that it protected certain South African interests, such as the Katse Dam water scheme.[117] Propping up a shaky regime could not be regarded as a legitimate response in terms of international law.[118] It was also pointed out that SADC had no clear guidelines for military responses to internal conflicts in SADC member countries.[119]

Several questions were raised:

- On what basis should SADC countries in general, and South Africa in particular, become involved in intervention operations, and was the SANDF's enforcement action in Lesotho legitimate?

- Should the UN Security Council grant permission for intervening in such cases? What about future responses to internal conflicts in terms of SADC objectives?

## 6.2 Co-ordinating military intervention: the United Nations (UN), OAU and SADC

It can be rightly argued that any justification for military intervention in the interests of peace should proceed from the assumption that such justification cannot be contradictory to the purpose and principles of the United Nations, as embodied in the Charter of the world body.[120] To this end, Article 24 of the UN Charter confers upon the UN Security Council primary responsibility for the maintenance of international peace and security. Article 52 deals with "regional arrangements" and states that nothing in the Charter precludes the existence of regional arrangements or agencies for dealing with matters relating to the maintenance of international peace and security. Yet, intervention operations should not be contemplated without UN authorisation, as Article 53 of the UN Charter clearly states that "no enforcement action shall be taken under regional arrangement or by regional agencies without the authorisation of the Security Council."[121]

Some analysts rightly contend that the internal affairs of many countries have become an important component of the new world order, making intervention a legitimate right. It can even be regarded as an obligation upon the international community whenever a threat to international peace arises. This implies that the broad community of nations has a legitimate right and responsibility to intervene when conditions require people to preserve peace.[122]

The question is: Given the sustained importance of the principles of sovereignty and non-interference in internal affairs, when should a situation in an African state be considered to have deteriorated to such an extent that an international and/or regional response is required on humanitarian grounds?

Until recently, intervention operations were conducted under the auspices of the United Nations and under the guise of peacekeeping: especially peace enforcement. The UN operation in Somalia is a typical example as it was essentially a peace making operation based on Chapter VII of the UN Charter.[123] However, recent interventions in Africa, specifically interventions in Sierra Leone,[124] the DRC and Lesotho, have been without UN endorsement.

It should be noted that the formulation of UN mandates is generally a time-consuming process that does not provide for swift intervention in internal crises. For example, in the conflicts in Angola and Rwanda, the UN forces were brought in at a fairly late stage of the proceedings.[125] Moreover, the OAU has found that even when Africans are prepared to provide the forces for deployment in UN operations in Africa, the Security Council has been reluctant to authorise such missions. One explanation is that some Security Council members are unwilling to commit resources to African operations that may continue for indefinite periods. This was the case in Congo Brazzaville, Sierra Leone and the Comoros.[126] In addition, some analysts argue that the current UN structure is not suitable for the proper conducting of intervention operations.[127]

Potential conflicts or *coups* need to be dealt with before they can take place or escalate beyond control. This was articulated by Colonel Robbie Hartslief, who suggested that "this kind of intervention (in Lesotho) should be accepted as a new kind of peace operation in Africa, because such operations may prevent a massive loss of lives and enormous economic damage". According to Hartslief, everything possible should be done to prevent civil war, and this can be achieved only if intervention takes place before armed conflict can occur. "The problem is that people romanticise peace operations. It would seem to me that firstly they want to have an outbreak of civil war, then a cease-fire, then an agreement which is acknowledged by the UN, and only then should the peace force move in."[128]

The principle behind the preceding viewpoint cannot be disputed. The Secretary-General of the UN, Kofi Annan, has stated himself that peacekeeping (in the broadest sense) can help prevent conflict from breaking out in the first place.[129] At the same time, he is also strongly committed to the view that Africa should rely upon political rather than military responses to problems,[130] and that conflicts in Africa can be solved only within the framework of compromises and tolerance.[131]

In the final analysis, peacekeeping is essentially a UN responsibility: it has to be endorsed by the world body and conducted in accordance with the internationalist ethos of the UN Charter. This implies that any justification for military intervention on the grounds that it is in the interest of peace should be in line with the UN Charter. In this vein, some analysts believe that intervention operations should be led by regional organisations or military alliances, or even a single nation, under the political authorisation of the UN.[132] However, the formulation of UN mandates should not inhibit swift intervention in internal crises, and regional or subregional organisations should provide clear guidelines for military responses to internal conflicts. No organisation should ever prop up a questionable government, and the legitimacy of a particular leader should be objectively assessed. In addition, no military intervention should ever go beyond the ambit of international law, since neither the international community nor regional groupings are in a position to interfere in a country's domestic affairs in unqualified terms.

It is also significant that the United Nations now seems prepared to form partnerships with willing regional organisations and alliances in Africa regarding operations for maintaining peace and security. This relates to the idea of shared responsibility between the United Nations and continental stakeholders for the effective management of conflict in Africa. Africa is the first continent where the United Nations and a regional organisation (the OAU) have made a concerted effort to manage conflicts in a regional context. However, many issues remain unclear as regards an ideal arrangement between the UN, the OAU and other roleplayers. If these issues remain unclear, the justification and motives of interventionists in regional conflicts are likely to be called into question, and consequently the military aspects of such operations are also likely to be subjected to a greater deal of criticism and scrutiny. *Operation Boleas* is a case in point as many reporters and analysts seemed to be unsure about the mission's exact intention and South Africa's foreign policy framework in respect of peacekeeping efforts.

It would be of great value if the relevant groupings (and countries) in Africa could develop a set of broad principles and responsibilities for preserving regional security. In particular they should determine clear ways of responding appropriately and speedily to threats to peace, in co-operation with the United Nations and other stakeholders. Such principles are needed to avoid a haphazard, reactive response and hurried decisions in reaction to unforeseen crises – especially as African countries and organisations are accepting more responsibility for conflict prevention and resolution on the continent. African governments should also not send a message to the world that Africans prefer different methods for dealing collectively with conflict than those accepted by the UN. The legal and moral basis for delegating responsibilities for maintaining peace and security in the African context therefore needs to be clarified.

## 7. PROSPECTS AND FUTURE CHALLENGES

South Africa shares a common destiny with Southern Africa. Domestic peace and stability will not be achieved while there is regional instability. However, the South African approach to conflict resolution in Africa has hitherto been strongly influenced by its own recent history and its relations with neighbouring states. South Africa's reputation for power projection into Southern Africa prior to its transition to democracy in 1994, has created suspicion about its intentions, and the government has to take this into account. The South African intervention in Lesotho in September 1998 may have strengthened or perpetuated negative perceptions in this regard.[133] Future involvement in intervention or enforcement action is accordingly constrained by the memory of the country's past military involvement in the region and by negative viewpoints as regards regional giantism or supremacy. Hence, South Africa will have to walk a tightrope in its relations with neighbouring countries. It will have to assume a leadership role in some cases, but will also have to be prepared to follow the lead of other countries on other issues.

The SADC intervention in Lesotho illustrated, in a very practical manner, the factors that need to be considered prior to subregional deployment in either peace missions or intervention operations. Firstly, using *Operation Boleas* as a test case, any future deployment in peace missions or similar operations will have to consider the following:[134]

- The extent to which all the major roleplayers within the government have been informed about and/or involved in the preparation and planning for the operation.
- The extent to which key members of the legislature have been informed about such impending action.

Secondly, in subregional deployment various factors need to be considered. For example, the legal and procedural mandates governing the participation of countries in Southern Africa should to be determined. In addition, the extent to which the different national interests of the countries in the region can be co-ordinated and streamlined into a common and cohesive subregional strategy will be of critical importance.

Some observers are rightly concerned about a militaristic ethos that pervades the conflict resolution strategies of some of the powers in Southern Africa, with special reference to the involvement of Zimbabwe, Namibia and Angola in the DRC. It is claimed that the foreign policy paradigms of these countries have shown little support for conflict resolution (and peace missions) as longer-term, political-diplomatic strategies and attempts to secure lasting peace and stability. In fact, it is pointed out that there is a clear divergence between the foreign policy paradigms of these countries on the one hand, and those of South Africa, Botswana, Mozambique and Tanzania on the other.[135] A sound normative and strategic basis for future subregional approaches towards conflict resolution will depend on the acceptance of democratisation, state restructuring and policy re-orientation as part of conflict resolution efforts in Southern Africa. In this regard, the Southern African community should show unambiguous support for state building and good governance as the cornerstone of efforts to promote collective security.

## 8. CONCLUSION

*Operation Boleas* went far beyond the scope of an insignificant operation conducted by the SANDF in a tiny neighbouring state. It was a milestone for the SANDF as it was the first time that the post-apartheid government in South Africa had deployed its troops on foreign soil in a combat situation — and it was done in the full glare of the media.

From a military point of view it would seem that, unlike many other previous multinational operations on African soil, the SANDF was not hampered by political uncertainty about the political and strategic objectives of the operation. It is quite clear that the intervention was intended to establish control over the South African-Lesotho border, to protect South African assets and to stabilise Maseru in order to create a safe environment in which Lesotho's problems could be negotiated. Accordingly, the military planners of *Operation Boleas* were able to define a clear mission, a battle concept and a desired result for the operation.

At the same time, there appears to be substantial evidence that the decision to send troops to Lesotho marked a radical change in the approach of the South African government which, after failing to persuade the quarrelling parties to sit down and talk to each other, suddenly called upon the SANDF to intervene in the mountain kingdom. This left the SANDF without a proper contingency plan, especially in the light of vagueness and uncertainty about South Africa's foreign policy framework regarding enforcement action. Moreover, the SANDF units were not fully combat-ready as time was too short for proper planning, deployment drills and rehearsals.

Stock-level planning for operational reserves was also not properly done, resulting in a strain on supplies.

On the positive side, *Operation Boleas* was apparently not really hampered by financial constraints in terms of its day-to-day requirements. Neither was the Combined Task Force troubled by serious difficulties as regards long-distance deployment; command-and-control arrangements; sound civil-military relations; linguistic problems and diverse military cultures; poor quality of the participating forces and a lack of command functionaries with proper managerial skills. In fact, the South African and Botswanan forces and their support systems rate among the best on African soil. And, most importantly, the Combined Task Force managed to withdraw ahead of schedule in May 1999 under relatively stable conditions and avoided becoming involved in an interminable conflict along the lines of the West African force Ecomog in Liberia and Sierra Leone.[136] It is especially laudable that a small training unit of 300 soldiers from South Africa and Botswana remained in Lesotho to assist with the training and restructuring of the LDF, in accordance with the principles of defence in a democracy[137] - but with a warning that further political intervention by the military on behalf of the opposition or the monarchy would not be tolerated. As one analyst put it: "The military is being reduced as a factor in Lesotho's politics."[138]

Yet, *Operation Boleas* did experience certain shortcomings and problems. The SANDF's assessment was overoptimistic and resulted in a force that was too weak to handle the operational requirements and especially the level of resistance on the part of LDF elements. However, this should not be made the scapegoat for the higher rate of casualties than had been expected since enforcement action is seldom "tidy" and the "fog of war" often plays a role in operational difficulties. In fact, the SANDF admitted that the deployment phase was marked by a few tactical errors.

Another shortcoming is the fact that the South African government was not in a position to convince the media of the merits of *Operation Boleas*. The media generally questioned the decision to intervene in Lesotho and maintained that a military solution was too easily opted for. It was claimed that efforts by the government to find a negotiated political settlement in Lesotho had not been exhausted and that the enforcement action did not reflect an approach that elevates persuasion, conciliation and non-violent coercion above the use of force. For a large part of the media the operation resembled a military invasion and occupation of the Kingdom of Lesotho. These critical claims and viewpoints pertaining to the political handling of the operation seemed to have negatively influenced the media's general attitude towards the military or operational aspects of the operation although some of the criticism cannot be slated as totally unjustified. However, from later reports it appears that a return to normality in Lesotho and progress in the party political negotiations (after months of instability) have tempered the initial negative reporting.

One cannot disagree with the Chief of the SANDF, General Nyanda, that the military objectives defined in the mandate were accomplished,[139] despite the fact that certain tactical errors were made and the degree of armed resistance encountered was greater than had been anticipated. It would be fair to state from a clinically military viewpoint that *Operation Boleas* had been successfully conducted, as it succeeded in stabilising the security situation in Lesotho, which has allowed the political parties to resume negotiations on the issue of governance. In addition, it safeguarded South Africa's interests in that country and prevented strategic installations from being taken over or destroyed by the rebel forces. However, the operation did not succeed in preventing the destruction and looting of property in central Maseru. From a political perspective South Africa involved itself in the internal politics of Lesotho and it is yet to be seen whether the operation has paved the way for fresh elections in pursuit of a medium and long-term political goal and settlement. Unfortunately, the peace process in Lesotho remains uncertainly poised. The prospects for rooting democracy in as poor and as conflict-ridden a country as Lesotho are limited at best. At the time of writing, the conditions for maximising democratic possibilities do not yet exist because of the divide over the form of the electoral system. Therefore, some observers argue that more external pressure and facilitation are required for the process to be completed. More time is probably needed as well as more peace-building efforts aimed at establishing a reasonable consensus between the conflicting political parties, and at achieving a realistic and viable timetable for an election.[140]

What has been highlighted by *Operation Boleas* is the need for an overarching political framework within which SADC countries – and South Africa in particular – can exercise judgement and undertake enforcement action. The challenge is to establish an acceptable basis for involvement or intervention in intrastate conflicts or threats to regional peace which at the same time respects the dignity and independence of the states concerned. Needless to say, regional enforcement action is difficult, risky and expensive. Such operations should therefore be in accord with international law and the broad principles for preserving regional security. Multinational operations in the name of peace and security reside in the interface between political and military affairs, and success in any operation of this kind depends upon a broad political process. The SANDF's involvement in the intervention in Lesotho clearly bears testimony to this.

## ENDNOTES

1. *Sowetan* (Johannesburg), 22 September 1998.
2. Sutton-Pryce, T, Baudin, C, and Allie, N, "Baptism of Fire for SANDF", *Salut*, November 1998, p 26.
3. SANDF Directorate Corporate Communication, "The SADC Intervention in Lesotho... a Military Perspective", *Salut*, July 1999, p 23.
4. *The Star* (Johannesburg), 6 October 1998.
5. SANDF Directorate Corporate Communication, *op cit*, p 23.
6. Originally four countries were requested to participate, namely Botswana, Mozambique, South Africa and Zimbabwe, but in the event only South Africa and Botswana were practically able to help.
7. Republic of South Africa, Department of Defence, *Bulletin*, No 57/98, 22 September 1998; *The Star* (Johannesburg), 14 October 1998.
8. *Ibid*, p 6.
9. *The Star* (Johannesburg), 25 September 1998.
10. Internet site http://www.mil.za/SANDF/Current %20Ops/Boleas/Boleas-2.htm, March 1999.
11. Presentation by Colonel Robbie Hartslief, Officer Commanding *Operation Boleas*, Maseru, 2 October 1998.
12. Internet site http://www.mil.za/SANDF/Current %20Ops/Boleas/Boleas-2.htm, *op cit*.
13. Internet site http://www.mil.za/SANDF/Current %20Ops/Boleas/Boleas-2.htm, *op cit*.
14. This stage of the operation was dubbed *Campaign Charon*.
15. Internet site http://www.mil.za/SANDF/Current %20Ops/Boleas/Boleas-3.htm, March 1999.
16. *Pretoria News* (Pretoria), 26 September 1998.
17. *The Star* (Johannesburg), 25 September 1998.
18. Heitman, H-R, "SANDF Blunder Means Longer Stay in Lesotho", *Jane's Defence Weekly*, 30 September 1998, p 5.

19. *Business Day* (Johannesburg), 25 September 1998.
20. *Ibid.*
21. *Pretoria News* (Pretoria), 26 September 1998.
22. *Business Day* (Johannesburg), 25 September 1998.
23. *The Star* (Johannesburg), 25 September 1998.
24. *The Star* (Johannesburg) 14 October 1998.
25. *The Star* (Johannesburg), 5 October 1998.
26. *Ibid.*
27. Bir, C, "Interoperability and Intervention Operations", *The Rusi Journal*, December 1997, p 22.
28. *Operation Boleas* was a SADC intervention operation in Lesotho that was conducted because of fears that a military *coup* was planned in that country. Hence it is technically incorrect to typify it as a multinational peace support operation, since such operations are normally associated with action occurring along a conflict-continuum between preventive diplomacy and post-conflict reconstruction and development. In this regard, peace support operations in the military sense generally entail post-conflict activities designed to strengthen and rebuild a country; peacekeeping activities that involve the containment, moderation and termination of hostilities within states, or the application of military force in accordance with UN Security Council authorisation in support of efforts to reach a political settlement. At the same time, the elements required for effective military action during peace support operations are likewise of relevance in the case of intervention operations.
29. Bir, C, *op cit*, pp 22-23.
30. Riza, S I, "Parameters of UN Peacekeeping", *The Rusi Journal*, June 1995, pp 19-20.
31. Gamba, V, and Potgieter, J, "The Challenges to Multifunctional Peace Support Operations", in Multifunctional Peace Support Operations: Evolution and Changes, *ISS Monograph Series*, No 8, January 1997, p 73.
32. Williams, R, "Peace Operations and the South African Armed Forces", *Strategic Review for Southern Africa*, Vol XVII, No 2, May 1995, pp 91-92.
33. Berdal, M R, "Whither UN Peacekeeping", *Adelphi Paper*, Paper 281, October 1993, p 27.
34. Sutton-Pryce, T, Baudin, C, and Allie, N, *op cit*, p 26.

35. Nyanda, S, "New Year Messages: Message from the CSANDF", *Salut*, January 1999, p 12.
36. *The Star* (Johannesburg), 6 October 1998.
37. Internet site http://www.mil.za/SANDF/Current %20Ops/Boleas/Boleas-6.htm, March 1999.
38. Internet site http://www.mil.za/SANDF/Current %20Ops/Boleas/Boleas-6.htm, *op cit*; Internet site http://www.mil.za/SANDF/Current%20Ops/Boleas/Boleas-7.htm, *op cit*.
39. Arnold, G, "The OAU and Peacekeeping in Africa", *New African*, January 1997, p 33.
40. Mwila, B Y, "Equipment Requirements in Africa", *African Armed Forces Journal*, November 1994, p 8.
41. Henk, D, "Peace Operations: Views from Southern and Eastern Africa", *U.S. Army Peacekeeping Institute Occasional Paper*, 1995, p 19.
42. Heitman, H-R, *op cit*, p 5.
43. *Pretoria News* (Pretoria), 3 November 1998.
44. *Beeld* (Johannesburg), 11 February 1999.
45. *Beeld* (Johannesburg), 9 March 2000.
46. *Pretoria News* (Pretoria), 3 November 1998.
47. Internet site http://www.mil.za/SANDF/Current %20Ops/Boleas/Boleas-6.htm, *op cit*.
48. Van Buren, L, "Botswana" Economy, *Africa South of the Sahara 1998*, 27th Edition, Europa Publications Limited, p 195.
49. Internet site http://www.mil.za/SANDF/Current %20Ops/Boleas/Boleas-6.htm, *op cit*; Internet site http://www.mil.za/SANDF/Current%20Ops/Boleas/Boleas-7.htm, *op cit*.
50. Heitman, H-R, *op cit*, p 5.
51. *Business Day* (Johannesburg), 25 September 1998.
52. Sutton-Pryce, T, Baudin, C, and Allie, N, *op cit*, p 26.
53. *The Star* (Johannesburg), 14 October 1998; Internet site http://www.mil.za/SANDF/Current%20Ops/Boleas/Boleas-7.htm, *op - cit*.
54. Internet site http://www.mil.za/SANDF/Current %20Ops/Boleas/Boleas-7.htm, *op cit*.
55. Williams, R, *op cit*, pp 91-92.
56. Gamba, V, and Potgieter, J, *op cit*, pp 62-63.

57. *The Star* (Johannesburg), 14 October 1998.
58. Sutton-Pryce, T, Baudin, C, and Allie, N, *op cit*, p 28.
59. Internet site http://www.mil.za/SANDF/Current %20Ops/Boleas/Boleas-7.htm, March 1999.
60. Gamba, V, and Potgieter, J, *op cit*, p 76.
61. Cilliers, J, and Malan, M, "From Destabilisation to Peace-keeping in Southern Africa: The Potential Role of South Africa", *Africa Insight*, Vol 26, No 4, 1997, p 341.
62. Internet site http://www.mil.za/SANDF/Current %20Ops/Boleas/Boleas-6.htm, *op cit.*
63. SANDF Directorate Corporate Communication, *op cit*, p 24.
64. Internet site http://www.mil.za/SANDF/Current %20Ops/Boleas/Boleas-6.htm, *op cit.*
65. *The Star* (Johannesburg), 25 September 1998.
66. *Pretoria News* (Pretoria), 3 November 1998.
67. Sutton-Pryce, T, Baudin, C, and Allie, N, *op cit*, p 26.
68. Internet site http://www.mil.za/SANDF/Current %20Ops/Boleas/Boleas-5.htm, March 1999.
69. Olonisakin, F, "African". Homemade' Peace-keeping Initiatives, *Armed Forces & Society*, Vol 23, No 3, Spring 1997, p 360.
70. *The Star* (Johannesburg), 14 October 1998.
71. *Beeld* (Johannesburg), 3 October 1998.
72. Based on the author's personal impressions after a visit to the South African forces in Lesotho on 2 October 1998.
73. Sutton-Pryce, T, Baudin, C, and Allie, N, *op cit*, p 27.
74. Berdal, M R, *op cit*, p 27.
75. Gamba, V, and Potgieter, J, *op cit*, p 73.
76. Anyidoho, H, "Lessons Learned during Peacekeeping Operations in Africa", in M Malan (ed), *Conflict Management, Peacekeeping and Peace Building: Lessons for Africa from a Seminar Past*, ISS Monograph Series, No 10, April 1997, p 44.
77. *Pretoria News* (Pretoria), 26 September 1998.
78. Heitman, H-R, *op cit*, p 5.
79. *Pretoria News* (Pretoria), 26 September 1998.
80. *Ibid.*
81. *Beeld* (Johannesburg), 3 October 1998.

82. Sutton-Pryce, T, Baudin, C, and Allie, N, *op cit*, p 27.
83. SANDF Directorate Corporate Communication, *op cit*, p 28.
84. Internet site http://www.mil.za/SANDF/Current %20Ops/Boleas/Boleas-6.htm, *op cit*; Internet site http://www.mil.za/SANDF/Current%20Ops/Boleas/Boleas-7.htm, *op cit*.
85. *The Star* (Johannesburg), 14 October 1998.
86. Shaw, M, "International Peacekeeping - Are There Lessons for South Africa?", *African Defence Review*, No 15, March 1994, p 14.
87. Anyidoho, H, *op cit*, p 45.
88. *The Star* (Johannesburg), 14 October 1998.
89. *The Citizen* (Johannesburg), 3 November 1998.
90. Internet site http://www.mil.za/SANDF/Current %20Ops/Boleas/Boleas-6.htm, *op cit*.
91. *Ibid*.
92. *Beeld* (Johannesburg), 3 October 1998.
93. Sutton-Pryce, T, Baudin, C, and Allie, N, *op cit*, p 28.
94. *Rapport* (Johannesburg), 18 October 1998.
95. Williams, R, "Challenges for South and Southern Africa: Towards Non-Consensual Peace Missions?" Paper presented at a Conference, *From Peacekeeping to Complex Emergencies? Peace Missions in Africa*, University of the Witwatersrand, Johannesburg, 25 March 1999, p 16.
96. *Business Day* (Johannesburg), 5 October 1998.
97. *The Star* (Johannesburg), 25 September 1998.
98. De Brito, M, "Relationship between Peacekeepers, Host Governments and Local Populations: A Mozambican Perspective", in Malan, M (ed.), Conflict Management, Peacekeeping and Peace Building: Lessons for Africa from a Seminar Past, *op cit*, pp 61-64.
99. Hundt, U A, "Coping with Peacekeeping", *Salut*, Vol 3, No 3, March 1996, p 38.
100. SANDF Directorate Corporate Communication, *op cit*, p 23.
101. Sutton-Pryce, T, Baudin, C, and Allie, N, *op cit*, p 26.
102. SANDF Directorate Corporate Communication, *op cit*, p 23.
103. Presentation by Colonel Robbie Hartslief, Officer Commanding *Operation Boleas*, Maseru, 2 October 1998.
104. SANDF Directorate Corporate Communication, *op cit*, p 27.
105. Berdal, M R, *op cit*, p 41.

106. Anyidoho, H, *op cit*, p 44.
107. Williams, R, *op cit*, pp 91-92.
108. Bir, C, *op cit*, p 23.
109. Hough, M, "Collective Security and its Variants: A Conceptual Analysis with Specific Reference to SADC and Ecowas", *Strategic Review for Southern Africa*, Vol XX, No 2, November 1998, p 36.
110. Berman, E G, and Sams, K E, "Constructive Engagement: Western Efforts to Develop African Peacekeeping", *ISS Monograph*, No 33, December 1998, p 9.
111. Hough, M, *op cit*, p 36.
112. *Beeld* (Johannesburg), 24 October 1998.
113. *The Star* (Johannesburg), 6 November 1998.
114. Cornwell, R, and Potgieter, J, "Africa Watch: A Large Peace of Africa", *African Security Review*, Vol 7, No 6, 1998, p 77.
115. Southern African Development Community, *Final Communiqué of the 1998 SADC Summit of Heads of State and Government*, Mauritius, 19 September 1998.
116. Berman, E G, and Sams, K E, *op cit*, p 9.
117. Hough, M, *op cit*, pp 37-38.
118. Barrie, G, "South Africa's Forcible Intervention in Lesotho", *De Rebus*, January 1999, p 47.
119. Hough, M, *op cit*, pp 37-38.
120. Malan, M, "Regional Power Politics Under Cover of SADC – Running Amok with a Mythical Organ", *ISS Papers*, Paper 35, October 1998, p 8.
121. United Nations, *Charter of the United Nations*, San Francisco, 1945.
122. Bir, C, *op cit*, p 24.
123. *Ibid*, p 24.
124. The military intervention of the Economic Community of West African States in Sierra Leone in 1997 had been *ad hoc* and not in accordance with a specific operating procedure.
125. Clapman, C, "The United Nations and Peacekeeping in Africa", Paper presented at a symposium on *International Peace and Security: The African Experience*, South African Military Academy, Saldanha, 21-23 September 1998, p 9.

126. Vogt, M, "Cooperation between the United Nations and the OAU in the Management of African Conflicts", Paper presented at a symposium on *International Peace and Security: The African Experience*, SA Military Academy, Saldanha, 21-23 September 1998, p 7.
127. Bir, C, *op cit*, p 25.
128. *Beeld* (Johannesburg), 3 October 1998.
129. Annan, K, "Statement by the UN Secretary-General before the Special Commemorative Meeting of the General Assembly Honouring 50 Years of Peacekeeping", Internet site http://www.un.org/Depts/DPKO/pk5060sg.htm.
130. Annan, K, "The Causes of Conflict and the Promotion of Durable Peace and Sustainable Development in Africa: Report of the Secretary-General", Internet site http://www.un.org/Depts/DPKO/pk5060sg.htm.
131. *Beeld* (Johannesburg), 7 October 1998.
132. Bir, C, *op cit*, p 25.
133. *Pretoria News* (Pretoria), 28 September 1998.
134. Williams, R, 1999, *op cit*, p 16.
135. *Ibid*, p 15.
136. *Business Day* (Johannesburg), 19 May 1999.
137. Republic of South Africa, Department of Defence, *Bulletin*, No 40/99, 24 May 1999.
138. Southall, R, "Uncertain Progress in Lesotho", *Conflict Trends*, Issue 4, 1999, p 20.
139. Nyanda, S, *op cit*, p 12.
140. Southall, R, *op cit*, pp 16;20.

## Chapter 8

# CONCLUSION: THE CHALLENGE OF MILITARY INTERVENTION

### Louis du Plessis

## 1. INTRODUCTION

What is clear at the turn of the century and the millennium is that African societies are in crisis. The crisis constitutes a series of grave problems of human survival and happiness. According to many observers, crisis in Africa has become a state of existence.[1] Others even maintain that the crisis in Africa is so extensive that it threatens to dissolve the glues that somehow still hold together various societies.[2]

In this book it is argued that a complex network of factors threatens Africa's security. Falola expresses this eloquently: "The threat to the majority of African countries is not external invasion, but the inability to ensure sustainable development. Food scarcity, environmental degradation, and ethno-religious nationalism are the real dangers to stability and survival."[3] Directly related to the developmental challenges is the growing inclination of African states to intervene militarily in the domestic affairs of neighbouring countries. Whether states intervene individually or regionally, leaders tend to justify their actions with many and varied arguments, ranging from a need to ensure stability or to alleviate suffering to a need to restore democracy. From an academic point of view it is crucial to try to derive some sense from the inclination to intervene.

In this chapter the findings on the nature of the conflict and military intervention in Africa are briefly summarised and a few final conclusions are drawn. Moving from the broader to the more specific levels, the analysis first focuses on the global situation, thereafter on the continental (African) situation and finally the case studies are analysed within a regional context. The last section provides a concluding view on the complex nature of intervention in African conflicts.

## 2. INTERVENTION IN GLOBAL CONTEXT

In the analysis of the nature and scope of intervention (Chapter 1) it is pointed out that since 1945 the majority of international conflicts have been internal wars, a trend that will most likely continue into the future. Especially in the so-called "third-tier" — ungovernable and failed — states, many substate groups will be fighting national governments that are unable to govern their territories effectively.[4] This inability to govern and the related weakness of many states, often in the developing world, form an essential background to the understanding of interstate interventions.

The phenomenon of intervention deviates from the internationally acknowledged norms of peaceful co-existence and non-intervention.[5] Furthermore, military intervention represents the most basic type of intervenient behaviour, most closely associated with war.[6] It was defined as "the planned and limited use of force for a transitory period by a state or group of states against a weaker state in order to change or maintain the target state's domestic structure or to change its external policies".[7] Traditional thinking, which is still regarded as generally valid, has always viewed *military intervention* as a tool of the powerful against the weak and of older, established states against new states. Since military intervention politicises warfare to a level not previously experienced, it has become extremely difficult to distinguish between coercive diplomacy, military intervention and limited war.

In the comprehensive anatomy of military intervention, *unilateral* intervention was distinguished from *collective* intervention, which is undertaken in the name of an intergovernmental organisation such as the United Nations. Whereas the modern international community does not approve of intervention by individual states and even considers this to be an illegal activity, collective intervention tends to be regarded as proper since it has been authorised by an international body with wider legitimacy.[8] In fact, there has been a normative shift from non-interventionism to benign interventionism. This shift does not imply that public explanations for intervening behaviour currently identify the real motives of interveners – on the contrary.

National interests, although not necessarily the defence of national security or territorial integrity, are likely to remain paramount as motivation for military intervention. For this reason military intervention will always be questioned and deemed suspect by non-beneficiary societies. Since the correlate principles of sovereignty and non-intervention form the basis of contemporary international relations, military intervention always requires justification. Justification covers an extremely wide range of public reasons and is linked to the legitimacy of armed intervention. Of importance is that the government under attack must specifically request military intervention from a potential intervener, while also having the clear support of the majority of its population.

Moreover, intervention may constitute a dangerous risk. Since intervention is easier to initiate than to terminate, successful interveners are those who prioritise alternate future long-term strategic goals and policies. Such interveners in particular ensure that they formulate realistic criteria for terminating an operation, namely a termination or exit strategy. A major risk is the potential escalation from an act of peaceful intervention to one of coercive intervention, or to a limited or even a major war. Another kind of risk is the economic cost that such an intervention may incur.

The international context of military intervention is also discussed from the point of view of international law (Chapter 2), in which the principle of non-intervention in the domestic affairs of other states is highlighted. A substantial framework is the *Declaration on the Inadmissibility of Intervention in the Domestic Affairs of States and the Protection of their Independence and Sovereignty*, in which the United Nations General Assembly declares succinctly that "no state shall organise, assist, foment, finance, incite or tolerate subversive, terrorist or armed activities directed towards the violent overthrow of the regime of another state, or interfere in civil strife in another state".[9]

Normal civil strife, which is often used as justification, is unacceptable as a valid reason for intervention. In a civil war in which state control is divided between warring factions, intervention or assistance could be contrary to international law. States are obligated to refrain from action that encourages any activity that would promote civil strife. According to modern international law, the reason is that states should refrain from intervening in civil wars in other states in order to minimise the internationalisation of conflict.

However, five reasons have been put forward which, it is said, justify the intervention of one state in the affairs of another. These are: a state's right to protect its citizens abroad, self-defence, self-determination, an existing treaty and humanitarian reasons. The two exceptions to the prohibition by the United Nations Charter on the use of force in another state are intervention with the consent of the state that is the target of such intervention and intervention for humanitarian purposes.[10]

It would appear that humanitarian forcible intervention under multilateral (mainly UN) auspices is currently viewed as permissible. The principle of state sovereignty has, however, not yet disintegrated to such an extent as to render unilateral forcible intervention for humanitarian reasons permissible under international law. If humanitarian intervention is ever to be justified, it would be justified only in extreme and very particular circumstances.[11] Crucial considerations are likely to include whether a state or condition of large-scale humanitarian distress demanding immediate relief does exit; whether the state is itself incapable of meeting the needs of the situation or is unwilling to do so or is possibly itself the cause of it; whether competent organs of the international community are unable to respond effectively or speedily enough; whether there is a practicable alternative course of action, whether the territorial state is likely to offer any active resistance; and whether the action taken is restricted both in time and scope to the needs of the emergency.

The challenge is to apply these international rules and practices to the types of conflict experienced in a continent such as Africa.

## 3. INTERVENTION IN CONTINENTAL CONTEXT

To investigate military interventions in domestic conflicts in Africa, a crucial distinction is made (in Chapter 3) between forms of *intra*societal and *inter*societal armed conflict, and a series of manifestations of sub-Saharan armed conflict is identified. These had (and still have) serious effects on human and animal life and on living standards.[12] One of the main arguments is that sub-Saharan violence cannot be understood without investigating the underlying demographic, political, geographical and ethnic realities. These societal characteristics, especially when viewed against the background of a modernising continent, provide some insight into the resilience of conflict and military intervention. All the well-intended efforts at effecting peace in conflict areas will be to no avail unless the societal characteristics are determined. This is especially true of the belligerent Central African subregion, stretching from northern Angola and Congo Brazzaville through the Democratic Republic of the Congo (DRC), Burundi, Rwanda and Uganda to Somalia, Ethiopia, Sudan and Eritrea.

It was argued that one of the most underestimated factors is that Africa experiences the world's highest population growth. This factor exerts tremendous pressure on stability and increases the competition for scarce resources.[13] This situation is aggravated by the parasitical authoritarianism of political leaders and the centralisation of the few assets that are available. As was pointed out by the Sipri analysts, Sollenberg and Wallensteen, a striking feature of Africa is the link between armed conflict and underdeveloped, weak states.[14]

Manifestations of sub-Saharan conflict and intervention are increasingly influenced by the rigidity of political boundaries and the concomitant, increasing power of ethnicity. It was pointed out that ethnocentrism was the underlying cause of secessionist tendencies in several countries, such as the DRC, Eritrea, Nigeria, Senegal and Tanzania. If African specialists, such as Berman, Alao and Olonisakin, are taken seriously, the first decades of the twenty-first century may see a growing influence of ethnic consciousness on conflict.[15]

From the point of view of the management of conflict — analysed by using a conflict triangle model — it was argued that the financial and strategic marginalisation of Africa by the developed world may, in a certain sense, be a mixed blessing. Although countries, such as the United States, France and Britain have reduced their aid packages to Africa and have been cautious about their involvement in African conflicts after burning their fingers in hostilities such as in Somalia, African states, on the other hand, have become more self-reliant in conflict management. In fact, the OAU as principal regional organisation (which for years followed a strategy of non-interference in conflicts) has revamped and revitalised itself in the 1990s. The organisation became involved in a series of well-planned negotiations, such as those to restore peace to conflict-ridden states (such as Liberia, Rwanda and Somalia), and took part in monitoring elections in many subregions of the continent. At the beginning of the 1990s the OAU developed a formal Mechanism for Conflict Prevention, Management and Resolution.

Slowly but surely several states began to jointly implement conflict resolution measures in their subregions. Some signed defence agreements. Nigeria, Ghana, Ethiopia, Kenya, Zimbabwe and Tanzania began to train soldiers for peace keeping. Moreover, a few countries conducted combined operations for what they defined as "intervention missions" in support of democratically elected governments against armed rebellions or planned military *coups*. It was concluded that long-term societal development inevitably influences the propensity for conflict and thus the manifestations of conflict in sub-Saharan Africa. At the same time, the changing approach of African political leaders contributes directly, often immediately, to conflict management, sometimes through international military intervention.

In the historical overview of military intervention in sub-Saharan Africa (Chapter 4) it becomes clear that several of the (eighteen) fully-fledged civil wars in the first three decades of independence were initiated internally, but resulted in external military intervention, mostly by armed forces from outside Africa. This intervention often resulted from political, economic and military competition between the East and the West, as was clear from the deployment of Cuban units in Ethiopia and East German and Cuban troops in Angola. Intervention by colonial powers also occurred in former colonies. Especially France utilised its military bases in, and defence agreements with, former colonies such as Senegal to maintain its influence and to intervene militarily to protect its interests in the seventies and eighties. Britain deployed troops in former colonies such as Kenya. Belgium intervened militarily on five occasions, mostly in Zaire/the DRC. In some instances African countries, such as Togo and Gabon, provided troops for a French intervention.

Some of the factors conducive to intervention were internal divisions in the target countries, prior commitments to supplying military assistance and the emergence, since the 1970s, of a number of regional African powers with superior military capabilities.[16] Other factors linked to the previously analysed countries with a propensity for conflict, are shared cross-border ethnic and religious affinities and the related disputes over artificial colonial borders.[17] While some instances of foreign intervention stabilised conflict, others have affected African security negatively, since they intensified and prolonged conflict, increased the number of casualties and refugees, increased physical destruction and eroded national sovereignty.[18]

*Conclusion: the challenge of military intervention*

While most principles contained in the Charter of the Organisation of African Unity emphasise the sovereign equality of African states and the principle of non-interference, it does seem that a shift in emphasis is taking place in the OAU, especially with reference to collective intervention for humanitarian purposes.[19] This shift is illustrated by the case studies of West, Central and Southern Africa.

Military intervention by African states in other African states, particularly where civil wars are being waged, either to support the government in power or the rebels (as well as the resulting counter-intervention), seems set to continue. Moreover, there appears to be a trend towards formalising possible intervention through the conclusion of mutual defence pacts.[20]

## 4. INTERVENTION IN REGIONAL CONTEXT

The case studies focus on the three most comprehensive examples of military intervention in sub-Saharan Africa at the end of the twentieth century. These are the West African interventions of ECOWAS (through ECOMOG) in Liberia and Sierra Leone under the leadership of Nigeria, the Central African interventions by several states in the DRC, and the Southern African intervention of SADC in Lesotho under the leadership of South Africa. For each of these strategically far-reaching military interventions, the essential course of events and a brief assessment of the outcomes will be given.

### 4.1 The West African experience

An analysis of the historical events in West Africa, including the justifications given for foreign involvement in domestic affairs, makes it possible to identify negative and positive results.

## 4.1.1 Course of events

The first case study (in Chapter 5) analyses the military intervention by the Economic Community of West African States (ECOWAS) to solve internal crises in Liberia and Sierra Leone. The key state role players in ECOWAS were Nigeria, Gambia, Ghana, Guinea and Sierra Leone itself, who remained in Liberia throughout the seven-year war. Two other neighbours who became involved for certain periods only were Côte d'Ivoire and Burkina Faso. Of these states, Nigeria played a dominant role throughout the seven years, providing seventy per cent or more of the soldiers and finance for the operations in both Liberia and Sierra Leone.

ECOWAS cited humanitarianism and the promotion of democracy as its chief motives for military intervention. In Liberia the appalling humanitarian tragedy was a main reason, and the Nigerian President, Ibrahim Babangida, defended the Liberian operation by *inter alia* the following outspoken statements, crucial to understanding this specific case and also the general pattern of justifying interventions:[21]

- "We are in Liberia because events in that country have led to the massive destruction of property and the massacre of thousands of innocent civilians."

- "Should Nigeria and other responsible countries in the sub-region stand by and watch the whole of Liberia turned into one mass graveyard?"

- "There are those who are waiting to see the Liberian crisis as a concrete indicator of Africa in disarray and despair, purposeless and without any direction or control."

- "In Liberia we are first and foremost reflecting the love we have for our respective countries, our sub-region, Africa, the Black world and mankind."

Uganda's President Yoweri Museveni who, at the time, was the chairman of the OAU, supported the role of ECOWAS and justified it under the principle of restoring governance. He argued that the principle of international non-interference applied to the actions of a state not interfering in another "functioning state" and that this principle did not apply to Liberia, because "there was no longer any central authority in that country".[22]

In the case of Sierra Leone, ECOWAS added the argument of democracy. The body maintained that it intervened in Sierra Leone to reinstate the democratically elected government of Ahmed Tejan Kabbah. However, the irony was that Nigeria, which spearheaded the intervention, was ruled by the military regime of General Sani Abacha.

In the broader international context, an underlying assumption for both interventions was that the more advanced Western states had turned their backs on the West Africans by not providing economic and military assistance. Some observers concluded that, in spite of the atrocities committed by all sides, vital national interests were still a decisive determinant in international relations as the great powers, in general, simply ignored the collapse in Liberia and Sierra Leone, because their vital national interests were not directly threatened. ECOWAS thus felt obliged to act alone.

### 4.1.2 Assessment of intervention

It is pointed out that the military operations, in the name of humanitarianism and democracy, had different kinds of results. Despite eloquent justifications, the ECOWAS missions defeated some of their initial goals, confirming that military interventions, even at the request of apparently legitimate governments, may involve serious risks. As the earlier exit of the United States from Vietnam and the Soviet

Union's from Afghanistan testified, intervening powers cannot solve all societal conflicts by way of superior firepower. The intervening armies experienced similar problems, especially in the Sierra Leone bush war. There were indications that in Sierra Leone the atrocities against the civilian population became both more frequent and more bizarre after the intervention. One reason may be that several faction leaders resisted the intervention forces, which they never perceived as impartial.

The interventions also internationalised the wars in the two countries and, by doing so, prolonged the conflicts, as well as the hardships of the citizens. The intervening powers militarised civil society in Liberia and Sierra Leone. Small arms proliferated, urban crime increased and thousands of young men were drafted into the wars as child soldiers, also in neighbouring countries. In Sierra Leone the presence of ECOMOG seemed to have exacerbated atrocities. After the government had been flushed out of Freetown in February 1998 the kidnapping, rape, maiming and amputations became more frequent and gruesome. Some even argued that ECOMOG appeared to be a mere cover for foreign exploitation.[23]

After the missions, the already weak economies in the intervening and troop-contributing countries deteriorated even further. Moreover, following the interventions there were very limited funds available for the disarmament of factions in Liberia and Sierra Leone and for the rehabilitation, resettlement and reintegration of ex-combatants, including thousands of child soldiers, into civilian society.

Many regarded and still regard military intervention as a manifestation of self-interest. While stronger states have used military intervention to interfere in the problems of vulnerable governments, smaller states still regard the regional powers in West Africa, such as Nigeria or Ghana, as untouchables, immune against intervention in their own domestic affairs by others. It is improbable, they argue, that smaller countries will ever take steps against possible renegade military governments of regional powers, such as Nigeria or Ghana. Military intervention is thus regarded as a vehicle mainly for stronger states. Since national power is an important factor in international relations, the strong may still interpret the law and justify operations to their own advantage.

Some results have been interpreted more positively, because the intervening states, as well as the target societies, benefited from the intervention in the longer term. For example it is generally acknowledged that ECOMOG succeeded in stabilising the intolerable humanitarian situation in Liberia, especially around Monrovia, the haven for hundreds of thousands of displaced persons. ECOMOG put a check on the most brutal and barbaric phase in the civil war by separating the warring factions in Monrovia. The military interventions also facilitated the initiation of peace processes in both Liberia and Sierra Leone, and many accords were signed. In Liberia ECOWAS also moderated during the general democratic elections.

From a psychological point of view, ECOWAS boosted the morale of the inhabitants in the West African subregion in particular and in other African states in general, and contributed to what is now referred to as the African renewal and renaissance, a movement that has reinforced the belief that Africans are their brothers' keepers and helpers.

ECOWAS has undoubtedly set an important precedent, namely that a military operation can be mounted by a subregional body without the prior approval of the United

Nations. Although the world body did not directly sanction the operations, they received retroactive approval from New York. The underlying point is that a subregional organisation can, in fact, be used successfully to reverse a successful *coup* and, in the long run, can contain a deadly civil war although longer-term stability cannot be guaranteed. African leaders, like their colleagues elsewhere in the world, were thus attuned to the changes that have taken place in international relations since the dismantling of the Berlin Wall and since concepts, such as sovereignty, non-interference and intervention have been redefined.

The indecisive events in Central Africa differed fundamentally from those in West Africa.

## 4.2 The Central African experience

The discussion (in Chapter 6) on military intervention in Central Africa illustrates how thousands of fighters from at least eight African states (and several insurgent groups) became involved in a war in the DRC, the outcome of which was still undecided at the turn of the century despite the signing of a ceasefire accord.

### *4.2.1 Course of events*

After President Mobutu Sese Seko fled from the capital and Laurent Kabila came to power in May 1997 as a result of military intervention by Rwanda and Uganda, a short period of peace followed. Like that of his predecessor, Kabila's power in and around Kinshasa rested on military force, foreign support and a patronage network. The exclusion of various groups from the benefits of this state patronage made it attractive to the excluded groups to attempt to take over Kinshasa. Frustrated by the perceived exclusion, local militias increasingly assisted Ugandan, Rwandan and Burundi rebel groups to develop into a restless anti-Kabila rebel alliance.

Similar to the 1996-1997 anti-Mobutu campaign, the struggle for power which started in 1998 was related to a series of constant - but interacting - factors, such as the diversity and growth of the Congolese population of 45 million; regional and ethnic consciousness among more than two hundred language groups; the effect of the grossly artificial eastern borders (where Tutsis and Hutus live in the eastern DRC, in western Tanzania, in Rwanda, in Burundi and in southern Uganda); the locals' ambitions for power and wealth; the limited reach of authoritarian state structures typical of sub-Saharan Africa; the isolation of the eastern Kivu provinces from central state services; and economic weakness.[24]

While Rwanda, Burundi and Uganda were increasingly supporting the rebel groups, using Congolese and Rwandan ethnic Tutsi fighters as the vanguard, other sub-Saharan states became involved. President Robert Mugabe of Zimbabwe decided to commit his troops to support the Kabila government for several reasons, among others, to ensure the repayment of the Kabila war debt of several million dollars and to safeguard the business interests of Zimbabwean leaders. The Angolan government wished, *inter alia*, to secure a stable eastern border against Unita's increasing insurgencies from Congolese bases. The DRC also received assistance from Namibia, Sudan and Chad and political support from a number of francophone West African countries.[25] These operations became one of the most spectacular examples in the twentieth century of military intervention by African governments in another African country.

Despite this wide-ranging military intervention in the DRC, the fighting was sporadic and the casualties relatively light.

However, forces from both sides perpetrated civilian massacres, and thousands of Congolese military and civilian refugees fled into neighbouring states ranging from Zambia to Congo Brazzaville.

After a year, a military stalemate and exhausted resources prompted the various parties involved in the conflict to participate in a ceasefire process. In July 1999 a milestone was reached when a ceasefire agreement was signed by all the governments involved in the conflict. By this time the Kabila alliance was largely on the defensive, with the rebel groups dominating the east and parts of the north, but they were still far from Kinshasa.

The ceasefire agreement envisaged that the Kabila government, the rebel groups, the unarmed opposition and civil society representatives would enter into an equal and open national dialogue, would agree on a constitution and new state institutions, and would participate in elections. At the turn of the century these plans have not yet materialised, while violations of the ceasefire agreement have, in fact, already occurred and may continue to do so.[26]

### 4.2.2 Assessment of intervention

The interventions in Central Africa differed from those in West Africa in so far as they were not monistic, but pluralistic. Influential governments became involved on different sides of the conflict. The Rwandan, Burundi and Ugandan intervention on the side of the rebels, and the Zimbabwean, Angolan and Namibian intervention on the side of the government highlighted the fact that no single Congolese role player was able to exert authority over this vast territory and its diverse population. In addition, the interventions weakened the already impoverished Congolese state structures.

The conclusion is that when foreign uniforms are no longer present in the Congolese forests, intense political struggles will continue to feature strongly in the patchwork of power zones. Neither military intervention nor the end of military intervention has solved the long series of economic and educational, political and ethnic challenges facing DRC society.

The type of intervention by forces of the Southern African Development Community (SADC) in Lesotho in many respects differs from both previous cases.

## 4.3 The Southern African experience

As far as the involvement of the SADC in Lesotho is concerned, it is also possible to accentuate some negative and positive implications.

### 4.3.1 Course of events

During 1998 mutinous members of the Lesotho Defence Force (LDF) seized arms and ammunition, expelled or imprisoned their commanding officers, hijacked government vehicles and virtually held the Prime Minister and other ministers hostage. After the Prime Minister, Pakalitha Mosisili, approached SADC for assistance, armed forces from South Africa and Botswana intervened in the Kingdom of Lesotho from September 1998 for seven months. The South African armed intervention became known as *Operation Boleas*.

When justifying the military intervention, the South African government emphasised the fact that it was increasingly being required of South Africa to play a role in regional peace-keeping; that the military faction in Lesotho threatened a democratically elected government; and that the basic aim of this military intervention in the name of SADC was to restore stability in Lesotho.[27] This was the first time that the new government had deployed armed forces on foreign soil.

## 4.3.2 Assessment of intervention

The provided framework for analysing the Lesotho intervention evaluates the consensus on the mandate, available resources, command and control arrangements, the standard of forces, meaningful intelligence, media coverage, civil-military relations, and the management of linguistic and cultural diversity. Problems, as well as successes, are discussed.

In assessing the operation, one of the negative factors identified, is the lack of contingency planning for the intervention. The South African government, having failed to persuade the quarrelling parties to sit down and talk to one another, suddenly called upon the SA National Defence Force (SANDF) to intervene in the mountain kingdom. At this stage the SANDF did not have a proper contingency plan and there was too little time for units to be rendered fully combat-ready.[28] An attendant shortcoming was that, as a result of inadequate intelligence reports, the SANDF's initial force was too weak to quickly overcome the armed resistance by LDF elements.[29] In addition, the initial stage of the intervention contributed to stimulating the destruction and looting of property in central Maseru by rebels and some other citizens. The intervening forces were unprepared to prevent and control the initial destruction.

In serious criticism in the media some strategic analysts claimed that the South African government had not exhausted all avenues for a negotiated settlement and had opted too easily for the use of force. Some defined the intervention as nothing more than the military invasion and occupation of a vulnerable neighbouring country in support of the government.

In assessing the military intervention, it was pointed out that the operation was intended to establish control over the border between South Africa and Lesotho, to protect South African assets and to stabilise the capital of Maseru in order to create a safe environment in which Lesotho's problems could be negotiated. A positive factor is that the South African and Botswana forces and their support systems are rated among the best on African soil.

The Combined Task Force managed to withdraw ahead of schedule in May 1999 under relatively stable conditions and thus avoided becoming involved in an interminable and intractable conflict along the lines of the West African ECOMOG in Liberia and Sierra Leone and the intervening armies in the DRC.[30] A training element of three hundred soldiers from South Africa and Botswana remained in Lesotho to assist with training and restructuring the Lesotho Defence Force, in accordance with the principles of defence in a democratic society.[31]

From a military point of view *Operation Boleas* had been successfully conducted as it did succeed in stabilising the security situation in Lesotho. The intervention safeguarded South Africa's interests in the country, and the stability enabled the political parties to resume negotiations on elections and governance.

## 5. THE COMPLEX CHALLENGE

The case studies illustrate both the dilemma of *classifying* and that of *justifying* military interventions. In the first case study, several members of ECOWAS, under Nigeria, intervened in Liberia and Sierra Leone for apparently humanitarian reasons, exacerbated the conflict, undermined their own weak economies, but stabilised the brutal conflicts in West Africa. In the second case study, several Central African states with totally different motives intervened in power struggles in the DRC; put nearly unbearable pressures on their own economies; and settled for a ceasefire that held the prospect of peaceful developments. In the third case study, South Africa supported by Botswana, suppressed a *coup* attempt in Lesotho, in the name of SADC, and some agreement on future democratic elections was reached.

The guidelines for military intervention become exceptionally complicated when applied to these three diverse case studies, to other African conflicts and to conflict in general. An underlying reason is that the resilience of strife in sub-Saharan Africa can be linked to a long series of societal characteristics. Among others, these are a never-ending competition for scarce resources as a result of having the world's highest population growth; the parasitical authoritarianism of political leaders; and the artificiality of borders that ignore natural geographical and ethnic features. Over the past decades this persistance and intractable societal conflict have given rise to political resistance and human suffering attended by all kinds of justifications for cross-border operations and military interventions by Eastern, Western and African armed forces. Moreover, while most principles contained in the *Charter of the Organisation of African Unity* emphasise the sovereign equality of African states and the principle of non-interference, it does indeed seem that a shift in emphasis is taking place in the OAU, especially with reference to collective intervention for humanitarian purposes.

African justification to intervene is reinforced by a growing international emphasis on the interdependence of societies and states. In an increasingly interdependent world, the divide between what is defined as "domestic" affairs and what is defined as affairs "external" to a state is often a very thin one. The growing emphasis on globalisation at the beginning of the twenty first century has internationalised the internal affairs of states even more. "Globalisation" implies that the important principles that guided international relations, such as sovereignty and non-interference, have been revised.

However, the tentative acceptance of some forms of intervention is still only valid in terms of international law. Intervention missions conducted within an international legal framework, and perceived as legitimate are likely to be supported by more states.[32] Legitimacy is heightened when intervention is planned under the auspices of regional or continental organisations, such as ECOWAS, SADC or the OAU. Likewise, legitimacy is virtually always questioned when regional security structures endorse the military intervention of individual states only *after* it has started. An example is SADC's retroactive endorsement of the intervention by Zimbabwe in the DRC. Similar questions were asked about labelling the intervention of the South African armed forces in Lesotho a regional SADC venture after only a series of telephone calls had been made between some heads of state.[33]

Some analysts argue that legitimacy furthermore demands authorisation by the United Nations. In terms of Article 53 in the *Charter of the United Nations*, "no enforcement action shall be taken under regional arrangement or by regional agencies without the authorisation of the Security Council".[34] However, although the interventions in Sierra Leone, the DRC and Lesotho took place without explicit and prior United Nations endorsement, the United Nations seemed prepared to accept the responsibility of regional and subregional organisations for maintaining security.

Because the correlate principles of sovereignty and non-intervention form the basis of contemporary international relations, military intervention always requires justification. Of importance is that the government under attack must specifically request military intervention from the potential intervener, while also having the clear support of the majority of its population. Normal civil strife, which is often given as a justification, is not accepted as a valid reason for intervention. States are furthermore obligated to refrain from action encouraging any activity that will promote civil strife.

If humanitarian intervention — also in sub-Saharan Africa — is ever to be justified, it will only be in extreme and very particular circumstances. Crucial considerations are likely to include whether large-scale humanitarian distress exists which demands immediate relief; whether a state is itself incapable of meeting the needs of a situation or is unwilling to do so or is perhaps itself the cause of it; whether competent organs of the international community are unable to respond effectively or speedily enough; whether there is a practicable alternative to the action to be taken; whether there is likely to be any active resistance on the part of the state; and whether the action taken is restricted both in time and scope to the needs of the emergency.

In may be concluded that, whereas the modern international community still does not approve of military intervention by single states and even considers it to be an illegal activity, regional intervention is more often regarded as appropriate, especially if it has been authorised and planned by an international body with widespread legitimacy, such as the OAU. This is even more true of intervention under the auspices of the United Nations. Military intervention in a conflict, like other human projects, can be acceptable in the long run only if it is based not on arbitrary decisions, but on normative principles and on the rule of law.

## ENDNOTES

1. Mbembe, A, and Roitman, J, "Figures of the subject in times of crisis", *Public Culture*, 7, 1995, pp 323-352.
2. Cornwall, R, "The collapse of the African state", *Paper presented at the SA Defence College*, Thaba Tshwane, Feb 1999, p 9.
3. Falola, T, "Foreword" in Oyebade, A, and Alao, A, (eds), *Africa After the Cold War — The Changing Perspectives on Security*, Africa World Press, Asmara, Eritrea, 1998, p xii.
4. Metz, S, "Deterring conflict short of war", *Strategic Review*, Vol 22(4), 1994, pp 9-13.
5. Rosenau, J, "The concept of intervention", *Journal of International Affairs*, Vol 22(2), 1968, p 167.
6. Tillema, H K, "Foreign overt military intervention in the nuclear age", *Journal of Peace Research*, Vol 26(2), 1989, pp 179 and 181; and Little, R, *Intervention: External involvement in civil wars*, Martin Robertson, London, 1975, p 11.
7. Otte, T G, "On intervention: Some introductory remarks", in Dorman, AM and Otte, TG (eds), *Military Intervention: From Gunboat Diplomacy to Humanitarian Intervention*, Dartmouth, Aldershot, 1995, p 3.
8. Laurd, E, "Collective intervention", in Bull, H (ed), *Intervention in World Politics*, Clarendon Press, Oxford, 1984, pp 157-158.
9. General Assembly Resolution 2131 (XX) 21 December 1965.
10. Elias, TO, "Scope and meaning of Article 2(4) of the United Nations Charter", in Brown, ED and Cheng, B (eds), *Contemporary Problems of International Law*, Stevens and Sons, 1988, p 72.
11. Jennings, R and Watts, A (eds), *Oppenheim's International Law*, Vol 1, Ninth Ed, Longman, Hawlow, 1992, p 443.
12. Du Plessis, L, "Challenge of peace", in Du Plessis, L, and Hough, M, *Protecting sub-Saharan Africa: the Military Challenge*, HSRC Publishers, Pretoria, 1999, pp 24-29.
13. "Geography and population", in Esterhuysen, P (ed), *Africa A-Z: Continental and Country Profiles*, Africa Institute of South Africa, Pretoria, 1998, pp 13-14.

14. Sollenberg, M and Wallensteen, P, "Major armed conflicts", in Sipri (Stockholm International Peace Research Institute), *Yearbook 1998: Armaments, Disarmament and International Security*, Oxford University Press, 1998, p 23.
15. Alao, A and Olonisakin, F, "Post Cold War Africa: Ethnicity, ethnic conflict and security", in Oyebade, A and Alao, A (eds), *op cit*, p 121.
16. MacFarlane, SN, "Africa's decaying security system and the rise of intervention", *International Security*, Vol 8(4), 1984, pp 129-135.
17. Copson, RW, *Africa's Wars and Prospects for Peace*, ME Sharpe, New York, 1994, pp 36 and 43.
18. MacFarlane, SN, "Intervention and security in Africa", *International Affairs*, Vol 60(1), Winter 1983/4, pp 56-57.
19. OAU, *Resolving Conflict in Africa*: Proposals for Action, 1992, p 17.
20. *Business Day* (Johannesburg), 26 August 1999.
21. Babangida, Pres I, "The Imperative Features of Nigerian Foreign Policy and the Crisis in Liberia", speech at a press conference at the Dodan Barracks in Lagos, October 31, 1990.
22. Museveni Y quoted in "ECOWAS Mediation in the Liberian Crisis", ECOWAS Secretariat, Lagos, p 8.
23. Yoroms, G, and Aning, EK, "From Economic to Political Integration: Towards an Analysis of ECOWAS Transition", in *Africa Peace Review*, Abuja, Vol 1 (2), October 1997, p 47.
24. Solomon, H, "From Zaïre to the Democratic Republic of the Congo: Towards post-Mobutuism", *Africa Insight*, Vol 27(2), 1997, pp 91-97.
25. *Africa Confidential*, 20 November 1998, pp 1-2; Africa Confidential, 23 October 1998, p 8; Cornwall, R, "Central Africa on the boil", *African Security Review*, Vol 8(1), 1999, pp 50-56.
26. *Cape Times* (Cape Town), 27 Augustus 1999.
27. SA Department of Defence, *Bulletin*, 57/98, 22 September 1998; *The Star* (Johannesburg), 14 October 1998.
28. Internet site http://www/mil.za/SANDF/Current %20Ops/Boleas/Boleas-6.htm, March 1999.
29. Heitman, H-R, "SANDF blunder means longer stay in Lesotho", *Jane's Defence Weekly*, 30 September 1998, p 5.
30. *Business Day* (Johannesburg), 19 May 1999.
31. SA Department of Defence, *Bulletin*, 40/99, 24 May 1999.

32. Bir, C, "Interoperability and Intervention Operations", *The Rusi Journal*, December 1997, p 23.
33. Berman, EG, and Sams, KE, "Constructive engagement: Western efforts to develop African peacekeeping", *ISS Monograph*, No 33, December 1998, p 9.
34. United Nations, *Charter of the United Nations*, San Francisco, 1945.

# Comments on a recent study on African armed forces

Du Plessis, L, and Hough, M (eds),
*Protecting sub-Saharan Africa: the Military Challenge,*
HSRC Publishers, Pretoria, 1999, 278 pp,
ISBN 0-7969-1900-3, R102

"This work on African security is an excellent product of different perspectives in the military and social sciences. It follows a strong scientific approach without ideological bias."

Evert Jordaan, in *Military Strategy – Book Reviews*

"This book by the Centre for Military Studies at the University of Stellenbosch and the Institute for Strategic Studies at the University of Pretoria is a worthy contribution to defence research and should be required reading for professionals, students and analysts in the peace and security field."

Cedric de Coning, in *South African Journal of International Affairs*

"The authors undertook substantial research and painted an accurate picture of contemporary sub-Saharan Africa. Information pertaining to equipment related analysis and equipment usability in most sub-Saharan African countries is accurate and informative."

James Machakaire, in *Accord Online*

"*Protecting sub-Saharan Africa* follows a very structured approach, by delineating the armed forces by type and then giving examples of each from selected countries. The inclusion of statistics makes it easy to understand the conclusions drawn by the authors, and is useful as reference guides."

Barry Klein, in *Military Strategy — Book Reviews*

"If one has any interest in sub-Saharan Africa and any possible related military matters, this is the book that will provide a clear insight. The contributors deal with facts - which may be a disappointing reality if previously it has been convenient to indulge in wishful thinking and fantasy."

Peter McIntosh, in *African Armed Forces Journal*